The Gods of the Nations

Evangelical Theological Society Studies
David W. Baker, editor

Listening to the Text: Oral Patterning in Paul's Letters
    John D. Harvey
The Gods of the Nations: Studies in Ancient Near Eastern National Theology, Second Edition
    Daniel I. Block

Daniel I. Block (D.Phil., University of Liverpool) is Associate Dean and John R. Sampey Professor of Old Testament Interpretation at Southern Baptist Theological Seminary. Dr. Block wrote the two-volume commentary on Ezekiel in the New International Commentary on the Old Testament and the volume on Judges and Ruth in the New American Commentary.

The Gods of the Nations

Studies in Ancient Near Eastern National Theology

Second Edition

Daniel I. Block

Foreword by Alan R. Millard

Baker Academic

A Division of Baker Book House Co
Grand Rapids, Michigan 49516

APOLLOS

© 1988, 2000 by Daniel I. Block

Published by Baker Academic
a division of Baker Book House Company
P.O. Box 6287, Grand Rapids, MI 49516-6287
and
Apollos (an imprint of Inter-Varsity Press)
38 De Montfort Street
Leicester LE1 7GP
England

First edition published 1988 by the Evangelical Theological Society

Printed in the United States of America

Library of Congress Cataloging-in-Publication Data

Block, Daniel Isaac, 1943–
    The gods of the nations / Daniel I. Block.— 2nd ed.
        p. cm. — (Evangelical Theological Society Studies)
    Includes bibliographical references (p.) and index.
    ISBN 0-8010-2201-0 (paper)
        1. Religion and state—Middle East—History. 2. Religion and state—
Biblical teaching. 3. Bible. O.T.—Theology. 4. Middle East—Religion. I. Title.
II. Evangelical Theological Society. Studies.

    BL1640.B57 2000
    291.1′77′09394—dc21
                                          99-087028

British Library Cataloging-in-Publication Data

A catalogue of this book is available from the British Library. ISBN: 0-85111-471-7

For information about academic books, resources for Christian leaders, and all new releases available from Baker Book House, visit our web site:
http://www.bakerbooks.com

In memory of my father and mother
Isaac and Ella Block
whose lives demonstrated to all
what it means to be the people of God.

Contents

Foreword

If foreigners visited ancient Israel, would they find a very different mental attitude? If they were near neighbors, would they see a great difference between their people and their Israelite neighbors?

If they were Moabites, for example, moving in the face of national disaster, drought, famine, or defeat, they would believe their patron god Chemosh was angry with their land, and they would find the Israelites believed their God was angry with them if they suffered in the same way. Times of prosperity, peace, and victory proved the favor of the appropriate deity. The Israelites they met would bear names with meanings that their God was king—supporting and providing for them, shepherding them, in fact, carrying out the functions expected of a human king—just as Moabite names acknowledged Chemosh. Yet the visitors would notice the absence of other divinities from the Hebrew names. None revered Astarte, for example, or the Sun or the Moon, and while they might find evidence that Israelites did worship other gods, they would note that there was no room for them in the official cult. Israelites were expected to be loyal to one God alone and to do his will. The visitors' surprise might grow as they were told about the claims of Israel's God. He was the God of Israel, yet he was not limited to the land he had given to his people; his position had its origin before the existence of the people, and if they were taken from their land, he would still be their God. He was the God of Israel, his special people, but he was supreme over the whole world; he assigned the lands of the nations (Deut. 32:8) and moved peoples from one place to another (Amos 9:7).

Is the study of these ideas merely an antiquarian exercise, research into long-dead societies that simply adds to the sum of modern knowledge? The continuing force of biblical concepts suggests otherwise. Basic to Israel's existence was the covenant that God made with her at Mount Sinai. In this, Israel was different from her neighbors. Although other nations understood that they should be loyal to their patron gods, there is no hint of an agreement of the sort described in the Bible, and no comparison can be made between those gods and Israel's God, who communicated consistently century after century and so gave grounds for hope of restoration after the people were exiled from their land.

Daniel Block has investigated national theology extensively in the Bible and in the ancient Near East, exploring these topics through explicit attitudes as well as through those expressed in personal names and titles. Given the long period of time and the wide geographical area involved, variations and contradictions may appear (and with the fragmentary state of many texts, differences of interpretation may arise); still, the result reveals remarkably similar and homogeneous concepts. That the biblical writings have much in common with those ancient texts is not surprising, for their writers lived in the same world, with the same fashions of thought and means of expression. There was no need for them to be different, and indeed their particular emphases would hardly have been intelligible had they expressed them in an alien style. All the more important, then, are the points of distinction between Israelite thought and belief and the thoughts and beliefs of her contemporaries. If these points of distinction were not very extensive so far as national theology is concerned, this study makes it clear that they were very deep, an integral part of the uniqueness of ancient Israel. No other nation claimed a consistently, divinely ordained history involving forecasts of blessing or judgment and fulfillment of those forecasts together with revealed moral standards by which the deity also acted.

Although this study limits itself to the Old Testament world, it is not hard to perceive how some of the ideas discussed persist and are translated in the New Testament, through the new covenant, into a spiritual dimension. Lessons taught to Israel, sadly rarely learned, still need to be taught and learned today among God's people—lessons of loyalty, constancy, and wholehearted faith.

In the decade since the first edition of this book was published, the author has demonstrated the high quality of his scholarship in other works, notably his commentary on Ezekiel, winning the esteem of his peers, while at the same time demonstrating his deep pastoral concern that the Old Testament should be read and understood as God's living word for the world.

Alan R. Millard
Liverpool, England
Summer 1999

Preface

The response to the original version of *The Gods of the Nations* has been encouraging. But that work was published more than ten years ago and has long since been out of print. In the meantime people interested in subjects discussed in the book have benefited from a wealth of new data and a vast array of articles and monographs related to topics discussed in the study. While my understanding of the issues has deepened, my views on most matters have not changed. Even so, modifications appear on virtually every page, and several chapters have been thoroughly reworked in light of the new discoveries. Members of the Ezekiel Seminar sponsored by the Society of Biblical Literature will recognize drastic changes in the last chapter in particular. The present discussion of the end of deity-nation relationships incorporates elements from a paper presented to the Ezekiel Seminar in 1996. I am grateful to John Strong and Maggie Odell for seeing to the publication of that paper in full in an upcoming volume of essays on Ezekiel. Elsewhere my revisions are less drastic, my concern being primarily to update some of the bibliography and to correct some stylistic lapses.

I am grateful to Baker Book House for their interest in republishing the volume and their encouragement to revise the manuscript where necessary. Special thanks are extended to James Weaver and Brian Bolger for taking the initiative on the project, to David Baker for editing this new series, and to Kenneth Turner, Oleg Turlac, and Michael Roy, my graduate assistants, who carefully read the revised manuscript and offered many helpful suggestions. I am especially grateful for the endorsement of my mentor, Professor Alan Millard, who has graciously written the foreword for this revised edition. The revision benefited greatly from his interpretive and bibliographic suggestions.

As grateful as I am for the support of all these individuals, responsibility for lapses in judgment and infelicities in expression rests entirely on my own shoulders. In all my efforts my prayer is that Jesus Christ, the Lord of the church, will be glorified through this offering I present for the consideration of all who seek to understand the Scriptures.

Daniel I. Block
Louisville, Kentucky
March 1999

Abbreviations

AB	Anchor Bible
ABD	D. N. Freedman et al., eds., *Anchor Bible Dictionary*, 6 vols. (New York: Doubleday, 1992)
AHw	W. von Soden, *Akkadisches Handwörterbuch*, 3 vols. (Wiesbaden: Harrassowitz, 1965–81)
AI	J. C. L. Gibson, *Aramaic Inscriptions Including Inscriptions in the Dialect of Zenjirli* (Oxford: Clarendon, 1975)
ANET	J. B. Pritchard, ed., *Ancient Near Eastern Texts Relating to the Old Testament*, 3d ed. with supplement (Princeton: Princeton University Press, 1969)
AnOr	Analecta orientalia
AnSt	*Anatolian Studies*
AOAT	Alter Orient und Altes Testament
ARAB	D. D. Luckenbill, *Ancient Records of Assyria and Babylonia*, 2 vols. (Chicago: University of Chicago Press, 1926–27)
AS	Assyriological Studies
AUSS	*Andrews University Seminary Studies*
BA	*Biblical Archaeologist*
BAR	*Biblical Archaeology Review*
BASOR	*Bulletin of the American Schools of Oriental Research*
BDB	F. Brown, S. R. Driver, and C. A. Briggs, eds., *A Hebrew and English Lexicon of the Old Testament* (Oxford: Clarendon, 1907)
BHS	K. Elliger and W. Rudolph, eds., *Biblia Hebraica Stuttgartensia* (Stuttgart: Deutsche Bibelstiftung, 1967–77)
BiOr	*Bibliotheca Orientalis*
BJRL	*Bulletin of the John Rylands University Library of Manchester*
BKAT	Biblischer Kommentar Altes Testament
BM	B. R. Foster, *Before the Muses: An Anthology of Akkadian Literature*, 2 vols. (Bethesda, Md.: CDL, 1993)
BWANT	Beiträge zur Wissenschaft vom Alten und Neuen Testament
BZAW	Beiträge zur Zeitschrift für die alttestamentliche Wissenschaft
CAD	*The Assyrian Dictionary of the Oriental Institute of the University of Chicago* (1960–)
CAI	W. Aufrecht, *A Corpus of Ammonite Inscriptions*, Ancient Near Eastern Texts and Studies 4 (Lewiston: Edwin Mellen, 1989)
CAT	M. Dietrich, O. Loretz, and J. Sanmartín, *The Cuneiform Alphabetic Texts from Ugarit, Ras Ibn Hani and Other Places*, 2d ed. (Münster: Ugarit-Verlag 1995)
CBQ	*Catholic Biblical Quarterly*

CCBW	*The Context of Scripture*, vol. 1, *Canonical Compositions from the Biblical World*, ed. W. W. Hallo and K. L. Younger Jr. (Leiden: Brill, 1997)
CIS	*Corpus Inscriptionum Semiticarum*
DBS	*Supplément au dictionnaire de la Bible*
DDD	K. van der Toorn et al., eds., *Dictionary of Deities and Demons in the Bible* (Leiden: Brill, 1995)
DNWSI	J. Hoftijzer and K. Jongeling, *Dictionary of the North-West Semitic Inscriptions*, 2 vols. (Leiden: Brill, 1995)
EA	El-Amarna
EI	*Eretz-Israel*
IEJ	*Israel Exploration Journal*
HALOT	W. Baumgartner et al., *Hebrew and Aramaic Lexicon of the Old Testament*, trans. M. E. J. Richardson et al., 5 vols. plus supplement (Leiden: Brill, 1994–)
HMI	J. C. L. Gibson, *Hebrew and Moabite Inscriptions* (Oxford: Clarendon, 1973)
HSM	Harvard Semitic Monographs
HSS	Harvard Semitic Studies
HUCA	*Hebrew Union College Annual*
IBD	J. D. Douglas, ed., *Illustrated Bible Dictionary*, 3 vols. (Wheaton, Ill.: InterVarsity Press, 1980)
IDBSup	K. Crim, ed., *Interpreter's Dictionary of the Bible, Supplementary Volume* (Nashville: Abingdon, 1976)
IEJ	*Israel Exploration Journal*
JANES	*Journal of the Ancient Near Eastern Society of Columbia University*
JAOS	*Journal of the American Oriental Society*
JBL	*Journal of Biblical Literature*
JCS	*Journal of Cuneiform Studies*
JNES	*Journal of Near Eastern Studies*
JPS	Jewish Publication Society
JSOT	*Journal for the Study of the Old Testament*
JSOTSup	Journal for the Study of the Old Testament Supplements
JSS	*Journal of Semitic Studies*
KAI	H. Donner and W. Röllig, *Kanaanäische und Aramäische Inschriften*, 3d ed., 3 vols. (Wiesbaden: Harrassowitz, 1971–76)
LCL	Loeb Classical Library
LXX	Septuagint
MT	Masoretic Text
NAC	New American Commentary
NCB	New Century Bible
NICOT	New International Commentary on the Old Testament
NIDOTTE	W. A. VanGemeren, ed., *New International Dictionary of Old Testament Theology and Exegesis*, 5 vols. (Grand Rapids: Zondervan, 1997)
NRSV	New Revised Standard Version
OTL	Old Testament Library

OTS	*Oudtestamentische Studiën*
PI	J. C. L. Gibson, *Phoenician Inscriptions* (Oxford: Clarendon, 1982)
POS	Pretoria Oriental Series
RA	*Revue d'assyriologie et de l'archéologie orientale*
RAI	Rencontre assyriologique internationale
RB	*Revue biblique*
SANE	Sources from the Ancient Near East
SBLDS	Society of Biblical Literature Dissertation Series
SBLMS	Society of Biblical Literature Monograph Series
SBLRBS	Society of Biblical Literature Resources for Biblical Study
SBT	Studies in Biblical Theology
SJT	*Scottish Journal of Theology*
SWBA	Social World of Biblical Antiquity
TDNT	G. Kittel and G. Friedrich, eds., *Theological Dictionary of the New Testament*, trans. G. W. Bromiley, 10 vols. (Grand Rapids: Eerdmans, 1964–76)
TDOT	G. J. Botterweck et al., eds., *Theological Dictionary of the Old Testament* (Grand Rapids: Eerdmans, 1974–)
THAT	E. Jenni and C. Westermann, eds., *Theologisches Handwörterbuch zum Alten Testament*, 2 vols. (Munich: Chr. Kaiser, 1971–76)
TLOT	E. Jenni and C. Westermann, eds., *Theological Lexicon of the Old Testament*, trans. M. Biddle, 3 vols. (Peabody, Mass.: Hendrickson, 1997)
UF	*Ugarit-Forschungen*
UNP	S. B. Parker, ed., *Ugaritic Narrative Poetry*, SBLWAW 9 (Atlanta: Scholars Press, 1997)
UT	C. H. Gordon, *Ugaritic Textbook*, AnOr 38 (Rome: Pontifical Biblical Institute, 1965)
VAB	*Vorderasiatische Bibliothek*
VT	*Vetus Testamentum*
VTE	*Vassal Treaties of Esarhaddon*
VTSup	Vetus Testamentum Supplements
WBC	Word Biblical Commentary
WSS	N. Avigad, *Corpus of West Semitic Stamp Seals*, rev. and ed. B. Sass (Jerusalem: Israel Exploration Society, 1997)
ZA	*Zeitschrift für Assyriologie*
ZAW	*Zeitschrift für die alttestamentliche Wissenschaft*
ZDPV	*Zeitschrift des deutschen Palästina-Vereins*

Introduction

The rise of a spirit of nationalism among minorities who perceive themselves to be oppressed has been one of the most important influences on recent political and historical evolution. To cite one example, Canadians are keenly aware of the vitality and the strength of the separatist movement in Quebec. This movement has its roots in a consciousness of the uniqueness of the people of Quebec among the majority of the Canadian population. Many elements have contributed to this sense of distinctiveness: a common history, a common cultural heritage, a sense of ethnic cohesion, the occupation of a specific geographic territory identifiable by recognized boundaries, separate political institutions, and perhaps most significant, a distinctive language, French. In the past most Quebecois have shared a Roman Catholic religious tradition, as opposed to the rest of the country, which is more pluralistic. However, the religious dimension of the separatist movement has not received nearly the attention, either by the media or by politicians, that it enjoys in the development of, say, Irish nationalism. The conflict in Ireland is usually presented as a religious conflict, with the Roman Catholics struggling to shake off the shackles of minority Protestant rule.

The secular nature of many of the recent nationalistic revolutions around the world stands in sharp contrast to ancient Near Eastern perceptions. Scholars have been making notes on nationalistic movements in the ancient world for decades. The superficiality of many of these observations, however, has prompted me in recent times to engage in a systematic study of the subject. I have discovered that in the ancient Near East, more specifically in Syria,[1] the region bounded by the Taurus Mountains to the north, the Arabian desert to the east, the Sinai desert in the south, and the Mediterranean to the west, the development of national self-consciousness could be rooted in several different factors.

Among the Aramaeans and Phoenicians geographical and political considerations seem to have been paramount. States developed around cities. Their size and power often depended upon the personal ability of

1. Here the name is used in its broader sense. Where the narrower significance is required, that is, for the region occupied by the Aramaeans, the designation Aram will be used.

17

the ruling dynasty to assert and extend its influence. It is of considerable interest that neither of these large linguistic, if not ethnic, groups was able to unite all those who shared similar cultural, historical, and political traditions to form a single nation-state. We may speculate that this might eventually have transpired had the Assyrians not appeared on the scene to shatter all hopes of national ambition with their policy of the mass deportation of entire populations from conquered regions to other regions of the empire. As it happened, however, the movement toward unification, hints of which have been recognized here and there, aborted. Consequently, we may never speak of the nation of Aram or the nation of Phoenicia, if by "nation" we mean, "An extensive aggregate of persons, so closely associated with each other by common descent, language, or history, as to form a distinct race or people, usually organized as a separate state and occupying a definite territory."[2] This contrasts sharply with the political evolution of southern Syria. According to the biblical record, the latter part of the second millennium B.C. witnessed the emergence of a series of medium-sized states, Edom, Ammon, Moab, and Israel, each of which encompassed, to a greater or lesser degree, those of similar ethnic and historical heritage. This at least would appear to have been the perception of the Hebrews, who have provided us with the most extensive records. This difference between the developments in the northern and southern regions of Syria has convinced Buccellati to make a distinction between "national" and "territorial" states:

> A territorial state is one where the people identify themselves as dwellers of a given territory. A national state, on the other hand, is one where the people are aware of their identity as a group on the basis of other factors than simple contiguity within the same territory. What are these factors? First of all, the conception of *kin relationship* among the members of this group: the people conceive of themselves as descendants from a common ancestor, and they trace their history back to him.[3]

Common to nationalistic sensitivities throughout the ancient world, however, was the religious dimension. The ancient Near Easterner's recognition of divine involvement in all of human history, individual as well as corporate, is quite incomprehensible in the modern secular world. But according to the religious conceptions of all ancient Near

---

2. *The Compact Edition of the Oxford English Dictionary* (Oxford: Oxford University Press, 1971), 1897, s.v. "nation."

3. Georgio Buccellati, *Cities and Nations of Ancient Syria: An Essay on Political Institutions with Special Reference to the Israelite Kingdoms,* Studi Semitici 26 (Rome: Istituto di Studi del Vicino Oriente, 1967), 13–14.

Easterners, the affairs of the world in general and people in particular were subject to the wills and the actions of the gods. The sphere of influence of these divinities varied greatly, ranging from the limited authority of household deities, as, for example, in the case of the *teraphim*,[4] to the universal sovereignty exercised by the cosmic gods, most notably the heads of pantheons, such as Enlil in Sumer and Akkad, El at Ugarit, and Zeus in Greece. Between these two extremes a host of intermediate gods was recognized. One group, defined essentially in functional terms, included divinities such as the storm god (Baal-Hadad) and the goddess of war (Anath). The authority of others, such as the god of the sea (Yamm at Ugarit) or the gods of the mountains, was subject to geographical qualification. Such perceptions are dramatically illustrated by the strategy of the Aramaeans at the battle of Aphek (1 Kings 10:22–25). A third category was especially associated with a specific group of people, be this a tribe, a city, or an entire nation. Gods that were acknowledged to enjoy this special relationship with a group of people have been variously designated as patron,[5] titular, or national deities, terms that are often too easily interchanged.

Individual deities frequently exercised authority over more than one sphere. In addition to being especially favored in specific places, and by specific groups of people, many of the local gods of the ancient Near East were essentially functional divinities who received particular veneration among specific groups of people. Examples of these would be Hadad/Adad, the storm god, revered as Rimmon/Ramman in Damascus, and Astarte/Ishtar, the goddess of love as well as war.

The objective of the present study is to determine how the relationships that existed between deities and nations were perceived by ancient Near Easterners. My investigation considers four primary questions: (1) How did these deity-nation ties originate? (2) How was this relationship expressed in everyday speech? (3) What was the nature of this relationship? (4) Under what circumstances and in what manner could such associations be terminated? The study concludes

---

4. Cf. Gen. 31:34–35, on which see E. A. Speiser, *Genesis: Introduction, Translation and Notes*, AB 1 (Garden City, N.Y.: Doubleday, 1964), 249–50; C. H. Gordon, "Biblical Customs and the Nuzu Tablets," *BA* 3 (1940): 1–12; A. E. Draffkorn, "*ILĀNI/ELOHIM*," *JBL* 76 (1957): 216–24. For more recent discussions of *teraphim* see K.-H. Deller, "Die Hausgötter der Familie Sukrija S. Huja," in *Studies on the Civilization and Culture of Nuzi and the Hurrians*, ed. M. A. Morrison and D. I. Owen (Winona Lake, Ind.: Eisenbrauns, 1981), 47–76; T. J. Lewis, "Teraphim," in *DDD*, 1588–601.

5. Or matron, as in the case of Ishtar of Avbela. The use of the term "patron" throughout this study reflects the overwhelming preference for masculine deities as the primary gods of cities and lords throughout the ancient Near East. In the absence of a word that represents both matronly and patronly interests, the word "patron" should generally be interpreted inclusively.

with an examination of one specific biblical text, Ezekiel 8–11, to illustrate the importance and implications of the findings for the interpretation of the Old Testament.

In any discipline, the investigator's zeal for analysis may cause one to isolate much too sharply elements that should be viewed synthetically. Seldom is an object merely the sum of its parts. The complexity of ancient Near Eastern perceptions of national identity renders this cautionary note especially important. It should not be surprising that the peoples of ancient Syria were not uniform in their views concerning what made a people a nation. In the picture that emerges, however, it quickly becomes clear that, among other factors, the territorial and theological factors were viewed as critical throughout the region, whether one is dealing with the Aramaeans to the north or the Israelites to the south. The three-dimensional nature of the northwestern Semitic perspective may be illustrated by a triangle in which each of the members represents one apex:

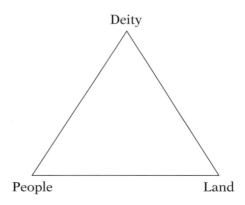

In this scheme of things each element is vital, not only because it is related to both of the other elements, but also because it has a significant bearing on the bond that unites the opposite members. So intertwined are the connections that it is often difficult to determine which bilateral association is to be considered the most significant. Consequently, as this study will show, it is impossible to examine the relationship of a god and his/her subjects in isolation from the ties of both deity and population to the land. Furthermore, a people's ties to its homeland cannot be understood without reference to some measure of divine involvement. In this study I attempt to explain why this is so and what effect it had on feelings of national self-consciousness.

The Origins of Deity-Nation Relations

In the attempt to understand ancient Near Eastern perceptions concerning a nation's or a people's relationship to its favored divinity, it seems logical to begin by exploring how such ties originated in the first place. Several different hypotheses may be proposed. First, the inhabitants of Syria in antiquity could have recognized the relationship between a divinity and his/her land as primary. In this case the ties between the god and the nation that occupied the land would have been viewed as secondary. Second, the relationship might first have been established between the deity and his/her people. Then the connections between the god and the land would have been treated as secondary. The ancient world provides evidence for both perceptions.

Significantly, the third possibility, that of a primary association between a people and its territory, with a resulting secondary involvement of the deity, seems to have been foreign to the northwestern Semites. This appears to be a uniquely modern and Western secular attitude toward nationality. The absence of this third alternative narrows the scope of this study. We need to examine only the first two perspectives.

The Priority of the Deity-Territory Tie

To date, no ancient Semitic text providing a detailed account of how specific gods came to be associated with specific lands has surfaced. Nevertheless, hints of the circumstances under which this was perceived to have transpired may be gleaned from several sources widely separated both geographically and chronologically. Two ancient Greek traditions deserve notice. Homer wrote:

> [W]e are three brothers born by Rhea to Kronos, Zeus, and I [i.e., Poseidon], and the third is Hades, lord of the dead men. All was divided among us three ways, each given his domain. I, when the lots were shaken, drew the grey sea to live in forever; Hades drew the lot of the mists and the

darkness, and Zeus was allotted the wide sky, in the cloud and the bright air. But the earth and high Olympus are common to all three.[1]

Although the text does not deal specifically with the division of the lands among the gods, one may make three observations: (1) Kronos, the highest deity, appears to have presided over this distribution; (2) the allocations were made by means of the lot; (3) the spheres apportioned to the gods were geographic rather than demographic. In spite of the epithet for Hades, "lord of the dead men," the text designates his domain as the netherworld, not the dead.

The seventh-century B.C. author Pindar described the division of the earth among immortals:

> But the tale is told in ancient story that, when Zeus and the immortals were dividing the earth among them, and the isle of Rhodes was not yet to be seen in the open main, but was hidden in the briny depths of the sea; and that, as the Sun-god was absent, no one put forth a lot on his behalf, and so they left him without any allotment of land, though the god himself was pure from blame. But when that god made mention of it, Zeus was about to order a new casting of the lot, but the Sun-god would not suffer it. For, as he said, he could see a plot of land rising from the bottom of the foaming main, a plot that was destined to prove rich in substance for men, and kindly for pasture; and he urged that Lachesis of the golden snood should forthwith lift up her hands and take, not in vain, the great oath of the gods, but consent with the Son of Cronus, that that island, when it had risen forth into the light of day, should forever be a boon granted to himself alone. And all these several words were fulfilled and fell out truly.

The text goes on to describe the marriage of the sun god to the nymph of the island, a marriage that produced seven sons. Three grandsons were eventually also born, each having his own city and calling his dwelling after his own name.[2] Again we observe the presence of a pre-

---

1. Iliad 15.189–93, as translated by R. Lattimore, *The Iliad of Homer* (Chicago: University of Chicago Press, 1951), 314. For the Greek text see W. Leaf, ed., *The Iliad*, 2d ed., 2 vols. (Amsterdam: Hakkert, 1971), 2:117–18. Cf. also the text and translation by A. T. Murray, *Homer, The Iliad*, LCL, 2 vols. (Cambridge: Harvard University Press, 1963), 1:120–21.

2. *Olympian Odes* 7.55–76. For the Greek text and translation see J. Sandys, trans., *The Odes of Pindar*, LCL (Cambridge: Harvard University Press, 1961), 76–79. This text has been overlooked by H. O. Forshey in his study of extrabiblical parallels to Deut. 32:8–9, "The Hebrew Root *NḤL* and Its Semitic Cognates" (Th.D. diss., Harvard University, 1973), 89–92. Forshey does, however, mention Hesiod's *Theogony* 881–85 in this context. But this text is not as significant for the discussion as he suggests, since it deals with the exaltation of Zeus and the distribution of honors among other members of the pantheon. For the Greek text see Hesiod, *Theogony*, ed. M. L. West (Oxford: Clarendon, 1966), 144. See also the text and trans-

siding officer, in this instance Zeus, and the employment of the lot as the means of distribution. More important, however, is the concern again with territories rather than peoples.

Nearer to our geographical area of concern is a Sumerian tradition according to which "Enlil, king of all the lands, the father of all the gods, marked off the boundary of Ningursu and Shara by his steadfast word," the latter being the patron deities of Lagash and Umma, respectively.[3] An Old Babylonian text, *Atra-Ḥasīs* I:1–18, provides an early Semitic account of the division of realms among the gods:

> When the gods like men
> Bore the work and suffered the toil—
> The toil of the gods was great,
> The work was heavy, the distress was much—
> The Seven great Anunnaki
> Were making the Igigi suffer the work.
> Anu, their father, was the king;
> Their counsellor was the warrior Enlil;
> Their chamberlain was Ninurta;
> And their sheriff Ennugi.
> The gods had clasped hands together,
> Had cast lots and divided.
> Anu had gone up to heaven,
> [. .] . . . the earth to his subjects.
> [The bolt], the bar of the sea,
> [They had given] to Enki, the prince.
> [After Anu] had gone up to heaven
> [And Enki] had gone down to the Apsu.[4]

The text resembles the Homeric citation in two respects. In the first place, its interest is not in the distribution of the various lands among the gods, but in the cosmic spheres of the high deities, Anu, Enlil, and Enki. To these divinities are allocated the heavens, the earth, and the

---

lation provided by H. G. Evelyn-White, *Theogony*, LCL (Cambridge: Harvard University Press, 1959), 142–43.

3. S. N. Kramer comments, "The sentence states the current belief that after the creation of the world, the two cities were allotted to the two gods as their personal possession and property, and that Enlil himself as the head of the gods had drawn the boundary lines between them" ("Sumerian Historiography," *IEJ* 3 [1953]: 224 n. 11).

4. For the Akkadian text and translation see W. G. Lambert and A. R. Millard, *Atra-Ḥasīs: The Babylonian Story of the Flood* (Oxford: Clarendon, 1969), 42–43. For a slightly different reading cf. W. von Soden, "Die erste Tafel des altbabylonischen Atrāhasis-Mythus. 'Haupttext' und Parallel-versionen," *ZA* 68 (1978): 54–55. For more recent English translations of the text see *BM* 1:159–60; S. Dalley, *Myths from Mesopotamia: Creation, the Flood, Gilgamesh, and Others* (Oxford: Oxford University Press, 1989), 9.

waters beneath the earth, respectively.[5] Second, here also the allotments are decided by casting lots (*isqum*, "lot").

Strictly speaking, the following second-millennium B.C. text from Ugarit deals with universal/cosmic gods (who elsewhere were recognized as patrons of particular cities), rather than the allocation of specific lands to their respective divinities; nevertheless *'nt* VI:12–17 seems to presuppose some such event.

idk.al.ttn/pnm	You must head off
tk.ḥqkpt/il.klh	To Memphis,[6] (to) the god of it all,
kptr/ksu.tbth	(To) Crete,[7] (which is) the throne (on which) he sits,
ḥkpt/arṣ.nḥlth	(to) Memphis (which is) the land of his own possession.[8]

This text portrays Egypt and Kaphtor (Crete) as the domain, the possession (*nḥlt*), of *Ktr wḥss*, the craftsman god, whom scholars identify with Ptah, the Egyptian counterpart.[9]

Eusebius provides the most important extrabiblical source for the origins of the territorial claims of the gods.[10] Although the written text originated in the Christian era, it is based upon the accounts of Sanchu-

---

5. So Lambert and Millard, *Atra-Ḥasīs*, 8. Although the text does not state specifically that this was the purpose of the lots, the context generally appears to suggest it. For a discussion of the allocations of regions to gods in Mesopotamian mythology see W. G. Lambert, "Myth and Mythmaking in Sumer and Akkad," in *Civilizations of the Ancient Near East*, ed. J. M. Sasson (New York: Scribner, 1995), 1:1827–29.

6. As in the Amarna correspondence, Egypt is identified here by the native name for Memphis. The Greeks later use it to refer to the Nile Valley. Cf. W. F. Albright, *From the Stone Age to Christianity: Monotheism and the Historical Process*, 2d ed. (Garden City, N.Y.: Doubleday, 1957), 216; idem, "Recent Progress in North Canaanite Research," *BASOR* 70 (1938): 22; H. L. Ginsburg, "Two Religious Borrowings in Ugaritic Literature," part II: "The Egyptian God Ptah in Ugaritic Mythology," *Orientalia*, n.s., 9 (1940): 39–44. G. R. Driver, *Canaanite Myths and Legends*, Old Testament Studies 3 (Edinburgh: Clark, 1956), 90, inserts *'m . ktr . wḥss* after this line. But J. C. L. Gibson, editor of the second edition (*Canaanite Myths and Legends*, 2d ed. [1977], 55 n. 1), prefers the text as it stands, interpreting the phrase literally, "Memphis of El, all of it."

7. Gibson (*Canaanite Myths and Legends*, 2d ed., 55 n. 2) rejects the common identification of *kptr* with Crete.

8. As translated by D. Pardee, "The Ba'lu Myth," in *CCBW*, 255. For the Ugaritic text and translation see also M. S. Smith, *UNP*, 119.

9. Cf. W. F. Albright, *Yahweh and the Gods of Canaan: A Historical Analysis of Two Contrasting Faiths* (Garden City, N.Y.: Doubleday, 1968), 135–38; idem, *Stone Age to Christianity*, 216; J. Gray, *The Legacy of Canaan: The Ras Shamra Texts and Their Relevance to the Old Testament*, VTSup 5 (Leiden: Brill, 1957), 137. On the deity Kothar/Koshar see M. S. Smith, "Kothar waḤasis, the Ugaritic Craftsman God" (Ph.D. diss., Yale University, 1985); D. Pardee, "Koshar," *DDD*, 913–17.

10. *Praeparatio Evangelica* 1.10.31–41. For the Greek text and a French translation see J. Sirinelli and E. des Places, trans. and eds., *La préparation évangélique*, Sources chrétiennes 206 (Paris: Cerf, 1974), 200. For the English translation see Eusebius, *Preparation for the Gospel*, trans. E. G. Gifford (1903; reprint, Grand Rapids: Baker, 1981), 37–47.

niathon, a Phoenician historian probably from the seventh century B.C.[11] In his recollection of the tradition, Eusebius notes that after Kronos had visited the various regions of the habitable world, he granted the Mediterranean city-states of Attica, Byblos, and Berytus to Athena, Baaltis, and Poseidon respectively, and the land of Egypt to Taautos.[12] The passage does not indicate the circumstances of the first three allotments, but the allocation of Egypt's territory follows Taautos's designing of the royal ensign for Kronos. It may have represented a reward for services rendered.[13]

Several common features may be recognized in these texts. First, none depicts a deity wresting territory from another deity or gaining it by military victory. On the contrary, in each instance the allotment appears to have proceeded under peaceful circumstances. Where the procedure is noted, the allocations are made either by lot[14] or as outright grants.[15] Second, in several the highest deity appears to have played the leading role.[16] Third, and most important for our discussion, in each case the relationships established are between deities and lands, without respect to the inhabitants of the land. The texts all portray the lands as the realms of the gods.

The Priority of the Deity-People Tie

The only available evidence for a prior and primary association of deity and people derives from the Hebrew Old Testament and writings based thereon. The most important witness to this view is undoubtedly Deut. 32:8–9. But the textual problems here are acute, and before I offer an interpretation of the passage, these difficulties need to be explained. The problems surface when we compare the Masoretic reading (MT) on the one hand and the Septuagint (LXX) and Vulgate renderings on the

---

11. So also O. Eissfeldt, *Ras Schamra und Sanchuniathon* (Halle: Niemeyer, 1939), 67–71. Albright (*Stone Age to Christianity*, 317 n. 57), although personally favoring the seventh-century date, indicates that the sixth century is also possible. Eusebius did not receive his information directly from Sanchuniathon but through the mediation of Philo of Byblos. The historical fragments of Philo are conveniently collected by F. Jacoby, *Die Fragmente der griechischen Historiker*, part 3C (Leiden: Brill, 1969), no. 790, 802–24. For a helpful study of Philo's history and the nature of its transmission see J. Barr, "Philo of Byblos and His 'Phoenician History,'" *BJRL* 57 (1974): 17–68.

12. Οἰκουμένη, rendered "terre habittée" by Sirinelli and des Places, *La préparation évangélique*, 200.

13. Cf. Barr, "Philo of Byblos," 29. The text does not indicate how this relationship began, but according to *Praeparatio Evangelica* 1.10.38, Tyre appears similarly to belong to Astarte.

14. *Atra-Ḥasīs* I:11–12; Homer, *Iliad* 15.189–93; Pindar, *Olympian Odes* 7.55–76.

15. Sanchuniathon.

16. Homer, Pindar, Sanchuniathon.

other. The discrepancies may be highlighted by juxtaposing MT with
the hypothetical *Vorlage* of LXX:

MT	LXX[17]
běhanḥēl ʿelyôn gôyim	*běhanḥēl ʿelyôn gôyim*
běhaprîdô běnê ʾādām	*běhaprîdô běnê ʾādām*
yaṣṣēb gěbulōt ʿammîm	*yaṣṣēb gěbulōt ʿammîm*
lěmispar běnê yiśrāʾēl	*lěmispar běnê ʾĕlōhîm*
kî ḥēleq yhwh ʿammô[18]	*kî ḥēleq yhwh ʿammô yaʿăqōb*
yaʿăqōb ḥebel naḥălātô	*ḥebel naḥălātô yiśrāʾēl.*

Translation of MT	**Translation of LXX**
When Elyon gave the nations their patrimony,	When Elyon gave the nations their patrimony,
When he separated the sons of man,	When he separated the sons of man,
He established the boundaries of the peoples	He established the boundaries of the peoples
According to the number of the **sons of Israel.**	According to the number of the **sons of God.**
For the portion of Yahweh is his people;	For the portion of Yahweh is his people Jacob,
Jacob is the allotment of his patrimony.	The allotment of his patrimony is Israel.

The first three lines are in complete agreement. Yahweh, who is here
identified by the lofty title Elyon,[19] not only separated the *běnê ʾādām*

---

17. The Greek text reads as follows:

    ὅτε διεμέριζεν ὁ ὕψιστος ἔθνη,
    ὡς διέσπειρεν υἱοὺς Αδαμ,
    ἔστησεν ὅρια ἐθνῶν
    κατὰ ἀριθμὸν ἀγγέλων θεοῦ,
    καὶ ἐγενήθη μερὶς κυρίου λαὸς αὐτοῦ Ιακωβ,
    σχοίνισμα κληρονομίας αὐτοῦ Ισραηλ.

18. *ʿammô* is commonly deleted for metrical reasons. See, for example, P. Skehan,
"The Structure of the Song of Moses in Deuteronomy (Deut. 32:1–43)," *CBQ* 13 (1951):
154 n. 6, who sees in *ʿammô* "a (purposeful?) duplication from vs. 8; the disappearance
of *Yiśrāʾēl* from vs. 9 (where LXX has it) is a reflex of its substitution for *ʾEl* in vs. 8. The
place of the caesura in vs. 9 is clearly dictated by considerations of metre and parallelism,
once these points are recognized." Cf. Forshey, "Hebrew Root *NḤL*," 137.

19. O. Eissfeldt argued that Elyon should be understood as a personal name of the
highest deity, the one who apportioned the nations to the members of the pantheon, including Yahweh ("El and Yahweh," *JSS* 1 [1956]: 25–27; idem, *Das Lied Moses Deuteronomium 32:1–43 und das Lehrgedicht Asaphs Psalm 78 samt einer Analyse der Umgebung des
Mose-Liedes* [Berlin: Akademie Verlag, 1958], 9 n. 1). It seems preferable, however, to interpret the two names as parallel designations of the same deity. So also W. F. Albright,
"Some Remarks on the Song of Moses in Deuteronomy XXXII," *VT* 9 (1959): 343; M. Tse-
vat, "God and the Gods in Assembly: An Interpretation of Psalm 82," *HUCA* 40–41 (1969–
70): 132 n. 28; Forshey, "Hebrew Root *NḤL*," 139 n. 78; E. E. Elnes and P. D. Miller Jr.,
"Elyon," *DDD*, 566.

into their respective *ʿammîm*; he also apportioned for each, as a politically identifiable entity,[20] a territorial possession, specifically establishing the boundaries (*gĕbulôt*) thereof.[21] The sense is clear: whatever territorial ties the nations enjoyed, these were to be attributed to Yahweh. This is in keeping with earlier notices in Deuteronomy concerning the inviolability of Mount Seir as the territory of the descendants of Esau (Deut. 2:5), Ar as the territory of the Moabites (Deut. 2:9), and the re-

20. On the political nature of *gôy*, see D. I. Block, *The Foundations of National Identity: A Study in Ancient Northwest Semitic Perceptions* (Ann Arbor: University Microfilms, 1983), 84–127, 493–509; idem, "Nations," *NIDOTTE* 4:966.

21. On the significance of *gĕbûl* see Block, *Foundations*, 319–27. Forshey has argued that the notion of Israel as the *naḥălat yhwh* dates to exilic times, after the territorial link with Yahweh had been severed. See "Hebrew Root *NḤL*," chaps. 3, 5; idem, "Segullah and Nachalah as Designations of the Covenant Community," *Hebrew Abstracts* 15 (1974): 86; idem, "The Construct Chain *naḥᵃlat yhwh/*ᵉlōhîm*," *BASOR* 220 (1975): 51–53. To defend this thesis Forshey must treat each reference to the people as *naḥălat yhwh* in one of two ways: either the text is dated late, or the expression applies to the land rather than the people. Although he dates Deuteronomy 32 during the time of the Assyrian crisis (contra Eissfeldt and Albright, who defend an eleventh-century B.C. date, but drawing support from G. E. Wright, "The Lawsuit of God: A Form-Critical Study of Deuteronomy 32," in *Israel's Prophetic Heritage*, James Muilenburg Festschrift, ed. B. W. Anderson and W. Harrelson [New York: Harper, 1962], 67, who dates the poem in the ninth century), Forshey treats this text in the latter way ("Hebrew Root *NḤL*," 136–38). However, this interpretation suffers because:

(1) The retention of *ʿammô* in v. 9a may be defended on metrical grounds. As it stands, MT consists of two perfectly balanced seven-syllable stichoi arranged in common chiastic parallelism. To delete *ʿammô* and then shift *yaʿăqōb* to the end of the first line and insert *yiśrāʾēl* at the end of the second to restore metrical balance (so Skehan, "Structure," loc. cit.; R. Meyer, "Die Bedeutung von Deuteronomium 32,8f. 43 [4Q] für die Auslegung des Moseliedes," in *Verbannung und Heimkehr*, W. Rudolph Festschrift, ed. A. Kuschke [Tübingen: Mohr, 1961], 199–200) is unnecessary.

(2) Although *ḥēleq*, *gĕbûlâ*, *ḥebel*, and *naḥălâ* are all associated with landed terminology, the allocation of lands is not the only subject treated in these verses. They also deal with the prior division of peoples and nations. The allocation of lands is a secondary development.

(3) Jacob, as an independent name, is never employed as a territorial designation (cf. Block, *Foundations*, 254–59).

(4) The succeeding verses (10–11) are clearly concerned with the community rather than the land of Israel. But cf. P. Winter, "Der Begriff 'Söhne Gottes' im Moselied Dtn. 32 1–43," *ZAW* 67 (1955): 40–48, who isolates v. 9 from the succeeding verses on internal grounds.

(5) The related texts (Deut. 4:20; 9:26–29; and 1 Kings 8:51, 53) are acknowledged by Forshey, "Hebrew Root *NḤL*," 178–79, as unambiguous references to the community (these, however, are all ascribed to a second deuteronomistic redaction and dated in the exile, Forshey, "Hebrew Root *NḤL*," 174–80). Deuteronomy 32:8–9 presents an intentional contrast: whereas the lands were assigned to their respective nations (not vice versa) and indirectly to their patrons, Yahweh reserved Israel, the people, for himself as his own possession.

For a summary of the issues related to the dating of Deuteronomy 32 see J. H. Tigay, *Deuteronomy*, JPS Torah Commentary (Philadelphia: Jewish Publication Society, 1996), 509–13. On pp. 514–15 Tigay discusses 32:8 in particular.

gion occupied by the Ammonites (Deut. 2:19). These Yahweh had given to their respective inhabitants as their *yĕruššâ*, "possession."[22]

So far MT and LXX agree. But in the statement concerning the principle on which the division of the nations and the allocation of their territories was based (v. 8d), the two recensions diverge. According to MT the number of nations isolated was determined by the number of the sons of Israel. In view of the prominence of the sons of Jacob in the patriarchal traditions, the association with the number twelve is natural.[23] Indeed, this is the figure adopted by the shorter paraphrase of the passage in Targum Neofiti I:

> When the Most High gave the nations inheritance, when he divided the languages of the sons of humankind, (he) set up boundaries for the nations according to the number of the tribes of the sons of Israel; for the portion of the Lord was his people, the children of Israel; Jacob the lot of his inheritance.[24]

More commonly, however, the figure has been related to the number of Jacob's descendants who accompanied him down into Egypt.[25] Thus the second, more expanded paraphrase of our text in Targum Pseudo-Jonathan reads:

> When the Most High gave the world as an inheritance to the peoples who came from the sons of Noah, when he divided the writings and languages among mankind, in the generation of the division, at that time, he cast lots on seventy angels, the leaders of the nations, with whom it was revealed to see the city; and at that time he established the borders of the nations according to the sum of the number of the seventy souls of Israel who went down to Egypt.[26]

This text conflates ideas derived from the Table of Nations (Genesis 10), the account of the Tower of Babel (Gen. 11:1–9), and the references to

---

22. On the significance of *yĕruššâ*, cf. Block, *Foundations*, 425–26; C. J. H. Wright, "ירש," *NIDOTTE* 2:547–48. It should be noted, however, that Yahweh's authority over international boundaries was not limited to this original occasion; they continued to be subject to his control (Isa. 10:13), as is witnessed by his action of "cutting off" from the land of Israel (2 Kings 10:32), and in transferring entire groups of people from one region to another. See here Amos 9:7. Cf. Acts 17:26.

23. Gen. 35:22–26; 49:28; Num. 1:44; 17:17, 21 (17:2, 6 Eng.); etc.

24. As translated by M. McNamara, *Targum Neofiti I: Deuteronomy. Translated with Apparatus and Notes*, Aramaic Bible 5A (Collegeville, Minn.: Liturgical Press, 1997), 151.

25. Cf. LXX, which has 75 in both instances. For a discussion of these texts see D. Barthélemy, "Les tiqquné sopherim et la critique textuelle de l'Ancien Testament," *Congress Volume: Bonn, 1962*, VTSup 9 (Leiden: Brill, 1963): 300–301.

26. As translated by E. J. Clarke, *Targum Pseudo-Jonathan: Deuteronomy. Translated with Notes*, Aramaic Bible 5B (Collegeville, Minn.: Liturgical Press, 1998), 90.

the number of Jacob's household (Gen. 46:26–27; Exod. 1:5). It also appears to incorporate notions from both variants of Deut. 32:8. Insofar as both paraphrases refer to the sons of Israel, however, they seem to be based upon the same tradition as MT.[27]

In 1951 Skehan argued for the priority of LXX, claiming that MT was the product of a pious Jew, living in a polytheistic world, in which the recognition of supernatural beings alongside God presented serious theological difficulties.[28] A fragment of Deuteronomy 32 from the fourth cave at Qumran, published in 1954 by the same author, has provided strong support for this view,[29] and most scholars are now convinced that LXX has preserved the original reading.[30] According to this recension, the *běnê ʾĕlōhîm*, whose number provided the basis for the division of the nations, should be seen as members of God's heavenly court, that is, the angels.[31] Consequently, each nation was perceived to have been identified with its own patron angel. According to verse 9, however, Israel's status was special. She was not to be supervised by an intermediary being as were the rest—Yahweh had selected her for his own personal care.

Support for this perspective, if not this reading of the text, is both ancient and widespread. The prose texts of Deuteronomy speak of the sun, moon, and stars as having been apportioned for all the people; Israel, on

27. Cf. also Rashi's commentary, s.v.: *"lmspr bny yśrʾl* According to the number of the children of Israel—i.e., because of the number of the children of Israel that were in the future to descend from Shem's sons, and in accordance with the number of the seventy souls of the children of Israel who went down to Egypt he firmly established the *gblt ʿmym"* (*Pentateuch with Targum Onkelos, Haphtorah and Prayers for Sabbath and Rashi's Commentary,* ed. A. M. Silbermann, 5 vols. [London: Shapiro, Valentine, 1946], 5:160).

28. Skehan, "Structure," 154. It has been suggested by O. Loretz, "Die Vorgeschichte von Deuteronomium 32,8f. 43," *UF* 9 (1977): 355–57, that this alteration was made in Hasmonean times. Cf. Barthélemy, "Les tiqquné sopherim," 297, where a detailed discussion is provided. For another defense of this position cf. Winter, "Begriff 'Söhne Gottes,'" 40–48.

29. P. Skehan, "A Fragment of the 'Song of Moses' (Deut. 32) from Qumran," *BASOR* 136 (1954): 12–15. Where MT has *bny yśrʾl,* the fragment has . . . *bny ʾl*[..... . This reading has been filled out to *bny ʾlym* by subsequent discoveries. See idem, "Qumran and the Present State of Old Testament Text Studies: The Masoretic Text," *JBL* 78 (1959): 21.

30. See Tigay, *Deuteronomy,* 514–15.

31. On which see F. M. Cross, "The Council of Yahweh in Second Isaiah," *JNES* 12 (1953): 274–77; P. D. Miller Jr., *The Divine Warrior in Early Israel,* HSM 5 (Cambridge: Harvard University Press, 1973), 12–23. Albright (*Stone Age to Christianity,* 297), suggested that these *běnê ʾĕlōhîm* were the stars. Cf. Job 38:7. Later, however, in "Remarks on the Song of Moses," 343 n. 1, he noted that the emphasis was not on the stars as such but on the angels, who function as members of the heavenly assembly. The expression *bn ʾlm* has surfaced in a recently discovered Ammonite text. See Kent P. Jackson, *The Ammonite Language of the Iron Age,* HSM 27 (Chico, Calif.: Scholars Press, 1983), 9–33, esp. 23–24. For a different interpretation see A. van Selms, "Some Remarks on the ʿAmmān Citadel Inscriptions," *BiOr* 32 (1975): 6.

the other hand, is not to be deluded into worshiping these heavenly bodies (Deut. 4:19–20; cf. 29:24–25 [29:25–26 Eng.]). The texts suggest that some correlation should be made between the *běnê ʾĕlōhîm* referred to in 32:8 and these heavenly bodies.[32] Speaking explicitly of the "prince (*śār*) of the kingdom of Persia" who was successful in delaying the arrival of the heavenly messenger for Daniel's assistance, Dan. 10:13 seems to be based on related notions.[33] In the apocryphal and pseudepigraphical writings these ideas appear repeatedly. For example, Ben Sirach comments, "For every nation he appointed a ruler; but Israel is the Lord's portion" (Sir. 17:17). Jubilees 15.30b–32 is even more specific:

> But he chose Israel that they might be a people for himself. And he sanctified them and gathered them from all of the sons of man because (there are) many nations and many people, and they all belong to him, but over all of them he caused spirits to rule so that they might lead them astray from following him. But over Israel he did not cause any angel or spirit to rule because he alone is their ruler and he will protect them and he will seek for them at the hand of his angels and at the hands of his spirits and at the hand of all of his authorities so that he might guard them and bless them and they might be his and he might be theirs henceforth and forever.[34]

In the New Testament, Paul reflects traditional Hebrew thought when he emphasizes to the Athenians the determinative role God has played in establishing all national-territorial associations: "[A]nd he

32. Note the use of *ḥēleq* in both contexts. In 4:19–20 the heavenly bodies are allotted (*ḥēleq*) to the peoples, whereas Yahweh takes Israel out of Egypt to be a people for his own possession (*ʿam naḥălâ*). In 32:8–9 the term *ḥēleq* is applied to Israel as the allotment of Yahweh. Skehan ("Structure," 155), observes that the former does not imply an endorsement on the part of the writer of the worship of the heavenly bodies; the language is mythological and poetic.

33. The reference to Michael as the prince who guards the sons of Israel (Dan. 10:13; 12:1) appears to contradict the Deuteronomic statement. The differences in perspective derive from the divergent aims of the texts. Deuteronomy 32:8 intends to highlight Israel's special status and the nation's special relationship with Yahweh, vis-à-vis the nations. In Daniel, Michael serves as the heavenly agent charged with the defense of Israel. Yahweh's role as their patron need not preclude the employment of other spiritual beings to care for his own.

34. Translation by O. S. Wintermute in *The Old Testament Pseudepigrapha*, ed. J. H. Charlesworth, 2 vols. (Garden City, N.Y.: Doubleday, 1983–85), 2:87. A late Hebrew version of the Testament of Naphtali 8:3–10:5 has each of the nations choosing its own deity, rather than Yahweh appointing the former to the latter. Abraham alone is said to have chosen Yahweh. It was after this matter had been taken care of that the territorial allotments were made, this time, however, by Yahweh. For the text see R. H. Charles, ed., *The Apocrypha and Pseudepigrapha of the Old Testament*, 2 vols., *Pseudepigrapha* (Oxford: Clarendon, 1913), 2:363. The Old Testament does occasionally refer to Israel as having chosen its deity(ies). In each case, however, they have apostatized from their national deity. Cf. Judg. 10:14; Isa. 41:24; Jer. 2:11–13.

made from one every nation of mankind to live on all the face of the earth, having determined their appointed times, and the boundaries of their habitation" (Acts 17:26).

If the fragment from 4Q and LXX do indeed preserve the original reading of Deut. 32:8–9, the persistence in later writings of the number seventy as the number of angelic beings and nations remains a problem.[35] Whereas those who followed the Masoretic tradition had a ready answer in the seventy descendants of Jacob, this solution is now precluded. The text itself provides no clue. Some have suggested that underlying this text is a Canaanite tradition that associates the *běnê ᵓělôhîm* with the seventy *banu Athirat*, "sons of Athirat," of the Ugaritic texts.[36] This interpretation is far-fetched, however, and it is preferable to search for a solution within Israel's own traditions. Although the biblical authors never speak specifically of seventy nations, it is more likely that we should associate Deut. 32:8 with the tradition that provides the background to the Table of Nations in Genesis 10. With a limited amount of adjustment we notice that the list contains the names of seventy nations.[37] The late version of the Testament of Naphtali, in which Nimrod is specifically associated with Cush,[38] as well as the longer paraphrase of Deut. 32:8–9 in Targum Pseudo-Jonathan,[39] demonstrates that people made this association in later times. In view of the use of the verb *pārad* in both texts, this connection may also be defended on internal grounds.[40]

35. For citations and discussion see Meyer, "Bedeutung," 204–7; Barthélemy, "Les tiqquné sopherim," 295–303.

36. *UNP*, 10.VI,46, p. 134. So R. Tournay, "Les psaumes complexes," part 1, *RB* 56 (1949): 53; Albright, "Remarks on the Song of Moses," 343; Barthélemy, "Les tiqquné sopherim," 295–97; M. S. Smith, *UNP*, 171 n. 135.

37. Nimrod is to be excluded since he is clearly presented as an individual, rather than a national figure. The same applies to the Philistines, who are mentioned only in an appended note. On the other hand, it may be unnecessary to demand an exact figure of seventy in the table. So also Umberto Cassuto, *A Commentary on the Book of Genesis*, trans. I. Abrahams, vol. 2, *From Noah to Abraham* (Jerusalem: Magnes, 1964), 175–76. Cassuto sees in the number seventy a perfect figure, reflective of an ideal creation. However, Barthélemy ("Les tiqquné sopherim," 296 n. 5), insists that the number of "begetters" and "sons" in the table is exactly seventy. For a fuller discussion see D. I. Block, "Table of Nations," in *International Standard Bible Encyclopedia*, rev. ed. (Grand Rapids: Eerdmans, 1988), 4:707–13.

38. 9:1–4. Cf. supra, n. 34. Nimrod's name appears only in the table (Gen. 10:8–9; 1 Chron. 1:10) and Mic. 5:5 (5:6 Eng.).

39. Cf. supra.

40. Deuteronomy 32:8 uses the Hiphil stem with Elyon as subject; Gen. 10:5 and 32 both have Niphal forms. Skehan's suggestion that the number may derive from the analogy of Moses and the seventy elders, similar in size to the Jewish Sanhedrin, is without objective support. Cf. his "Structure," 162–63. Cf. also the reference to the seventy shepherds of Israel in 1 Enoch 89:59; E. Isaac, "I (Ethiopic Apocalypse of) Enoch," in *Old Testament Pseudepigrapha*, ed. Charlesworth, 1:68.

If one assumes the originality of the tradition reflected by LXX and the 4Q fragment renderings of Deut. 32:8–9, the chronological sequence of events appears to have run as follows: (1) Originally the heavenly court consisted of Yahweh, the presiding deity, and a host of lesser beings identified variously as *běnê ʾĕlōhîm*, "the sons of God," princes, or angels. (2) God divided humankind (*běnê ʾādām*) into a series of peoples/nations whose total corresponded to the number of members in the heavenly court. One of the latter was designated as the patron and guardian over each of the former. (3) Israel, however, received special treatment inasmuch as Yahweh selected her for his own direct care; she would need no intermediary patron. (4) For each of the nations Yahweh allocated a specific geographical region to be possessed and occupied. According to this interpretation, the priority of the deity-people over the deity-land association, a notion unique to Israel, is confirmed.[41]

Conclusion

The Israelite perspective, which understood Yahweh to have established a relationship with them as a nation independent of and prior to their association with the land belonging to Yahweh, appears to have broken new ground in ancient Semitic thought.[42] The evidence of extra-biblical sources not dependent upon the Old Testament points to a view that is quite different: Deities were primarily attached to specific geographic territories and only secondarily concerned with the inhabitants of those areas. This geocentricity in national theology mirrors political perceptions.

The evidence is admittedly less than complete for the northwestern Semites. Nevertheless, they appear to have followed the pattern of the Mesopotamians in viewing neighboring regions primarily as lands to be conquered and annexed (particularly if those regions were hostile),[43] rather than as peoples to incorporate into the empire. But humans shared this disposition with the gods. The primary concern of deities was the land ascribed to them; the identity of the inhabitants of those lands seems to have been relatively immaterial.

41. So also F. Dreyfus, "Le thème de l'héritage dans l'Ancien Testament," *Revue des sciences philosophiques et théologiques* 42 (1958): 30–31.

42. However, one should note that the Hebrews possessed long-standing traditions of their title to the land, based on God's promises to the fathers. For a discussion of this issue see Claus Westermann, *The Promises to the Fathers: Studies on the Patriarchal Narratives*, trans. D. E. Green (Philadelphia: Fortress, 1980), 143–49. He lists the relevant biblical texts on p. 143.

43. Thus A. R. Millard in private communication.

This stands in sharp contrast to the national theology of the Israelites. Although these perspectives may have gained acceptance among those who apostatized in their faith, orthodox Yahwists acknowledged the God of Israel as a deity who had called a people to himself to be his people. He was not merely a divinity who had acquired a plot of real estate and then accepted as his own whatever population happened to inhabit his land.

The effects of this radical shift in the interpretation of the origin of the association between deity and people on other aspects of national theology and historiography are apparent throughout the Old Testament. Indeed, they spill over into the New, where the church, the new Israel, becomes the people of God. But the pursuit of this fascinating topic would take us far beyond the scope of the present investigation.

The Expression of the Deity-Nation Relationship

It is difficult to determine the nature of popular religion in ancient Syria, outside Israel.[1] Because much of the preserved evidence derives from official circles, the extent to which they express general sentiments is unclear. What appear in the inscriptions to be presented as patron deities may have been nothing more than the favorite gods of individual kings, dynasties, or priestly/religious functionaries. Kilamuwa's ninth-century B.C. inscription from Zenjirli identifies the gods of two of his predecessors, "Baʿl-ṣamad who belongs to Gabbar,"[2] and "Baʿl-ḥamman who belongs to BMH." The text concludes with an invocation to *rkb ʾl bʿl bt*, "Rakab-El, lord of the dynasty."[3] Similarly, Ben-Hadad of Damascus identified Melqart as "his lord" on the Melqart Stela.[4] In the bilingual inscription on the skirt of Hadad-yisʿi, king of Gozan, this official refers to Hadad of Sikan as "the great lord, the lord of Hadad-yisʿi, king of Gozan."[5]

1. Cf. J. Teixidor, *The Pagan God: Popular Religion in the Greco-Roman World* (Princeton: Princeton University Press, 1977), 3–61. For a more recent attempt at describing late monarchic piety in Israel see R. Albertz, *A History of Israelite Religion in the Old Testament Period*, vol. 1, *From the Beginnings to the End of the Monarchy*, trans. J. Bowden, OTL (Louisville: Westminster/John Knox, 1994), 186–95.

2. *bʿl smd ʾš lgbr*. See *KAI* 24:15; and *ANET*, 655.

3. *KAI* 24:16; *ANET*, 655. An eighth-century B.C. successor to Kilamuwa, Barrakab, also speaks of Rakab-El as "my lord" (*mrʾy rkbʾl*), *KAI* 216:5; *ANET*, 655.

4. *KAI* 201:3, *lmrʾh lmlqrt*. Cf. *ANET*, 655.

5. *mrʾ rb mrʾ hdysʿy mlk gwzn*. The editio princeps is provided by A. Abou-Assaf, P. Bordreuil, and A. R. Millard, *La statue de Tell Fekherye et son inscription bilingue assyro-araméenne*, Etudes Assyriologiques, Editions recherche sur les civilisations 7 (Paris: A.D.P.F., 1982), 23–24, line 6. The Akkadian parallel text reads *bēli rabî bēlīšu ᴵadad-it-ʾi šakin māti* ᵃ*guzani* (Abou-Assaf, Bordreuil, and Millard, *La statue de Tell Fekherye*, 62). For additional studies see, among many others, A. R. Millard and P. Bordreuil, "A Statue from Syria with Assyrian and Aramaic Inscriptions," *BA* 45 (1982): 135–42; V. Sasson, "The Aramaic Text of the Tell Fakhriyah Assyrian-Aramaic Bilingual Inscription," *ZAW* 97 (1985): 86–103; J. C. Greenfield and A. Shaffer, "Notes on the Akkadian-Aramaic Bilingual Statue from Tell Fekherye," *Iraq* 45 (1983): 109–16; idem, "Notes on the Curse Formulae of the Tell Fekherye Inscription," *RB* 92 (1985): 47–59; F. M. Fales, "Le double bilinguisme de la statue de Tell Fekherye," *Syria* 60 (1983): 233–50.

Occasional hints of this dynastic connection with deity also occur in the Old Testament. Reflecting the cultural influences of his neighbors, King Ahaz of Judah rationalized his construction of a Damascene style altar in Jerusalem with, "Because the gods of the kings of Aram helped them, I will sacrifice to them that they will help me" (2 Chron. 28:23). In a later context, in typical Assyrian fashion, Sennacherib spoke of "the god of Hezekiah" (2 Chron. 32:17).

Unfortunately, most of the ancient inscriptions now available were produced at the request of monarchs. Consequently, the information concerning popular religion that they provide is limited. Nevertheless, some hints of the religious sensitivities of the common people may be gleaned from the epigraphic material. The present chapter examines the use of genitive constructions and personal names as clues to general perceptions, and investigates several of the epithets used by ancient Near Easterners to refer to patron deities.

Genitival Constructions

The relationship between a nation and its deity/deities was commonly expressed by means of two types of genitive constructions: bound or construct forms, and pronominal suffixes attached to nouns. We shall examine these briefly in turn.

Bound Forms

The most general construct forms associating nations and gods in the Old Testament are the expressions *ʾĕlōhê haggôyim*, "the gods of the nations," and *ʾĕlōhê hāʿammîm*, "the gods of the peoples." The former occurs six times, the latter seven.[6] Although the connotations of the singular *gôy*, "nation," and *ʿam*, "people," are quite different, the plural forms are often interchanged with little or no shift in meaning.[7] This semantic overlap is confirmed by the displacement of *ʾĕlōhê hāʿammîm*, "gods of the peoples," in Deut. 6:14 and 13:8 with *ʾĕlōhê haggôyim*, "gods of the nations," in the same expression in 29:17, as well as the interchange of the two words within the context of 2 Chronicles 32.[8] Be-

---

6. *ʾĕlōhê haggôyim*: Deut. 29:17 (29:18 Eng.); 2 Kings 18:33 (//Isa. 36:18); 19:12 (//Isa. 37:12); 2 Chron. 32:13, 14, 17. *ʾĕlōhê hāʿammîm*: Deut. 6:14; 13:8; Judg. 2:12; Ps. 96:5 (// 1 Chron. 16:26); 1 Chron. 5:25; 2 Chron. 32:19.

7. Cf. D. I. Block, *The Foundations of National Identity: A Study in Ancient Northwest Semitic Perceptions* (Ann Arbor: University Microfilms, 1983), chaps. 1 and 2.

8. This is confirmed also by LXX, which usually translates both expressions with θεῶν τῶν ἐθνῶν. The three exceptions are Judg. 2:12; 1 Chron. 5:25; 2 Chron. 32:19. The Targums understood the phrases identically, rendering both *ʾĕlōhê hāʿammîm* and *ʾĕlōhê haggôyim* with *ṭʿwt ʿmmyʾ* throughout. See A. Sperber, ed., *The Bible in Aramaic*, 4 vols. printed in 5 (Leiden: Brill, 1959, 1962, 1968, 1973).

cause the Chronicler's record of the speeches of Sennacherib through Rabshakeh illustrates the matter so well, several segments deserve quotation here.

> "Do you not know what I and my fathers have done to all the peoples of other lands? Were the *gods of the nations of those lands* at all able to deliver their lands out of my hand? Who among all the *gods of those nations* that my fathers utterly destroyed was able to deliver his people from my hand, that your God should be able to deliver you from my hand? Now therefore do not let Hezekiah deceive you or mislead you in this fashion, and do not believe him, for no *god of any nation or kingdom* has been able to deliver his people from my hand or from the hand of my fathers. How much less will your God deliver you out of my hand? . . . Like the *gods of the nations of the lands* who have not delivered their people from my hands, so the God of Hezekiah will not deliver his people from my hand." . . . And they spoke of the God of Jerusalem as they spoke of the *gods of the peoples of the earth,* which are the work of men's hands. (2 Chron. 32:13–15, 17, 19)

Singular forms, frequent in both the Old Testament and in extrabiblical texts, make the association of deities and lands specific. The basic form, *ʾĕlōhê hāʿām,* "the gods of the people," occurs in 2 Chron. 25:15. Construct forms identifying Yahweh as "God of Israel" or "God of the Hebrews" appear more than one hundred times in the Old Testament.[9] The expressions are similar in form to those that identify Ashtoreth as "the god(dess) of the Sidonians," Chemosh as "the god of Moab," and Milcom as "the god of the sons of Ammon" in 1 Kings 11:33. Elsewhere reference is made to "the gods of Egypt" (Exod. 12:12; Jer. 43:12, 13), "the gods of the Amorites" (Josh. 24:15; Judg. 6:10), "the gods of Aram" (Judg. 10:6), "the gods of the sons of Seir" (2 Chron. 25:14), "the gods of Edom" (2 Chron. 25:20). Extrabiblical counterparts to this expression abound. Especially to be noted here are "the gods of TḤPNḤS," in the sixth-century B.C. Saqqara papyrus;[10] "the gods of Byblos," in the Yehawmilk inscription;[11] "the gods of KTK and the gods of Arpad," in the Sefire treaty;[12] "all the gods of YʾDY," in the Panammuwa text from Zenjirli.[13] Similar expressions are also common in Neo-Assyrian writings. To cite but one example, after listing more than a dozen deities by name, the prologue to the Vassal Treaties of Esarhaddon adjures all the

---

9. Cf. A. Even-Shoshan, *A New Concordance of the Bible,* Ridgefield edition (Jerusalem: Kiryat Sepher, 1981), 69–71.

10. *KAI* 50:3 (Phoenician).

11. *KAI* 4:4, 7; *ANET,* 653. See also the longer text *KAI* 10:16; *ANET,* 656.

12. *KAI* 222 B:5–6.

13. *KAI* 215:22.

gods of the cities Ashur, Calah, Arbela, Kalzi, Harran, Assyria, Babylon, Nippur, Sumer, and Akkad as guarantors of the pact. To emphasize the universal scope of the treaty, the Assyrian overlord appeals finally to "all the gods of every land" and "the gods of heaven and earth."[14]

The last reference cited above illustrates the fundamental difference between general northwest Semitic and Mesopotamian perspectives on the one hand, and the Israelite viewpoint on the other. Expressions like "God of Israel" and "God of the Hebrews," with a gentilic or eponymic national designation in the genitive position, stress the association between deity and the population. But all the extrabiblical citations associate the divinity primarily with a geographic locality. The expression *ʾĕlōhê hāʾāreṣ*, "the gods of the land," occurs three times in 2 Kings 17:26–27, and is quite appropriate on the lips of Assyrians. However, it is used by an Israelite only in Deut. 31:16, where it refers to the gods of the promised land. The narrator's comment, "They spoke of the God of Jerusalem as they spoke of the gods of the peoples of the earth" (2 Chron. 32:19), accords well with the theological perceptions and other expressions used in this context.

The reverse construction, with the name of the deity in the genitive position, expresses the association as well. Judges 20:2 and 2 Sam. 14:13 speak of Israel as *ʿam ʾĕlōhîm*, "the people of God"; elsewhere the nation is identified as *ʿam yhwh*, "the people of Yahweh." The presence of the expression in the Song of Deborah and Barak in Judg. 5:11 testifies to its antiquity. In this text, as well as in 2 Sam. 1:12, Ezek. 36:20, and Zeph. 2:10, "the people of Yahweh" are seen in relation to foreign nations. Second Samuel 6:21 (David) and 2 Kings 9:6 (Jehu) refer to kings appointed over "the people of Yahweh." The phrase appears three more times, in Num. 11:29, 17:6 (16:41 Eng.), and 1 Sam. 2:24. A foreign counterpart to this expression is found in *ʿam kĕmôš*, "the people of Chemosh," which occurs in Num. 21:29 and Jer. 48:46.

Other bound forms confirm this distinction between Israelite and extra-Israelite usage. Typical of the north Syrian conception is the phrase "lands of Dagan," found in a Phoenician text.[15] In spite of the vast amount of Hebrew source material, the counterpart, "land of Yahweh," occurs only twice in the entire Old Testament, and that in two different forms, *ʾereṣ yhwh* in Hos. 9:3 and *ʾadmat yhwh* in Isa. 14:2. These

---

14. *ANET,* 534–35. See also the reference to ᵈ*bēʾli rakabbi ša* ᵃˡ*samalla* in R. F. Harper, *Assyrian and Babylonian Letters,* vol. 6 (Chicago: University of Chicago Press, 1902), 633:7. Cf. L. Waterman, *Royal Correspondence of the Assyrian Empire,* 4 parts (Ann Arbor: University of Michigan Press, 1930–36); part 1: *Text and Transliteration* (1930), 440; *KAI* 216:5; *ANET,* 655.

15. *KAI* 14:19, *ʾrṣt dgn.* Donner and Röllig (*KAI* II [3d ed., 1973], 20) translate "Kornländer." On the deity Dagan/Dagon, see J. F. Healey, "Dagon," *DDD,* 407–13.

observations accord with the manner in which deity-nation links were thought to have been established, as discussed in the previous chapter.

Pronominal Suffixes

A second common genitival method of expressing the deity-nation association involves the attachment of pronominal suffixes to a designation for the deity or the nation. The Israelites frequently identified Yahweh as "our God"; others referred to him as "your [singular and plural] god."[16] The same could be said for other deities. In Judg. 11:24 Jephthah asks of the Ammonite leaders, "Will you not possess what *Chemosh your god* [sic] gives you to possess?"[17] Judges 16:23 speaks of Dagon as "your god," that is, belonging to the Philistine lords. Especially impressive in this context is Ruth's immortal resolution recorded in Ruth 1:16, "Your people shall be my people, and your god my god." This Moabite woman recognized that if she would alter her ethnic ties she must also transfer her allegiance to the deity of the people to whom she committed herself.

These specific cases illustrate the principle that is clearly reflected in several prophetic texts. In Isa. 8:19 the prophet admonishes the Israelites that a people should consult "its god" when in distress. Speaking for the nation, Micah declares:

> For all the peoples walk
> each in the name of its god,
> But we will walk in the name of Yahweh our God
> for ever and ever. (Mic. 4:5)

Jeremiah appears to have drawn on a well-known maxim when he stresses rhetorically the importance of fidelity to one's national deity:

> Has a nation changed gods,
> even though they are no gods?
> But my people have changed their glory
> for that which does not profit. (Jer. 2:11)[18]

Conversely, the perspective of the divinity is frequently reflected in the Old Testament by Yahweh referring to the Israelites as "my people" (ʿammî). In the presence of Yahweh the Israelites in turn identify themselves as "your people" (ʿamměkā). To each other they are "his people"

---

16. See Even-Shoshan, *Concordance*, s.v. ʾĕlôhîm.

17. Chemosh was the god of Moab, not Ammon.

18. The suffix is missing from ʾĕlôhîm but its presence on kābôd in line three implies that in the mind of the author it was also attached to "gods."

(*ʿammô*).[19] Similar connections are assumed for other nationalities. Jeremiah 49:1 speaks of the Ammonites as "his people" (*ʿammô*), that is, those belonging to Milcom. In the text quoted above from 2 Chron. 32:14–17 the Assyrian official boasts that just as none of the gods has been able to deliver "his people" (*ʿammô*) from the power of the Assyrians, so Yahweh will be unable to save "his people" Israel.

Personal Names

In recent decades our understanding of the religious beliefs of ancient Semites has been greatly enhanced by the study of onomastics. In contrast to our own culture, in which names are often selected arbitrarily or simply on euphonic grounds, in the ancient Near Eastern world names borne by individuals were much more than mere means of identification. Names generally expressed some aspect of the personality or character of the person who bore or of the person who gave the name. Many Semitic names expressed theological ideas, particularly when they incorporated divine names. These theophoric names were in effect expressions of faith, reflecting the spiritual allegiance of the bearer.[20] Since many of the persons bearing theophoric elements can be identified as ordinary people, as opposed to royal and religious officials, the study of onomastics provides the researcher with the most reliable data for determining the religious beliefs of ancient Near Easterners in general and the extent of popular devotion to reputed national deities in particular.

Israel

The onomastic evidence for popular devotion to Yahweh in Israel is both abundant and clear.[21] The Old Testament evidence indicates that names bearing the theophoric element *Yah* are to be found in all periods of the nation's history, beginning with the exodus and conquest traditions, and extending to the end of the biblical period and beyond.[22]

19. Well over half the occurrences of *ʿam* with pronominal suffixes involve Israel as the people of Yahweh. For further discussion and tabulation see Block, *Foundations*, 18–20.

20. For a detailed analysis of theophoric names in Israel see J. D. Fowler, *Theophoric Personal Names in Ancient Hebrew: A Comparative Study*, JSOTSup 49 (Sheffield: Sheffield Academic Press, 1988).

21. See J. H. Tigay, "Israelite Religion: The Onomastic and Epigraphic Evidence," in *Ancient Israelite Religion: Essays in Honor of Frank Moore Cross,* ed. P. D. Miller Jr. et al. (Philadelphia: Fortress, 1987), 157–94.

22. Cf. Jochebed (*ywkbd*), Exod. 6:20; Joash (*ywʾš*), Judg. 6:11–12; Jonathan (*yhwntn*), Judg. 18:30; Joshua (*yhwšwʿ*), Exod. 17:9ff. S. Norin contended that *yhw-* at the beginning of personal names is an innovation of a late "Deuteronomistic" editor. See "Jô-Namen and Jᵉhô-Namen," *VT* 29 (1979): 87–97. This conclusion contradicts that of O.

These names derive from all regions of the nation[23] and represent a broad economic and social spectrum. Only a few representative examples need to be cited here. No fewer than thirteen individuals in the Old Testament bear the name Johanan, "Yahweh has been gracious." Excluding religious personnel, the name identifies two of David's mighty men (a Benjaminite, 1 Chron. 12:5, and a Gadite, 12:13), a porter in David's time (1 Chron. 26:3), a Judaite captain (2 Chron. 17:15), an Ephraimite (2 Chron. 28:12), a Jewish captain after the fall of Jerusalem (2 Kings 25:23), a returnee from exile (Ezra 8:12), an Israelite of Ezra's time (Ezra 10:28), and a son of Tobiah (Neh. 6:18). Similar frequencies and distributions may be found for other names: Jonathan, Jehoshaphat, Joshua, Joel, Abijah, Obadiah, Azariah, and many more.[24] Yahwistic names also occur with great frequency in extrabiblical inscriptions, seals, and stamps.[25] Judging by the popularity of names bearing Yahweh as the theophore, there can be no doubt that his devotees were to be found in every stratum and region of the nation.[26]

Eissfeldt, "Renaming in the Old Testament," in *Words and Meanings: Essays Presented to David Winton Thomas,* ed. P. R. Ackroyd and B. Lindars (Cambridge: Cambridge University Press, 1968), 77, who notes that *yhwšwᶜ* is always used in the older strands of the Pentateuch, whereas *hwšᶜ* occurs only in P (the latest strand). Norin's position has been effectively refuted by A. R. Millard, "*YW* and *YHW* Names," *VT* 30 (1980): 208–12.

 For a statistical analysis of theophoric names in the Old Testament see J. H. Tigay, *You Shall Have No Other Gods: Israelite Religion in the Light of Hebrew Inscriptions,* HSS 31 (Atlanta: Scholars Press, 1986), 5–9. For an analysis of theophoric names in Israelite inscriptions see Tigay, *You Shall Have,* 47–73. According to Tigay's calculation Yahwistic names outnumber pagan names 557 to 35. For a discussion of Yahwistic names in fifth-century Achaemenid Nippur see M. W. Stolper, "A Note on Yahwistic Personal Names in the Murašû Texts," *BASOR* 222 (1976): 25–28. For the most recent listing of Yahwistic (with *yh, yw,* and *yhw*) names in Israelite seals, see *WSS,* 502–4. Of special interest is a cache of fifty-one bullae discovered in the ruins of a building destroyed in 586 b.c. Of the more than fifty names preserved on the bullae, over 50 percent have the theophoric ending *yhw-*. See Yigal Shiloh, "A Group of Hebrew Bullae from the City of David," *IEJ* 36 (1986): 16–38; Yigal Shiloh and David Tarler, "Bullae from the City of David: A Hoard of Seal Impressions from the Israelite Period," *BA* 49 (1986): 196–209. For a discussion of Yahwistic names in fifth-century Achaemenid Nippur, see M. W. Stolper, "A Note on Yahwistic Personal Names in the Murašu Texts," *BASOR* 222 (1976): 25–28.

 23. Based on extrabiblical evidence, D. Diringer and S. P. Brock ("Words and Meanings in Early Hebrew Inscriptions," in *Words and Meanings,* 41) suggest that North Israelite names end in *yw-,* rather than *yh-* or *yhw-.*

 24. See Fowler, *Theophoric Personal Names,* 32–38; cf. the older work by M. Noth, *Die israelitischen Personennamen im Rahmen der gemeinsemitischen Namengebung,* BWANT 3/10 (1928; reprint, Hildesheim: Olms, 1980), 101–14.

 25. The preexilic examples are conveniently listed by Millard, "*YW* and *YHW* Names." See also Shiloh, "Group"; Shiloh and Tarler, "Bullae"; and Stolper, "Yahwistic Personal Names." For a complete listing see *WSS,* 502–4.

 26. But not all theophoric names in Israel were Yahwistic. Tigay (*You Shall Have,* 7–8) estimates that 11 percent of the names in the Old Testament were probably pagan, bearing elements like "Baal" (Ishbaal) and "Haddu" (Hadoram).

Edom

No Edomite deities are named in the Old Testament. The only reference to Edomite gods occurs in 2 Chron. 25:20, where they are referred
to with the vague expression *ĕlōhê *ĕdôm, "the gods of Edom." Nevertheless, it is commonly agreed that the chief deity of this nation was
Qos/Qaus.[27] Qos has surfaced as the theophoric element of two of the
three known Edomite royal names from the period 840–582 B.C.[28] In recent years at least twenty personal names incorporating the divine
name have surfaced on seals and ostraca from Edom and Judah.[29]
Among these are names like *qwsg[br]*, "Qos is powerful"; *qwsʿnl*, "Qos
has answered [me]"; *bdqws*, "by the hand of Qos"; *pqʿqws*, "asked of
Qos"; *qwsbnh*, "Qos has built"; *qwsny*, a hypocoristic for *qwsntn*, "Qos
has given"; and the hypocoristic *qwsʾ*. Rarely does the inscription hint
at the social class of the bearer of the name, but most of these probably
represent nonroyal and nonpriestly individuals. *qwsg[br]*, further identified as *mlk ʾ[dm]*, "king of E[dom]," and probably to be equated with
Qausgabri in Neo-Assyrian sources, is an obvious exception.[30] On the
other hand, a lay or common status is assured for at least one person,
qwsʿnl, whose status is clarified on a seal from Tell el-Kheleifeh as *ʿbd
hmlk*, "servant of the king."[31]

Names with Qos as the theophore persist through the Persian period,
as witnessed by the biblical name like Barkos ("son of Qos," Ezra 2:53;
Neh. 7:55) and possibly Qushaiah, "Qos is Yahweh" (1 Chron. 15:17),
the latter representing a syncretistic linkage of the Israelite and
Edomite patron divinities.[32] From Achaemenid cuneiform sources we
learn of *qu-ú-su-šá-ma-aʾ*, "Qos has heard"; *qu-ŭ-su-ia-da-aʾ*, and *qu-ú-
su-ya-da-ʿ*, both "Qos has known"; *qu-su-ya-a-ha-bi*, "Qos has given";

27. The name appears in the following blessing formula preserved on a seventh- to
early sixth-century B.C. Edomite ostracon: *whbrhtk lqws*, "I bless you by Qaus," on which
see I. Beit-Arieh and B. Cresson, "An Edomite Ostracon from Horvat ʿuza," *Tel Aviv* 12
(1985): 96–101; J. R. Bartlett, *Edom and the Edomites*, JSOTSup 77 (Sheffield: Sheffield
Academic Press, 1989), 221–22. On this deity see T. Vriezen, "The Edomite Deity Qaus,"
OTS 14 (1965): 330–53; Bartlett, *Edom and the Edomites*, 200–207; E. A. Knauf, "Qos,"
DDD, 1272–78.

28. *Qa-uš-ma-la-ka* (*ANET,* 282), *Qa-uš-gab-ri* (*ANET,* 291). On these historical char-
acters see Bartlett, *Edom and the Edomites*, 128–30, 138–40.

29. Bartlett (*Edom and the Edomites*, 204–5) lists twenty-eight names. A listing of *qws*
names on seals is also provided by Avigad and Sass in *WSS*, 529. For a discussion of these
Qos names, see F. Israel, "Supplementum Idumeum I," *Rivista Biblica* 35 (1987): 337–56.

30. Cf. C.-M. Bennett, "Fouilles d'Umm El-Biyara: Rapport préliminaire," *RB* 73
(1966): 399–401; Bartlett, *Edom and the Edomites*, 213.

31. See N. Glueck, *The Other Side of the Jordan*, rev. ed. (New Haven: American
Schools of Oriental Research, 1970), 134; Bartlett, *Edom and the Edomites*, 214.

32. Cf. J. R. Bartlett, "The Moabites and Edomites," in *Peoples of Old Testament Times*,
ed. D. J. Wiseman (Oxford: Clarendon, 1973), 245; idem, *Edom and the Edomites*, 201.

and possibly *qu-us-da-na-ʿ*, "Qos is judge."[33] But the popularity of Qos in southern Judah in late Persian times is confirmed especially by the frequency with which the name appears in the Aramaic ostraca discovered at Arad and Beersheba. Of the thirty names occurring on the latter, at least one-third contain this theophore.[34]

Evidence of the persistence of the cult into Nabataean times is to be found in names like *ʾrqs*, "Qos is light," *qwsʿdr*, "Qos has helped," *qwsntn*, "Qos had given," and *qwsmlk*, "Qos is king."[35] These names agree with Josephus, who notes that Herod the Great's ancestry was traced back to Kostabaros, a member of the priestly family in the service of Qoze.[36]

Since all of this evidence is relatively late, it is not clear how early Qos had been adopted as the primary Edomite deity. The possible presence of theophoric names prefixed with *qws* in a topographical list of Ramses II at Karnak may indicate an early date for the cult. Oded has argued that the five names mentioned identify Edomite chiefs or clans.[37]

While the evidence is admittedly incomplete, the relatively high proportion of confirmed Edomite names having Qos as the theophoric element from early to late times, and the absence of other similarly attested deities, strongly suggest that the worship of this god was sufficiently popular for him to have been considered a "national" deity.

Moab

Information on Chemosh, the most prominent divine element in Moabite personal names, is sketchy. Of the known Moabite royal

---

33. On these names see Bartlett, *Edom and the Edomites*, 204; Knauf, "Qos," 1274.

34. See J. Naveh, "The Aramaic Ostraca from Tel Beersheba (Seasons 1971–1976)," *Tel Aviv* 6 (1979): 182–95, who discusses *qwsnhr*, "Qos is light" (28:2); *qwsynqm*, "Qos will avenge" (33:3); *qwsbrk*, "Qos will bless"; *qwsmlk*, "Qos is king" (33:4; 42:3[?]); *qwsʿwt*, "Qos has helped" (34:1); the hypocoristic *qwsy* (34:3); *qwsʿdr*, "Qos has helped" (34:6); *qwswhb*, "Qos has given" (36:1); *qws[.*. . . (36:6); *b[r]qws* ([?] 37:1); *qwsgbr*, "Qos is powerful" (37:4); *qws[.*. . . (41:4); *qwshbn*, meaning unknown (41:6); see also Bartlett, *Edom and the Edomites*, 204. Note also from Arad, [*qws*. . . (1:1), . . .]*qws* (10:1), *qwsynqm*, "Qos will avenge" (20:1); . . .]*qws*, (21:1), *qwsbh* (32), *qwsp[.*. . . (43:1), on which see J. Naveh, "The Aramaic Ostraca from Tel Arad," in *Arad Inscriptions*, ed. Y. Aharoni, Judaean Desert Studies (Jerusalem: Israel Exploration Society, 1981), 153–76. Cf. also a Thamudic reference to *h-qws ʿbd*, "O Qos, be generous" (E. A. Knauf, "Zwei thamudische Inschriften aus der Gegend von Ǧeraš," *ZDPV* 97.2 [1981]: 188–92.)

35. See Bartlett, *Edom and the Edomites*, 206, for references.

36. *Antiquities* 15.7.8ff. Another Kostabaros is named in 20.9.4. For theophoric names with Qos in Greek sources, see Bartlett, *Edom and the Edomites*, 206–7.

37. B. Oded, "Egyptian References to the Edomite Deity Qaus," *AUSS* 9 (1971): 47–50. For further references to Qos in Egyptian inscriptions see Knauf, *DDD*, 1273–75.

names five indicate an association with this deity.[38] Although the discovery of several Moabite seals bearing *kmš* as the theophoric element has yielded little additional information, the following names have surfaced: *kmššdk*, "Chemosh is righteous"; *kmšyhy*, "Chemosh may live"; *kmšʾl*, "Chemosh is god"; *kmšʿm*, "Chemosh is a paternal kinsman"; *kmšntn*, "Chemosh has given"; *kmšʾš*, "Chemosh has rewarded"; and *kmšdn*, "Chemosh has judged."[39] The identification of *kmšʿm* and *kmšʾl* as scribes (*hspr*) and the Mesopotamian origin of *kmšntn* suggest a measure of popularity of the cult among laypeople. Egyptian sources attest three names bearing "Chemosh" as the theophoric element. In addition to *kmššdq*, "Chemosh is righteous," and *kmšyhy*, "Chemosh may live," which have already been cited as occurring in Moabite seal inscriptions, *kmšplṭ*, "Chemosh has saved," has also surfaced. Although virtually identical in form to the royal name cited above, one individual from the time of the Persian Cambyses, *Ka-mu-šu-šar-uṣur*, is named in an Achaemenid cuneiform text.[40] The presence of the theophore suggests the individual was Moabite, perhaps an exile,[41] but this cannot be confirmed. The most that can be said with confidence is that Chemosh was widely recognized from Egypt to Mesopotamia.

Ammon

It is clear from the Old Testament that the Israelites considered Milcom/Malkam to be the patron deity of the Ammonites.[42] In contrast to the Edomite and Moabite onomastic evidence, however, one would hardly have known this from attested Ammonite names. Because these names display an overwhelming preference for ʾIl/ʾEl, the chief god in

38. The father of Mesha, *kmšyt* (*KAI* 181:1), as restored by Gibson, *HMI*, 77, on the basis of the El-Kerak inscription; *Ka-am-mu-su-na-ad-bi*, "Chemosh is generous to me" (*ANET*, 287); *Ka-mu-šu-i-lu*, "Chemosh is god"; *Ka-mu-šú-šar-uṣur*, "Chemosh protect the king"; *Ka-am-aš-ḫal-ta-a*, of uncertain meaning (*ANET*, 298). On these names see H.-P. Müller, "Chemosh," *DDD*, 359–60. The other known kings of Moab are Mesha, Shalman (Akkadian Salamanu), Eglon, Balak, and Musuri. For discussion see A. H. van Zyl, *The Moabites*, POS 3 (Leiden: Brill, 1960), 180–84; J. M. Miller, "Moab," *ABD* 4:885–92.

39. Cf. N. Avigad, "Ammonite and Moabite Seals," in *Near Eastern Archaeology in the Twentieth Century: Essays in Honor of Nelson Glueck*, ed. J. A. Sanders (Garden City, N.Y.: Doubleday, 1970), 289; S. Timm, *Moab zwischen den Mächten* (Wiesbaden: Harrassowitz, 1969), 162–83; Müller, "Chemosh," 360.

40. See further van Zyl, *Moabites*, 39.

41. Cf. N. Avigad, "Seals of Exiles," *IEJ* 15 (1965): 222–32. For a seal inscribed simply *kmš*, see R. Hestrin and M. Dayagi-Mendels, *Inscribed Seals: First Temple Period* (Jerusalem: Israel Museum, 1979), no. 114. Cf. also N. Avigad, "New Moabite and Ammonite Seals in the Israel Museum," *EI* 13 (1977): 109.

42. The name of the deity is vocalized *milkôm* in 1 Kings 11:5, 33 and *malkām* in 2 Kings 23:13; Jer. 49:1, 3; Zeph. 1:5; and perhaps in 2 Sam. 12:30 (= 1 Chron. 20:2).

the Canaanite pantheon, Tigay comments, "[I]f one assumes that the Ammonites were polytheists, this would indicate that other important deities could go largely unmentioned in the onomasticon of their worshippers."[43] In this comment Tigay assumes that ʾIl/ʾEl was the chief god of the Ammonites as well, and that Milcom was merely a title of ʾIl/ʾEl.[44] But this interpretation has been rightly questioned, and most scholars agree that El was but one of several divinities worshiped alongside Milcom by the Ammonites.[45] Even so, it is extraordinary that to this day none of the known Ammonite royal names bears this element,[46] and that as late as 1980 no certain personal names incorporating Milcom as the theophoric element were attested.[47]

In the meantime, however, the latter situation has changed somewhat. But it is still remarkable that although more than ninety Ammonite personal names are now known,[48] only four or five incorporate Milcom as the theophore. Certain examples include *mlkmʾwr*, "Milcom is light";[49] *mlkmgd*, "Milcom is fortune";[50] *mlkmyt*, "May Milcom come";[51] and *mlkmʿz*, "Milcom is mighty."[52] A possible fifth name is *bd-mlkm*, "by/in the hand of Milcom," though the nature of the first two letters is disputed.[53] The onomastic evidence is obviously limited, but it supports the earlier contention that Milcom was the patron deity of the Ammonites.[54]

---

43. Tigay, "Israelite Religion," 171.

44. Ibid., 187 n. 66. This interpretation is rightly questioned by W. Aufrecht, *CAI*, xviii.

45. For discussion of Ammonite religion and Milcom's place in it see U. Hübner, *Die Ammoniter: Untersuchung zur Geschichte, Kultur und Religion eines transjordanischen Volkes im 1. Jahrtausend v. Chr.*, Abhandlungen des Deutschen Palästina-Vereins 16 (Wiesbaden: Harrassowitz, 1992), 247–82, esp. 247–68. On Milcom in particular see E. Puech, "Milcom," *DDD*, 1076–80.

46. The known royal names include Nahash, Hanun, Shobi, Shanib, Zakur, Yariḥ-Ezer, Pudu-ilu/Budu-ilu, ʿAmminadab I, Hiṣṣal-El, ʿAmminadab II, Baalis/Baal-Yasha. See J.-M. de Tarragon, "Ammon," *ABD* 1:195.

47. See J. Naveh, "The Ostracon from Nimrud: An Ammonite Name-List," *Maarav* 2.2 (1979–80): 166.

48. The number is based on the list provided by Hübner, *Die Ammoniter*, 125–29.

49. Hübner, *Die Ammoniter*, seal #88; *CAI* #129. The seal, which was discovered in 1984 at Tell el-ʿUmeiri, created quite a stir because the full inscription (*lmlkmʾwr ʿbd bʿlyšʿ*, "belonging to Milcomʾur servant of Baʿlyašaʿ") appears to name an Ammonite king known from Jer. 40:14 as Baalis. On the significance of the inscription see L. Geraty, "Baalis," *ABD* 1:556–57.

50. Hübner, *Die Ammoniter*, seal #89; *CAI* #127.

51. Hübner, *Die Ammoniter*, ostracon #1:1; *CAI* #147:1.

52. Hübner, *Die Ammoniter*, seal #72; *CAI* #136.

53. Hübner, *Die Ammoniter*, seal #154. He prefers to read *br mlkm*, "son of Milcom," or *ʿbd mlkm*, "servant of Milcom," suggesting this may have been the seal of a priest (*Die Ammoniter*, 118–19).

54. Though Ammonites were not the only ones naming Milcom as the theophore of personal names. For a listing of seal inscriptions bearing the element see *WSS*, 511.

Aram

For determining the nature of popular religion in Aram the onomastic evidence for national divinities is even less helpful than it has been in the foregoing. The worship of a host of different gods in Aram is reflected in the multiplicity of theophores appearing in personal names. Among these are El,[55] Rakkab,[56] Adān,[57] Hadad,[58] Rammān,[59] and Baʿalat.[60] It is clear from other sources that the most important of these was the weather god Hadad, who was worshiped in different localities in various manifestations. The Damascene kings venerated him as Hadad-Rimmōn/Rammān.[61] However, evidence of popular devotion in Damascus to this deity is lacking. Greenfield has gathered about a dozen names bearing the theophore Rammān, but little more may be concluded from these than that this form of the weather god enjoyed widespread recognition. The extent to which the citizenry of Damascus accepted this deity as the state god cannot be determined.[62]

Phoenicia

It is apparent from the personal names of ancient Phoenicians that no single deity commanded the devotion of all of the people.[63] Some of

55. E.g., Hazael, *KAI* 202 A:4; 232; Matiʿel, *KAI* 222 A:1–3, and passim; 223 C:14.

56. Barrakab, *KAI* 215:1, 19; 216:1; 218; 221:3. Cf. *KAI* 24:16; 25:4–6; 214:2, 3, 11, 18; 215:22; 216:5; 217:7–8, where this god is named Rakib-El. He is probably to be identified with ᵈbē-ʾ-li ra-kab-bi ša ᵃlsa-ma-al-la in Harper, *Assyrian and Babylonian Letters*, 633:7. On Rakib-El see K. van der Toorn, "Rakib-El," *DDD*, 1296–97.

57. *Adan-lu-ram*, *KAI* 203. On Adon/Adan see K. Spronk, "Lord," *DDD*, 994–98.

58. Bar-Hadad, *KAI* 201:1–2; 202 A:4, 5 (= Ben-Hadad, 1 Kings 15:18; 20:1ff.; 2 Kings 13:14–19); Hadadezer, 2 Sam. 10:16–19 (= Akkadian Adad-ʾidri, *ANET*, 278); Hadad-yisʿi, Tell Fekheriyeh statue. On Hadad see J. C. Greenfield, "Hadad," *DDD*, 716–26.

59. Sidqi-Rammān, *CIS* II, 97; Tabrimmon, 1 Kings 15:18. Rimmôn/Rammānu, "the thunderer," is actually an epithet of Hadad. Cf. Greenfield, "Hadad," 720.

60. ʿbdbʿlt, *KAI* 204.

61. On which see J. C. Greenfield, "The Aramaean God Rammān/Rimmōn," *IEJ* 26 (1976): 195–98; idem, "Aspects of Aramaean Religion," in *Ancient Israelite Religion: Essays in Honor of Frank Moore Cross*, ed. P. D. Miller Jr. et al. (Philadelphia: Fortress, 1987), 67–78.

62. Although it is nowhere stated that Tabrimmon was ever king in Damascus, it has been suggested that his father, Hezion, was the founder of the dynasty. See Abraham Malamat, "The Aramaeans," in *Peoples of Old Testament Times*, 143. Benjamin Mazar's conclusion that Rimmon was a common name among the Aramaeans after Damascus became the metropolis of Aram is possible but cannot be confirmed. See "The Aramaean Empire and Its Relations with Israel," in *Biblical Archaeologist Reader*, vol. 2, ed. D. N. Freedman and E. F. Campbell (Garden City, N.Y.: Doubleday, 1964), 139 n. 23 and 140 n. 26.

63. On the Phoenicians see V. Krings, ed., *La civilisation phénicienne et punique* (Leiden: Brill, 1995), especially F. Israel, "L'onomostique et la prosopographie," 215–21, and C. Bonnet and P. Xella, "La religion," 316–33.

the theophores employed include Ba‘al,[64] El,[65] Eshmun,[66] Melqart,[67] and Milk.[68] However, their usage does not always agree with what is known from other sources about the primary gods of some of the major cities. Ba‘alat seems to have been the dominant divinity at Byblos,[69] yet her name is not found in any personal names discovered to date from that place.

The worship of Melqart is known to have been quite widespread,[70] yet he seems to have been a favorite in Tyre. The name itself, apparently a conflation of *mlk qrt*, "king of the city,"[71] suggests some type of patron status, but the extent of popular adherence to this cult is impossible to establish from the onomastic evidence. If anything, the evidence is negative. Few Phoenician names with this element have been discovered.[72]

In Sidon, Eshmun enjoyed considerable support, especially from the ruling dynasty. At least two kings near the middle of the first millennium b.c. bore the name Eshmun‘azar.[73] Several foundation stones of *bd‘štrt*, Bod‘astarte, another royal personage, have been found, identifying the building being constructed/dedicated as "the temple of his god, ’Eshmun the holy prince."[74] It should also be observed, however, that Tabnit, the son of the first Eshmun‘azar, identifies both himself and his father as priest of Astarte.[75] Furthermore, all of these inscrip-

---

64. See F. L. Benz, *Personal Names in the Phoenician and Punic Inscriptions,* Studia Pohl 8 (Rome: Biblical Institute Press, 1972), 90–100, 288–90.

65. Ibid., 266–67.

66. Ibid., 70–73, 278–79. See also S. Ribichini, "Eshmun," *DDD,* 583–87.

67. Benz, *Names,* 347–48. See also S. Ribichini, "Melqart," *DDD,* 1053–58.

68. Benz, *Names,* 344–45. On *mlk* as a theophore in Phoenician (and Punic) names see G. C. Heider, *The Cult of Molek: A Reassessment,* JSOTSup 43 (Sheffield: JSOT Press, 1985), 179–81.

69. Cf. the title *b‘lt gbl,* in *KAI* 4:3–4; 5:2(?); 6:2; 7:3–4; 10:2, 3, 7, 8, 10, 15. For the publication of a fifth-century b.c. statuette bearing the inscribed name *b‘lt gbl* see E. Gubel and P. Bordreuil, "Statuette fragmentaire portant le nom de la Baalat Gubal," *Semitica* 35 (1985): 5–11. The expression ^d*bēltu ša* ^{al}*gubla* occurs frequently in the Amarna letters. See J. A. Knudtzon, *Die El-Amarna Tafeln,* 2 vols., VAB 2 (Leipzig: Hinrichs, 1915), 2:1583. Cf. S. B. Mercer, *The Tell El-Amarna Tablets,* 2 vols. (Toronto: Macmillan, 1939), 2:901, for references. On Baalat see also E. T. Mullen Jr., "Baalat," *DDD,* 263–65.

70. See Benz, *Names,* 347–48.

71. Unless *qrt* refers to the netherworld. See W. F. Albright, *From the Stone Age to Christianity: Monotheism and the Historical Process,* 2d ed. (Garden City, N.Y.: Doubleday, 1957), 307. For a recent tentative defense of this position, see Heider, *Cult of Molek,* 175–79.

72. Cf. *bdmlqrt,* which parallels the seal inscription *bdb‘l,* "in/by the hand of Baal," on which see Nahman Avigad, "Some Decorated West Semitic Seals." *IEJ* 35 (1985): 1–3. *bd* is discussed by Benz, *Names,* 283–86. Most of the names with the theophore *mlqrt* are Cypriot or Punic.

73. *KAI* 13:2; 14:1, 2, 13, 14, 15; 16. In *KAI* 14:17–18, Eshmun is described as *šr qdš,* "holy prince," and *b‘l ṣdn,* "lord of Sidon." *KAI* 36:5 is from Cyprus.

74. *KAI* 15; 16.

75. *KAI* 3.

tions are royal; they reveal nothing about the religious commitments of the common folk.

To summarize, as a gauge of popular recognition of national deities the evidence provided by personal names is inconsistent. Apart from occasional aberrations, in Israel, from which the most names for analysis are available, the acknowledgment of Yahweh as the national God was almost universal. But the data for the surrounding peoples is much more limited. Nevertheless, the names from Edom, Moab, and Ammon seem to point in similar directions, with Qos, Chemosh, and Milcom, respectively, being favored in these lands. Our knowledge of the Phoenician and Aramaean situations suffers from the known complexities of their recognized pantheons, and the tendency of functional deities to be worshiped in widely separated regions, albeit as local manifestations. If one speaks in primarily ethnic terms, neither group as a whole seems ever to have united around the worship of a single god. At best, favorite divinities seem to be associated with specific sites, rather than as patron gods of the nations.

Divine Epithets

In addition to genitive constructions and personal names, a third clue to the ancient understanding of the relationship between a nation and its patron deity is found in the epithets by which ancient Near Easterners referred to the divinities that they considered to be their patrons. Five expressions appear frequently in the texts: *ʾAdon*, *Baʿal*, *Melek*, *Mareʾ*, and *Roʿeh*. These titles will be examined briefly in turn.

ʾAdon

The root *ʾdn*, popularized in Greek mythology in the form Adonis, appears to have been a distinctly Amorite term taken up in Canaanite, Phoenician, and Hebrew. In its ordinary secular sense the word means "lord, master,"[76] but it was applied to both divine and human masters. A second-millennium text from Mari contains the earliest attested ascription of the title to a god.[77] The composite personal name Aduna-Adad suggests that this deity was acknowledged as the lord of the individual bearing the name.[78] In one Ugaritic text, the high god El addresses one

---

76. See O. Eissfeldt, "אָדוֹן *ʾādhôn*," *TDOT* 1:59–72; E. Jenni, "אָדוֹן," *THAT* 1:31–38 (= *TLOT* 1:23–29); K. Spronk, "Lord," *DDD*, 994–98.

77. H. B. Huffmon, *Amorite Personal Names in the Mari Texts: A Structural and Lexical Study* (Baltimore: Johns Hopkins University Press, 1965), 20, 159. Cf. also Aduna, king of Irqata in el-Amarna tablets 75:25; 140:10. See W. L. Moran, trans., *The Amarna Letters* (Baltimore: Johns Hopkins University Press, 1992), 145, 226; Knudtzon, *Die El-Amarna Tafeln*, 2:1556.

78. So also Eissfeldt, "אָדוֹן *ʾādhôn*," 1:60.

of the lesser gods (probably Yamm) and declares, *at.adn.tpᶜr,* "You are proclaimed lord (of the gods?)."[79] However, because this text is concerned with the relative ranks among the gods, rather than the relationship between a deity and his human subordinates, the citation has little significance here other than to illustrate the early use of the term. An eighth-century B.C. graffiti inscription from Hamath reads: *ᵓdnlrm skn [b]yt mlkh,* "Adanluram, the minister of the house of the king."[80] Phoenician texts contain several references to the god Adon. The two earliest, from the tenth century B.C., use the feminine form to identify Baalat, apparently the patron deity of Byblos, as *ᵓdt gbl,* "mistress of Gebal/Byblos."[81] In his fifth-century inscription, Eshmunᶜazar of Sidon ascribes to Baal, who has given him Dor and Joppa, the lofty, if impersonal, title *ᵓdn mlkm,* "lord of kings."[82] The same expression appears in a second-century B.C. Umm el-ᶜAwamid text. But the opening phrase, *lᵓdn lbᶜl šmm,* "to Adon, to Baal Shamem," reflects a more personal relationship between deity and king.[83] A late altar inscription from Byblos makes this association quite explicit, adding the suffix, *ᵓdnn,* "our lord."[84]

In the Old Testament Yahweh is often identified as Adon. As the universal lord his titles include *ᵓădōnê hāᵓădōnîm,* "lord of lords" (Deut. 10:17; Ps. 136:3), and *ᵓădôn kol-hāᵓāreṣ,* "lord of all the earth" (Josh. 3:11, 13; Mic. 4:13; Zech. 4:14; 6:5; Ps. 97:5). Exodus 34:23 reads, *hāᵓādōn yhwh ᵓĕlōhê yiśrāᵓēl,* "the Lord, Yahweh, God of Israel"; Isa. 1:24, *hāᵓādōn yhwh ṣĕbāᵓôt ᵓăbîr yiśrāᵓēl,* "the Lord, Yahweh of hosts, the Mighty One of Israel." Psalm 114:7 parallels *ᵓādôn* with *ᵓĕlôah yaᵓăqōb,* "the God of Jacob." Psalm 135:5 juxtaposes Yahweh and *ᵓădōnênû,* "our Lord." The form *ᵓădōnāy,* "my Lord," is enigmatic but it appears over four hundred times, more than three hundred of which occur in association with the personal name Yahweh.[85] Perhaps the clearest indication of a sense of relationship is found in the personal name Adonijah, "my lord is Yahweh."

---

79. As translated by Spronk, "Lord," 996. Cf. *UNP* 7.III.17 (= ᶜnt x:IV:17), p. 89, where M. S. Smith translates, "You, O Lord, you proclaim [his name]."

80. *KAI* 203; *AI,* 17–18. For the most recent publication of the Hamath graffiti see B. Otzen, "Appendix 2. The Aramaic Inscriptions," in *Hama 2,* ed. P. J. Riis and M.-L. Buhl (Copenhagen: National Museum, 1990), 267–318.

81. *ᵓdtw, KAI* 6:2; 7:4. Cf. Astarte, identified as *ᵓdty,* "her mistress," on the seventh-century B.C. Ur ivory, *KAI* 29:2.

82. *KAI* 14:18.

83. *KAI* 18:1, 5.

84. *KAI* 12:3. *ᵓdn* also appears as the theophore in two Ammonite personal names: *ᵓdnnr,* "my lord is (the) light" (*CAI* 40:1; Hübner, *Die Ammoniter,* seal #14); *ᵓdnplṭ,* "my lord has delivered" (*CAI* 17:1; Hübner, *Die Ammoniter,* seal #15).

85. For a discussion of Adonai see Eissfeldt, "אָדוֹן *ᵓādhôn,*" 1:62–72; Spronk, "Lord," 997–98.

The foregoing survey of the use of *ʾdn* reveals that when ancient Near Easterners addressed a deity as Adon, they had one of two ideas in mind: either the god was lord of the universe and/or the gods, or the god was a personal or national master.

Baʿal

Bʿl was a common Semitic root also meaning "lord." As numerous genitives indicate, however, this term connoted ownership, rather than mastery or sovereignty as in the case of Adon above.[86] As a *baʿal* a man could be the owner of his wife (i.e., a husband),[87] a member of the aristocracy,[88] or a partner in a covenant.[89]

The root *bʿl* was used as an appellative for many gods in the ancient world. Titles like *bʿl šmm*, "lord of the heavens,"[90] and *bʿl pn ʾrṣ*, "lord of the surface of the earth,"[91] reflected a deity's cosmic lordship. Placing a geographic name in the genitive position, as in *bʿl ṣpn*, "lord of Zaphon,"[92] *bʿl ḥrn*, "lord of Haran,"[93] and *bʿl krntryš*, "lord of KRN-TRYSH,"[94] expressed a god's sovereignty over a specific locality. Especially noteworthy are *mlqrt bʿl ṣr*, "Melqart, lord of Tyre,"[95] and the phrase's feminine counterpart, applied to the patron goddess of Byblos, *bʿlt gbl*, "mistress of Gebal."[96]

Baal occurs as a divine name more than seventy times in the Old Testament. It is not always clear whether the storm god par excellence is in view or merely a local manifestation of the deity. The latter seems to be the case when geographic genitives follow Baal: for example, Baal-Peor, Baal-Hazor, Baal-Gad, Baal-Hermon, Baal-Meon, Baal-Shalisha, Baal-Tamar, and Baal-Zaphon.[97] A cosmic lordship may be suggested by

---

86. In Akkadian, *bēl bīti*, "owner of a house"; *bēl eqli*, "owner of a field." In Phoenician, *bʿl bqr*, "owner of cattle"; *bʿl ṣʾn*, "owner of sheep." In Hebrew, *bʿl hbyt*, "owner of the house" (Exod. 22:7). In Aramaic *bʿl rkb*, "owner of the chariot"; *bʿl ksp*, "owner of the money." For additional examples and discussion see J. C. de Moor, "בַּעַל *baʿal*," *TDOT* 2:181–82; J. Kühlewein, "בַּעַל," *THAT* 1:327–33 (= *TLOT* 1:247–51); W. T. Koopmans, "בעל," *NIDOTTE* 1:681–83; W. Herrmann, "Baal," *DDD*, 249–63.

87. Gen. 20:3. Cf. also the extrabiblical occurrences cited by Hoftijzer and Jongeling, *DNWSI* 1:182–84.

88. Judg. 9:2; 20:5; for extrabiblical citations, see *DNWSI* 1:183–84.

89. Baal-berith, Gen. 14:13; Judg. 9:2–3. See M. J. Mulder, "Baal-berith," *DDD*, 266–72; T. J. Lewis, "Baal-Berith," *ABD* 1:550–51.

90. *KAI* 4:3/4; 18:1, 7; etc.

91. *KAI* 27:14/15. The text is admittedly uncertain.

92. For Ugaritic citations and discussion see H. Niehr, "Baal-Zaphon," *DDD*, 289–93; cf. de Moor, "בַּעַל *baʿal*," 2:187.

93. *KAI* 218.

94. *KAI* 26A II:19.

95. *KAI* 47:1.

96. *KAI* 4:3/4.

97. See Even-Shoshan, *Concordance*, 196, for references.

names like Bamoth-Baal and Kiryath-Baal, in which the divine title appears in the genitive position.[98] These place-names are not the only indications of Baal worship in Israel. An allegiance to this deity seems also to be reflected in several personal names: Ish-Baal, "man of Baal" (1 Chron. 8:33), Merib-Baal, "Baal strives" (? 1 Chron. 8:34), Jerub-Baal, "may Baal contend,"[99] Baal-yada, "Baal knows" (1 Chron. 14:7), and Baal-Yah, "Yahweh is Baal" (1 Chron. 12:6).[100] Hosea 2:18–19 (2:16–17 Eng.) illustrates poetically the extent to which Yahweh had been "baalized" in popular religious thought in the eighth century B.C.:

> "And in that day," declares Yahweh,
> "You will no longer call me 'My husband' (*ʾîšî*),
> And no longer will you call me 'My Baal' (*baʿlî*),
> For I will remove the names of the Baals from her mouth,
> And they shall be mentioned by name no more."

As in the case of Adon, the application of an appellative like *bʿl* to the storm god, known otherwise by his personal name Hadad, or to any other deity reflects an attitude of subjection to the god on the part of the devotee.

Melek

In the ancient Near East gods were often described in royal terms.[101] This was especially true of the highest divinities, whose status and function were usually interpreted in cosmic, rather than nationalistic, terms. Thus expressions like "king of the gods,"[102] "king of the Anunnaki,"[103] "king of the Igigi,"[104] "king of the lands,"[105] and "king of the universe entire"[106] are common in Mesopotamian

---

98. Cf. Even-Shoshan, *Concordance*, s.v., for references.

99. Or perhaps "let Baal prove himself great" (Judg. 6:32). For discussion see J. A. Soggin, *Judges: A Commentary*, trans. J. Bowden, OTL (Philadelphia: Westminster, 1981), 124–25; D. I. Block, *Judges and Ruth*, NAC (Nashville: Broadman & Holman, 1999), in loc.

100. It is also possible that the name is intended as a verbless clause of classification, in which case it would mean simply "Yah is lord." So BDB, 128; *HALOT* 1:145. Cf. F. I. Andersen's Rule 3, discussed in *The Hebrew Verbless Clause in the Pentateuch*, Journal of Biblical Literature Monograph Series 14 (Nashville: Abingdon, 1970), 42–45. On these and other names involving "Baal," see Fowler, *Theophoric Personal Names*, 57–63.

101. Cf. G. V. Smith, "The Concept of God/the Gods as King in the Ancient Near East and the Bible," *Trinity Journal*, n.s., 3 (1982): 18–38.

102. Of Anu(m), *ANET*, 383, line 34; 462, lines 381–91; of Marduk, *ANET*, 68, VI:38; 309–10, 315; of Sin, *ANET*, 311–12.

103. Of Anu(m), *ANET*, 164.

104. Of Ashur, *ANET*, 285.

105. Of Enlil, *ANET*, 159. Cf. S. N. Kramer, *Sumerian Mythology*, 3d ed. (Philadelphia: University of Pennsylvania Press, 1972), 45.

106. Of Marduk, *ANET*, 66–67.

sources. In the Ugaritic texts El is depicted as king of the pantheon,[107] but when Baal is promoted to the office the latter also gains authority over the gods.[108] In a much later Phoenician text, *mlk⸣*, "the king," serves as an epithet of Baal-Shamayn.[109] A few titles like "king of the abyss"[110] and "king of the deep"[111] perceive the kingship more territorially, but it is clear that these are not perceived as designations for national patrons.

Hints of territorial claims do, however, surface occasionally. The prologue to the Code of Hammurabi describes Marduk as having "an enduring kingship in Babylon."[112] But even here this may merely indicate the location of his throne, since the text emphasizes his dominion over much broader cosmic and pantheonic spheres.[113] Nebuchadnezzar II's claim, "Marduk my king,"[114] need similarly indicate no more than a recognition of his personal subjection to the cosmic ruler.

Perhaps the clearest example of a localized jurisdiction is the title "king of the land," applied to Ninurta, patron of Kur.[115] From northwest Semitic texts, the designation of the Baal of Tyre as Melqart (i.e., *mlk qrt*), "king of the city," seems equally localized.[116] On the other hand, *qrt*, "city," may also be interpreted as a euphemism for the netherworld, since Melqart is elsewhere equated with the Mesopotamian Nergal.[117] Personal names incorporating *mlk* as the theophore appear in several names from Byblos. Yehawmilk (*yhwmlk*), "may Milk give life," appears as the son of Urimilk (*⸣rmlk*), "Milk is light," in a fourth- to fifth-century B.C. text.[118] The name of the Ammonite deity Milcom/Malkam, discussed earlier, is rooted in the same appellative.

107. For references to El bearing the title *mlk* see W. Herrmann, "El," *DDD*, 524. Cf. M. H. Pope, *El in the Ugaritic Texts*, VTSup 2 (Leiden: Brill, 1955), 25–32; E. Jacob and H. Cazelles, "Ras Shamra et l'Ancien Testament," *DBS* 9:1434–35.
108. Cf. Smith, "God/the Gods as King," 26–27.
109. Hatra 16:1, 2. Cf. *DNWSI* 2:639, for additional examples of *mlk⸣* employed as an epithet of divinities.
110. Of Enki, Kramer, *Sumerian Mythology*, 60.
111. Of Ea, *ANET*, 390.
112. *ANET*, 164.
113. Cf. *ANET*, 66–67.
114. *ANET*, 307. Cf. the earlier reference to "Marduk my lord," ibid.
115. Kramer, *Sumerian Mythology*, 81.
116. So also M. Höfner in *Die Religionen Altsyriens, Altarabiens, und der Mandäer*, ed. H. Gese et al. (Stuttgart: Kohlhammer, 1970), 193–98. Unless *qrt* refers to the netherworld. See Albright, *Stone Age to Christianity*, 307; Heider, *Cult of Molek*, 175–79.
117. Cf. S. Ribichini, "Melqart," *DDD*, 1053.
118. *KAI* 10:1. Cf. Benz, *Names*, 344–45, for many more Phoenician and Punic names incorporating the theophore *mlk*. The name is reminiscent of the recently discovered Ammonite name *mlkm⸣r*. See Hübner, *Die Ammoniter*, seal #88. For a discussion of the seal, see L. Geraty, "Baalis," *ABD* 1:556–57.

The Old Testament provides several additional divine names incorporating the root *mlk*. In 2 Kings 17:31 the compound forms Adrammelek and Anamelek identify the gods of Sepharvaim.[119] The name Molek is used on several occasions in connection with child sacrifices.[120] His identification as "the detestable idol of the sons of Ammon" in 1 Kings 11:7 suggests some association with the Ammonite patron divinity. Speaking of the valley of Hinnom, in which persons were causing children to pass through the fire to Molek, Jer. 32:35 seems to connect the name with the Canaanite fertility deity. In several texts Molek is preceded by the article, which may indicate a basic appellative significance, "the one who rules."[121]

The treatment of Yahweh as king in the Old Testament parallels in many respects the extrabiblical usage, but it deviates from the latter as well.[122] Sometimes the designation of Yahweh as king describes his authoritative position in the heavens, as in Ps. 95:3–5:

> Yahweh is a great God,
> And a great king above all gods,
> In his hand are the depths of the earth;
> The heights of the mountains are his also.
> The sea is his, for he made it;
> For his hands formed the dry land.

This is also true of Ps. 103:19–20:

> Yahweh has established his throne in the heavens,
> And his kingdom rules over all.
> Bless Yahweh, you his angels,
> You mighty ones, who perform his word,
> Obeying the voice of his word!

119. On which see Ran Zadok, "Geographical and Onomastic Notes," *JANES* 8 (1976): 116–17.

120. Lev. 18:21; 20:2, 3, 4; 2 Kings 23:10; Jer. 32:35. For a discussion of the form of the name see Heider, *Cult of Molek*, 223–28.

121. For further discussion see M. Weinfeld, "The Worship of Molech and of the Queen of Heaven and Its Background," *UF* 4 (1972): 133–54; idem, "Burning Babies in Ancient Israel: A Rejoinder to Morton Smith's Article in *JAOS* 95 (1975) pp. 477–479," *UF* 10 (1978): 411–13; and the article by M. Smith cited, "On Burning Babies," *JAOS* 95 (1975): 477–79. A well-illustrated discussion of child sacrifice at Carthage, including the *mulk* sacrifice, is provided by L. E. Stager and S. R. Wolff, "Child Sacrifice at Carthage— Religious Rite or Population Control?" *BAR* 10.1 (1984): 30–51. These studies have now been superseded by the full-length investigation of Heider, *Cult of Molek*, who argues that the worship of Molek was of Canaanite origin and was associated with the cult of the dead. Cf. Heider, "Molech," *ABD* 4:895–98; idem, "Molech," *DDD*, 1090–97.

122. Cf. Smith, "God/the Gods as King," 26–27.

> Bless Yahweh, all you his hosts,
> You who serve him, that do his will!

In other contexts the title *mlk* signifies his rule over the entire earth,[123] its people,[124] or its nations.[125] Even though orthodox Israelites perceived Yahweh as the universal monarch, the treatment of Zion as the seat of his rule is analogous to the treatment of Marduk as king in Babylon.[126] In view of this pronounced cosmic emphasis, the attention given to Yahweh as a more localized king over Israel is striking. Expressions like "Yahweh was king in Jeshurun" (Deut. 33:5), "Yahweh, king of Israel" (Isa. 44:6),[127] and "the king of Jacob" (Isa. 41:21) are particularly noteworthy.[128] The psalmist declares in Ps. 10:16:

> Yahweh is king forever,
> Nations have perished from *his* land.

Elsewhere Israel is identified as the people belonging to Yahweh the king,[129] or Yahweh is referred to as the king who belongs to the nation.[130] The most explicit statements are provided by Samuel in 1 Sam. 12:12, "Yahweh your God was your king,"[131] and Isa. 43:15, "I am Yahweh, your Holy One, the Creator of Israel, your king." In Ezek. 20:33, Yahweh declares, "I shall be king over you." Obviously Israel's prophets perceived no contradiction in treating Yahweh as cosmic monarch and national king at the same time.[132]

123. E.g., Ps. 24:7–10 (*melek hakkābôd*); 47:3, 8 (47:2, 7 Eng.); 93:1; 97:1; 98:6 (cf. v. 4); Jer. 10:10; Zech. 14:9. Cf. also Ps. 48:3 (48:2 Eng.).
124. Ps. 99:1.
125. Ps. 22:29 (22:28 Eng.); 47:9 (47:8 Eng.); Jer. 10:7, "O King of the nations"; Mal. 1:14, "I am a great king! My name is feared among the nations." Cf. "the king whose name is Yahweh of hosts," in the contexts of oracles against Egypt (Jer. 46:18), Moab (48:15), Babylon (51:57). Cf. also Zech. 14:16–17.
126. Ps. 68:25 (68:24 Eng.); Isa. 24:23. Notice the emphasis on the eternal nature of Yahweh's kingdom in Ps. 29:10; 145:1–3; 146:10; Jer. 10:10; Dan. 2:44; 3:33; 4:31 (4:34 Eng.); 6:27 (6:26 Eng.); 7:27.
127. Cf. Zeph. 3:15, "The king of Israel, Yahweh is in your midst."
128. Cf. Ps. 44:5 (44:4 Eng.), "You are my king, O God/Command victories for Jacob." Also Ps. 146:10, and v. 5.
129. Ps. 29:10; Isa. 52:7.
130. Ps. 149:2.
131. Cf. 1 Sam. 8:7, "They [Israelites] have rejected me from being king over them."
132. Ps. 48:3 (48:2 Eng.); Isa. 24:23. Recent decades have witnessed numerous studies on divine kingship in general and the kingship of Yahweh in particular. See, for example, I. Engnell, *Studies in Divine Kingship in the Ancient Near East* (Uppsala: Almqvist, 1943); H.-J. Kraus, *Die Königsherrschaft Gottes im Alten Testament* (Tübingen: Mohr, 1951); J. H. Eaton, *Kingship and the Psalms*, SBT 2d series no. 3 (London: SCM, 1976); B. C. Ollenburger, *Zion, the City of the Great King*, JSOTSup 41 (Sheffield: Sheffield Academic Press, 1987).

Theophoric names bearing the element Yahweh add one more dimension to the general picture.[133] Malkijah (*mlkyhw*) seems to have become especially popular in the seventh century B.C.[134] Gray suggested long ago that this may have occurred in revolt against the claims being made by Mesopotamian names such as "Nabu is king" or "Ashur is king," the pressure of which must have been increasingly felt during this period.[135] Other names of this type include Abimelek, Elimelek, Ahimelek, Malkishua, Nathanmelek, Ebedmelek, Malkiram, and Malkiel. Even though these names do not identify Yahweh as the king of Israel, they confirm the perception of the deity as the patron king.[136]

By ascribing royal titles to their gods, the people of the ancient Near East expressed their expectation that divine patrons would fulfill functions normally carried out by human monarchs: vanquishing enemies,[137] providing care and security,[138] and dispensing justice.[139]

Mare'

The fourth northwest Semitic epithet for deity, *mr'*, which also means "lord,"[140] appears to be unique to Aramaic dialects. In several inscriptions the term is applied to the Assyrian overlords of the Aramaean kings.[141] Some familiar divine epithets, such as *mr' šmy'*, "lord of heaven,"[142] and *mr' 'lm*, "eternal lord,"[143] suggest a cosmic significance. Several kings identify their personal/dynastic gods as their lords. Bar-Hadad of Damascus treats Melqart, usually recognized as the patron of Tyre, as *mr'h*, "his lord."[144] From Sam'al, Barrakab credits *mr'y rkb'l*, "my lord Rakab-El," and *mr'y tgltplysr*, "my lord Tiglath-Pileser," with putting him on the throne.[145] Barrakab II confessed *mr'y b'lhrn*, "My

133. On Israelite theophoric names involving *mlk*, see Fowler, *Theophoric Personal Names*, 50–53.

134. The name is common in the Old Testament (cf. BDB, 575), but it has also surfaced on several seal inscriptions. See Fowler, *Theophoric Personal Names*, 350, for references.

135. Cf. George B. Gray, *Studies in Hebrew Proper Names* (London: Adam and Charles Black, 1896), 120.

136. For references see BDB, s.v.

137. Ps. 44:5–8 (44:4–7 Eng.).

138. Ps. 29:10–11.

139. Ps. 96:10 (= 1 Chron. 16:31); 99:1; Mic. 4:7. Cf. Smith, "God/the Gods as King," 33ff.

140. See *DNWSI* 2:682–69 for references. In the early-ninth-century B.C. Tell Fekheriyeh bilingual inscription, *mr'* occurs opposite Akkadian *bēl*, lines 6, 17, 18.

141. See *KAI* 215:11ff.; 216:3, 5, 6; 217:2, 3/4. Cf. Gibson, *AI* 14:11ff.; 15:3, 5, 6; 16:2, 3/4.

142. See A. Cowley, *Aramaic Papyri of the Fifth Century B.C.* (1923; reprint, Osnabrück: Otto Zeller, 1967), 30:15, as in Dan. 5:23.

143. As a title for Baal-Shamayn. See *DNWSI* 2:686, for references.

144. *KAI* 201:3.

145. *KAI* 216:5–6.

lord is Baal-Haran."[146] The usage that comes nearest to suggesting a national/state deity is provided by the Tell Fekheriyeh statue. After designating Hadad as *mrʾ rb mrʾ hdysʾy mlk gwzn*, "the great lord, the lord of Hadad-yisʾi, the king of Gozan,"[147] the deity is called *mrʾ ḥbwr*, "lord of Habur."[148]

The Old Testament uses *mrʾ* of Yahweh only in the cosmic sense. Daniel 2:47 identifies him as *mārēʾ malkîn*, "lord of kings." In 5:23 he is *mārēʾ šěmayyāʾ*, "lord of heaven."

Roʿeh

In Mesopotamia the motif of the divine shepherd is ancient, going back to Sumerian times. The title seems to have been especially appropriate for Dumuzu, to whom it is often applied.[149] In the "Lamentation over the Destruction of Ur" (Ningal Lament) the first song, which is thirty-five lines long, bemoans the destruction of Sumer by listing more than twenty deities who have "abandoned their stable; their sheepfold has been abandoned to the wind."[150] Particularly illuminating is an excerpt from an Akkadian hymn to Shamash, the sun god:

> O Shamash
> . . . .
> Leaning over the mountains, you inspect the earth,
> You balance the disk of the world in the midst of heaven
>   (For) the circle of the lands.
> You make the people of all lands your charge,
> All those king Ea, the counsellor,
>   has created are entrusted to you.
> You shepherd all living creatures together,
> You are herdsman, above and below.
> You cross regularly through the heavens,
> Every day you traverse the vast earth.[151]

This compares with the much later Babylonian Theodicy, which closes with, "The shepherd Shamash will pas[ture] people as a god should."[152] In Yahdun-Lim's dedicatory inscription for the temple devoted to Sha-

146. *KAI* 218.
147. Abou-Assaf, Bordreuil, and Millard, *La statue de tell Fekherye*, 23, line 6.
148. Ibid., line 16.
149. Cf. H. Ringgren, *Religions of the Ancient Near East*, trans. J. Sturdy (Philadelphia: Westminster, 1973), 11–16.
150. *ANET*, 456; *CCBW*, 535–36.
151. As translated by Foster, *BM* 2:537. Cf. *ANET*, 387–88.
152. As translated by B. R. Foster, *CCBW*, 495. Cf. W. G. Lambert, *Babylonian Wisdom Literature* (Oxford: Clarendon, 1960), 88–89, line 297.

mash, this god is identified as "the shepherd of all the blackheaded."[153] The personal name, "Shamash is my shepherd," is reminiscent of "Yahweh is my shepherd," for all who are familiar with Psalm 23.[154] It is closely related in sense to another personal name, "Marduk has provided me with pasture."[155] Elsewhere he is identified as *rê'i teneššēti*, "the shepherd of the people."[156]

To date no Northwest Semitic text has yielded a reference to deity being called a divine shepherd. This does not mean the notion was absent. On the contrary, the prominence of the divine shepherd-king ideology in the Old Testament suggests that this method of characterizing the role of the divine patron must have been common throughout the region.[157] Psalm 80 represents the most instructive biblical text. In this composition the psalmist appeals passionately to Yahweh to apply his patron status and come to the aid of the nation.[158] His role as shepherd has obvious royal overtones:

> Give ear, O Shepherd of Israel,
>> You who lead Joseph like a flock;
> You who are enthroned above the cherubim,
>> Shine forth!
> Before Ephraim, Benjamin, and Manasseh,
>> Stir up your might;
>>> And come to deliver us!
> O God! Restore us!
>> Let your face shine on us
>> That we may be saved! (80:2–4 [80:1–3 Eng.])

153. *ANET,* 556. On the issue see L. Dürr, *Ursprung und Ausbau der israelitischen Heilandserwartung* (Berlin: Schwetschke & Sohn, 1925), 121–22.

154. Cf. J. J. Stamm, *Die akkadische Namengebung,* Mitteilungen der vorderasiatisch-ägyptischen Gesellschaft 44 (Leipzig: Hinrichs, 1939), 214.

155. Ibid., 189.

156. Cf. Dürr, *Ursprung und Ausbau,* 121. Cf. the references to the gods as shepherds cited in von Soden, *AHw,* 2:977–78. It is striking that the title of shepherd is frequently applied to the heads of pantheons, with the remainder of the gods being viewed as the flock (e.g., Marduk, in Enuma Elish VII:131, *ANET,* 72), or as leaders of the heavens. On the deity Sin see A. Jeremias, *Handbuch der altorientalischen Geisteskultur* (Leipzig: Hinrichs, 1913), 242–43. For similar views on Amun and Osiris in Egypt cf. J. Jeremias, "ποιμήν, ἀρχιποίμην, ποιμαίνω," *TDNT* 6:486–87. For a study of the gods as shepherds see I. Seibert, *Hirt-Herde-König: Zur Herausbildung des Königtums in Mesopotamien* (Berlin: Akademie Verlag, 1969), 15–16.

157. On the subject of Yahweh as shepherd see J. G. S. S. Thomson, "The Shepherd-Ruler Concept in the OT and Its Application in the NT," *SJT* 8 (1955): 406–18; J. Jeremias, "ποιμήν," 6:485–88; J. A. Soggin, "רעה," *THAT* 2:793 (= *TLOT* 3:1246–48).

158. Cf. H.-J. Kraus, *Psalms 60–150,* trans. H. C. Hilton (Minneapolis: Augsburg, 1989), 141: "The underlying metaphor provides a characteristic expression for the close God-people relation and emphasizes the lordship of the guiding God over his people."

This divine shepherd-king ideology surfaces again in Ps. 95:3–7:

> For Yahweh is a great God,
>   And a great king above all gods.
> Come, let us worship and bow down,
>   Let us kneel before Yahweh our maker,
> For we are the people of his pasturing (*ʿam marʿîtô*),
>   That is the flock of his hand (*ṣōʾn yādô*).

The application of the term *rōʿeh* to Yahweh in the Blessing of Jacob demonstrates the antiquity of the notion in Israel.[159] In Gen. 49:24 the name appears as a designation for God alongside "Mighty One of Jacob" (*ʾăbîr yaʿăqōb*), "Stone of Israel" (*ʾeben yiśrāʿēl*), "God of your father" (*ʾēl ʾābîkā*), and "Almighty" (*šadday*).[160]

Divine shepherd imagery is common in the prophets as well. Micah 2:12–13 conjoins royal rule and pastoral care:

> I will surely gather all of you, O Jacob,
>   I will surely assemble the remnant of Israel.
> I will bring them together
>   Like sheep in a fold;
> Like the flock in the midst of its pasture,
>   They will throng with men.

The final strophe in the book begins on a similar note:

> Shepherd your people with your staff,
>   The flock of your patrimony (*ṣōʾn naḥălātekā*),
> Which lives alone in the forest,
>   In the heart of the fertile garden.
> Let them feed in Bashan and Gilead,
>   As they did in the days of old. (7:14)[161]

The fullest description of the pastoral role of Yahweh is provided by Ezekiel 34, a text that contrasts the irresponsible exploitation of the flock by human rulers with the genuine care of Yahweh.[162]

159. Cf. G. Wenham, *Genesis 16–50*, WBC 2 (Dallas: Word, 1994), 468–71, for discussion.

160. On the date of the text cf. F. M. Cross and D. N. Freedman, *Studies in Ancient Yahwistic Poetry*, SBLDS 21 (Missoula, Mont.: Scholars Press, 1975), 70.

161. For additional references to the divine shepherd of Israel see Gen. 48:15; Isa. 40:11; Hos. 4:16; Ps. 23; 28:9.

162. For full discussion of this text see D. I. Block, *Ezekiel 25–48*, NICOT (Grand Rapids: Eerdmans, 1998), 273–309.

Human Epithets

The foregoing discussion has focused on the role of the gods in ancient Near Eastern perceptions of divine-human relationships. The use of epithets like "lord," "master," and "king" for deity highlights the sovereignty of the deity over the human subjects. When we turn our attention to the role of the human subjects in these associations we observe the flip side of the notion that a divine patron was an owner or ruler of the people. Nations and peoples that recognized a divine suzerain would view themselves as his or her subjects and servants. At the individual level this subjection is expressed by personal names in which the term *ᶜebed*, "servant," occurs as a *nomen regens* with some divine name appearing as the *nomen rectum*. In a general sense this is reflected in names like *ᶜbdᵓl*, "servant of El," forms of which occur in Aramaic,[163] Phoenician,[164] Edomite, and Hebrew.[165] The connection is rendered specific in Hebrew names like Obadiah, "servant of Yahweh";[166] in Edomite *ᶜbdqws*, "servant of Qos,"[167] in Ammonite *ᶜbdᵓ*, "servant of I[l],"[168] and *ᶜbdᵓdd*, "servant of Adad";[169] in Phoenician *ᶜbdbᶜl*, "servant of Baal," *ᶜbdmlqrt*, "servant of Melqart," *ᶜbdᵓšmn*, "servant of Eshmun," *ᶜbdᶜštrt*, "servant of Ashtart," and so on.[170]

The Old Testament employs the phrase "servants of Yahweh" (*ᶜōbĕdê yhwh*) of the deity's devotees in general,[171] as well as of specific individuals in particular.[172] It is used also of those who serve Yahweh in a cultic sense, such as the Levitical singers in the temple worship,[173] and especially the prophets.[174]

Of particular interest here is the treatment of the nation of Israel as the *ᶜebed yhwh* in Isaiah 40–55. Several texts treat this status as a special

163. *ᶜbdᵓly*, "servant of my god," *KAI* 246:1.
164. *ᶜbdᵓlm*, "servant of divinity," *KAI* 18:1, 2; 28:3. For a discussion of such names see Benz, *Names*, 229–30.
165. *ᶜabdîᵓēl*, "servant of God," 1 Chron. 5:15.
166. Very common in the Old Testament and on Hebrew seals. See Fowler, *Theophoric Personal Names*, 353. Cf. Abednego, "servant of Nebo," which may be a corruption of the Babylonian name of Azariah, Dan. 1:7.
167. Bartlett, *Edom and the Edomites*, 203, 205, 206.
168. *CAI* 50; 53; 144:1:5.
169. *CAI* 131.
170. For these and many more see Benz, *Names*, 371.
171. See BDB, 714, for references.
172. Of the patriarchs: Exod. 32:13; Deut. 9:27; of Abraham: Gen. 26:24; Ps. 105:6, 42; of Isaac: Gen. 24:14; of Jacob/Israel: Ezek. 28:25; 37:25; 1 Chron. 16:13; of Moses: Exod. 14:31; Josh. 18:7; etc.; of Joshua: Josh. 24:29; Judg. 2:8; of Caleb: Num. 14:24; of Job: Job 1:8; 2:3; 42:7–8; of David: 2 Sam. 3:18; 7:5, 8, 26; etc.; of Hezekiah: 2 Chron. 32:16; of Zerubbabel: Hag. 2:23; of Eliakim: Isa. 22:20.
173. Ps. 113:1; 134:1; 135:1.
174. 2 Kings 9:7; 17:13, and many more. Cf. BDB, 714.

privilege, based upon the gracious election and redemption of the nation by their patron deity. Thus Isa. 41:8–16:

> But you, Israel, my servant,
>> Jacob, whom I have chosen,
>> The offspring of Abraham, my friend;
> You whom I have taken from the ends of the earth,
>> And called from its farthest corners,
> Saying to you, "You are my servant,
>> I have chosen you and not cast you off."
> Fear not, for I am with you;
>> Do not be anxious for I am your God.
> I will strengthen you;
>> I will help you;
> I will uphold you with my righteous right hand.

This is echoed in 44:1–5:

> But now hear, O Jacob, my servant;
>> Israel, whom I have chosen:
> Thus says Yahweh who made you
>> And formed you from the womb,
>> And will help you:
> "Fear not, O Jacob, my servant;
>> And you Jeshurun whom I have chosen.
> . . . .
> This one will say, 'I belong to Yahweh';
>> And that one will call himself by the name of Jacob,
> And another will write on his hand, 'Belonging to Yahweh';
>> And will surname himself by the name of Israel."[175]

Some texts emphasize the special mission of this servant, namely, that of being a witness to Yahweh (43:10), serving as a light and bringing salvation to the nations (42:1–6; 49:17).[176] Several of these references to Israel as the servant of Yahweh occur in strongly polemical

---

175. Note also 44:21–23:
> Remember these things, O Jacob,
>> And Israel, for you are my servant;
> I have formed you, you are my servant,
>> O Israel, you will not be forgotten by me.
Cf. 45:4; Jer. 30:10; 46:27–28; Ps. 136:22.

176. In several of these Servant Songs the vision appears to move from the ideal Israel to the messianic figure who embodies Israel. The resolution of this complex problem is beyond the scope of this discussion. See the commentaries.

anti-idolatry contexts (cf. 42:17; 43:11–12; 44:9–20; 45:5), highlighting the exclusive nature of this deity-nation association.

At the same time, if the divine patron was viewed as a shepherd, then the people must have looked upon themselves as the god's flock. This idea has already surfaced in some of the texts referred to above. Several terms reflect this sense: *ʿēder*, "herd,"[177] *ṣōʾn*, "flock,"[178] and *marʿît*, "pasturage."[179] Soggin has correctly observed that when the divine patron is referred to as a shepherd, *rōʿeh*, that term clearly serves as a variant expression for the royal title, *melek*.[180]

Limitations to the Concept of National Deities

The foregoing discussion suggests that as a rule in the ancient Near East the relationship between a deity and his or her particular people was not viewed as a casual association. On the one hand, the use of divine titles like *Baʿal*, *Melek*, *ʾAdon*, and *Mareʾ* indicates that the people acknowledged the sovereignty of the god and their subjection to that god, even as they were subject to any earthly monarch. For their part, the people were the god's servants. The relationship between deity and subjects may be characterized as a feudal type of relationship in which the god functioned as the divine overlord and the subject people represented the vassals. On the other hand, the identification of the divinity as *Roʿeh* adds a pastoral dimension to the association between deity and people. This epithet recognizes the divinity's role as the defender and provider of the people. The gods were responsible for the welfare and security of their devotees.[181]

However, this raises several important questions. Does the assumption of patron deities who bore responsibility for the welfare of their people demand a one-to-one correspondence between deities and peoples? Were such relationships perceived to be exclusive? Is it appropriate to speak of each nation as having its own "national god"? Or are there limitations to the notion of national divinities?

---

177. Isa. 40:11; Jer. 13:17 (*ʿēder yhwh*); 31:10; Zech. 10:3 (*ʿedrô*).

178. Jer. 23:1–4; Ezek. 34:6–16, 31; Mic. 7:14; Zech. 9:16; Ps. 77:21 (77:20 Eng.); 78:52; 79:13; 80:2 (80:1 Eng.); 95:7; 100:3.

179. The expression usually refers to pasturing, shepherding, as in the form *ṣōʾn marʿîtî* in Jer. 23:1 and Ezek. 34:31; cf. Ps. 74:1; 79:13; 100:3. By metonymy the expression may also designate the flock, as in Jer. 10:21, and perhaps Ps. 95:7. The latter may, however, be textually unsound. See the note in *BHS*.

180. *THAT* 2:793 (= *TLOT* 3:1248). A helpful study of the metaphorical use of animal names for leaders and nobles has been provided by P. D. Miller Jr., "Animal Names as Designations in Ugaritic and Hebrew," *UF* 2 (1970): 177–86. This study needs to be expanded to the use of animal names as collectives for people.

181. See esp. Ezekiel 34.

This issue may be pursued by asking two basic questions: (1) Would "national deities" tolerate the worship of other gods by their subjects? (2) Would the "national deity" look with favor upon the homage of persons, individuals or groups, who did not belong to his/her own people? Would his/her sovereignty and care be extended to outsiders?

The Problem of Rival Deities

Information on the issue of rival deities is most complete for Mesopotamia. In Nebuchadnezzar's Babylon, for example, the eight city gates were named after different gods. Even more striking is the fact that temples dedicated to Adad, Shamash, Ninurta, Ishtar, and numerous other deities existed simultaneously in the city. Obviously Marduk did not have a monopoly on the devotion of the residents of the city.[182] Indeed, judging by the personal names of the most important Neo-Babylonian rulers, Nabu was the acknowledged divine patron of the dynasty at the same time that Marduk was accepted as the god of the city.[183] In their epithets Neo-Assyrian kings regularly expressed a dependence upon several members of the Assyrian pantheon.[184]

The same phenomenon may be observed in Syria. Temples dedicated to both Baal and Dagan have been discovered in the important second-millennium city of Ugarit.[185] From the Aramaean texts of the first millennium B.C. we note that at YᵓDY Panammuwa acknowledged in his accomplishments the assistance of Hadad, El, Resheph, Rakab-El, and Shemesh.[186] Zakkur of Hamath depended upon the support of Baal-Shamayn, Ilwer, Shemesh, and Shahar.[187] Bar-Hadad of Damascus identified Melqart as his lord where Hadad-Rimmon would have been

182. For a discussion of the city plan and the temples in the time of Nebuchadnezzar (605–582 B.C.), see D. J. Wiseman, *Nebuchadnezzar and Babylon*, Schweich Lectures 1983 (Oxford: Oxford University Press for the British Academy, 1985), 42–73. Cf. idem, *IBD* 1:159. On the religion of the Babylonians, see W. G. Lambert, "The Babylonians," in *Peoples of Old Testament Times*, 184–87; also H. W. F. Saggs, *The Greatness That Was Babylon: A Sketch of the Ancient Civilization of the Tigris-Euphrates Valley* (London: Sidgwick & Jackson, 1962), 299–358. On the correlation between the history of Babylon and the importance of Marduk see D. I. Block, "Chasing a Phantom: The Search for the Historical Marduk," *Archaeology in the Biblical World* 2 (1992): 20–43.
183. Cf. Nebuchadnezzar, Nabonidus, Nabopolassar. So also C. R. North, *The Second Isaiah* (Oxford: Clarendon, 1964), 163. However, the theophore Marduk is found in the names of most of Nebuchadnezzar's sons. For a discussion of the issue see Wiseman, *Nebuchadnezzar and Babylon*, 9–12. On the gods in Babylon see A. R. George, *House Most High: The Temples of Ancient Mesopotamia* (Winona Lake, Ind.: Eisenbrauns, 1995).
184. Note, for example, Ashurbanipal, who names Ashur, Sin, Shamash, Adad, Ishtar, Belit, Bel, Ninorta, Nergal, and Nusku. See the Rassam Cylinder, *ARAB*, 2:§766.
185. On which see J. C. Courtois, "Ras Shamra: Archéologie," *DBS* 9:1195–97.
186. *KAI* 214:2–3; Gibson, *AI* 13:2–3.
187. *KAI* 202 B:20–28; *AI* 5 B:20–28.

expected.[188] As witnesses to his treaty with Matiᶜel of Arpad, Bargayah of KTK appealed to Millissu, Marduk, Zarpanitu, Nabu, Teshmet, Erra, Nusku, Nergal, Las, Shamash, Nur, Sin, Nikkal, NKR, Kadditu, Hadad, El Elyon, and all the gods of the country and the cultivated land.[189] The Phoenician religious scene was equally complex. Each major city seems to have favored not one but several members of the pantheon. The following typical groups have been recognized: El, Baalat, and Adonis in Byblos; Baal, Astarte, and Eshmun in Sidon; Melqart and Astarte in Tyre.[190]

It is obvious that in none of these regions did the religious commitments of the people approach anything like the monotheism evident in the orthodox Yahwism of the Old Testament. In most localities one deity tended to emerge above the remainder, but the rest were still recognized officially and unofficially. Therefore the situation could at best be characterized as territorial henotheism.

Even though the extrabiblical evidence from the south Syrian Transjordanian states is less complete, the data concerning Edom, Moab, and Ammon point in a similar direction. The witness of the Old Testament is consistent. According to Judg. 10:6 the apostasy of the Israelites involved the worship of "the Baals and the Ashtaroths, and the gods of Aram, and the gods of Sidon, and the gods of Moab, and the gods of the Ammonites, and the gods of the Philistines." Since the Baals and the Ashtaroths probably refer to a variety of local manifestations of these divinities, in this context *ʾĕlōhê* should also be understood in the plural sense.[191]

Although Chemosh was the primary god of the Moabites, according to Num. 22:41 Balak the king brought Baalam to the high place of Baal. Balak's subsequent sacrifice at the top of Peor (Num. 23:28–30) may well have been to the same deity as the one to which the Israelites apostatized in Num. 25:1–18.[192] The place-names Beth-Baal-Meon and Bamoth-Baal also betray some association with the cult.[193] Whether

---

188. *KAI* 201:3; *AI* 1:3.

189. *KAI* 222 A:8–11; *AI* 7 iA:8–11.

190. S. Moscati, *The World of the Phoenicians*, trans. A. Hamilton (London: Weidenfeld & Nicolson, 1968), 31–33.

191. So also J. Gray, *Joshua, Judges and Ruth*, NCB (1967; reprint, Grand Rapids: Eerdmans, 1986), 329–30, contra H. Orlinsky, "Nationalism-Universalism and Internationalism in Ancient Israel," in *Translating and Understanding the Old Testament: Essays in Honor of Herbert Gordon May*, ed. H. T. Frank and W. L. Reed (Nashville: Abingdon, 1970), 217.

192. Hos. 9:10 describes this as a shameful event.

193. Josh. 13:17. This seems to be the full form of Baal-Meon, referred to in Num. 32:38; Ezek. 25:9; 1 Chron. 5:8. Cf. also Jer. 48:23, which has Beth-Meon, and Num. 32:3, which reduces it to Beon.

one should view these names as local manifestations of the deity Baal or the worship of Chemosh under the epithet of Baal is uncertain. Scholars have established that the Moabite cult shared many features with the Baalism of Canaan.[194] This ambivalent attitude toward other deities is reflected also in the inscription of Mesha, which juxtaposes Ashtar-Chemosh with Chemosh,[195] and in Moabite personal names like Shalamanu, which incorporates the divine name Shalem/Shalam.[196]

Information regarding the Ammonite pantheon is contradictory. While Milcom appears to have been the divine patron of the nation, the preferred theophore in personal names is overwhelmingly El/Il. Other divine names attested in personal names include Adad, Adon (though this may be a title rather than a divine name), Baal, Gad, Mawt, Nanay, Shamash, and Yariḥ.[197]

In Edom, Qaus seems also to have had some competition, a fact hinted at in the Old Testament, which condemns Amaziah for worshiping Edomite gods (plural).[198] Baal,[199] El,[200] Eshmun,[201] and Hadad[202] occur in individuals' names. Archaeologists' discovery of female figurines suggests also the presence of the cult of the fertility goddess.[203]

The evidence from the northern and Transjordanian regions pointing to the simultaneous veneration of several divinities apart from the patron is clear.[204] But what was the situation in Israel? The writers of the

194. See van Zyl, *Moabites*, 193–202.

195. Ashtar is the masculine counterpart of the more familiar feminine Astarte. For discussion see Gibson, *HMI*, 81; J. Gray, "The Desert God ʿAṮṮR in the Literature and Religion of Canaan," *JNES* 8 (1949): 72–83.

196. On which see H. B. Huffmon, "Shalem," *DDD*, 1428–31. On the religion of the Moabites see further J. M. Miller, "Moab," *ABD* 4:891–92.

197. Based on the list of personal names provided by Hübner, *Die Ammoniter*, 125–29, and Aufrecht's glossary, *CAI*, 356–76. Cf. also K. P. Jackson, *The Ammonite Language of the Iron Age*, HSM 27 (Chico, Calif.: Scholars Press, 1983). The names of the known kings of Ammon are (in chronological order) Nahash, Hanun, Shobi, Shanib, Zakur, Yariḥ-Ezer(?), Pudu-Ilu/Buduilu, ʿAmminadab I, Hissal-El, ʿAmminadab II, Baalis/Baal-Yashaʿ. Cf. J.-M. de Tarragon, "Ammon," 1:195.

198. 2 Chron. 25:14–15. The singular interpretation is precluded since the suffixes on *lipnêhem* and *lāhem* are plural.

199. Baal-ḥanan (1 Chron. 1:49–50), *šʿdbʾl, bʿlyt[n], ʾšbʿl* (ostraca, Bartlett, *Edom and the Edomites*, 218–19).

200. Mehetab-el (1 Chron. 1:50), *šmʿʾl* (seal inscription, Bartlett, *Edom and the Edomites*, 214).

201. *ʿbdʾš[m]n* (ostracon, Bartlett, *Edom and the Edomites*, 218).

202. Hadad (Gen. 36:35; 1 Chron. 1:50 [spelled Hadar in Gen. 36:39]; 1 Kings 11:14–15).

203. Nelson Glueck, *The Other Side of the Jordan*, rev. ed. (New Haven: American Schools of Oriental Research, 1970), 186.

204. With reference to the Ammonite religion, Hübner (*Die Ammoniter*, 247–69) speaks of a "limited polytheism" (*begrenzte Polytheismus*).

Old Testament create the impression that Yahweh's demand for exclusive allegiance was constantly threatened by the seductive attractions of alien gods, especially the Canaanite divinities. The problem surfaces already at Sinai (Exodus 32), and reappears at the end of the desert wanderings (Numbers 25). It plagues the Israelites during the settlement period (Judg. 6:25–32; 8:27; 17–18), at the height of the united nation's power and influence (1 Kings 11:1–8), at the time of the division into northern and southern kingdoms (1 Kings 12:25–32), throughout the history of the northern kingdom (e.g., 1 Kings 16:29–34), and for much of the history of the kingdom of Judah (e.g., 2 Kings 21:1–9). Because these accounts are all preserved in polemical anti-idolatry contexts, and because the records have been preserved and transmitted by triumphant Yahwists for whom any compromise with Yahweh's demand for exclusive allegiance was a mark of depravity, many dismiss this evidence as biased and unreliable polemical literary products of a later age. However, the biblical portrait of Israel's spiritual condition is being increasingly illuminated by extrabiblical discoveries. While some continue to downplay the extent of Israel's departure from the worship of Yahweh,[205] we are faced with a growing body of evidence suggesting that syncretism was indeed a threat throughout the nation's history in the land of Canaan.[206]

Onomastic Evidence

I noted earlier that the overwhelming majority of Israelite theophoric personal names express an underlying devotion to Yahweh. However, one may remark some notable exceptions both within the Old Testament and in the extrabiblical sources. From the former, a name like Samson (Hebrew *Šimšôn*, "little sun") looks suspiciously derivative from Shamash/Shemesh, the widely used Semitic name for the sun god.[207] In the Old Testament scholars have found nine names identify-

205. Tigay, for example (*You Shall Have*, 91), argues that "relatively few Israelites worshipped gods other than YHWH."
206. The problem has been discussed at length in several monographs beginning with W. F. Albright, *Yahweh and the Gods of Canaan: A Historical Analysis of Two Contrasting Faiths* (Garden City, N.Y.: Doubleday, 1968), 153–264. Cf. also G. W. Ahlström, *Aspects of Syncretism in Israelite Religion* (Lund: Gleerup, 1963); and F. Stolz, "Monotheismus in Israel," in *Monotheismus im alten Israel und seiner Umwelt,* ed. O. Keel, Biblische Beiträge 14 (Fribourg: Schweizerisches Katholisches Bibelwerk, 1980), 163–74. More recent analyses are provided by M. S. Smith, *The Early History of God: Yahweh and Other Deities in Ancient Israel* (San Francisco: Harper & Row, 1987), 147–57; R. Albertz, *A History of Israelite Religion in the Old Testament Period,* trans. J. Bowden, 2 vols., OTL (Louisville: Westminster/John Knox, 1994), esp. 1:82–91, 146–56.
207. Some insist it means no more than "sunny" or "sunlit." Cf. E. Lipiński, "Shemesh," *DDD,* 1446; Fowler, *Theophoric Personal Names,* 167.

ing fifteen different individuals involving *Ba'al* as the theophore. The presence of this element need not by itself indicate syncretistic notions. In some of these names *Ba'al* probably functions as an epithet for Yahweh, synonymous with *'Adon*, "lord," with no pagan connotations whatsoever. Included in this category would certainly be names like *bĕ'alyâ*, "Yahweh is my lord," and perhaps also *bĕ'elyādā'*, "The lord [i.e., Yahweh] knows."[208] But it is difficult to interpret *yĕrubba'al*, Jerubbaal, this way. Not only does the name occur in an explicitly syncretistic cultural and textual context; despite the explanation given in Judg. 6:32, the common use of forms like this calls for a meaning something like "Let Baal contend [for him]," that is, stand up for the one who bears the name.[209] This interpretation of the name is supported by the Deuteronomistic historian's deliberate alteration of the name to *yĕrubbešet*, Jerubbesheth (2 Sam. 11:21). The same is true of *'išba'al*, "man of Baal." It is admittedly possible that Baal here serves as an epithet for Yahweh, that is, "man of the lord [i.e., Yahweh]." Here again, however, the Hebrew historian directs us to the preferred interpretation. In Kings the name is consistently rendered *'îš-bōšet*, Ishbosheth, which translates "man of shame."[210] The biblical author interpreted *mĕrîbba'al*, Meribbaal, "Baal is [my] advocate," similarly, replacing this intolerable form with an enigmatic *mĕpîbōšet*, Mephibosheth (2 Sam. 4:4; 9:6; etc.; cf. 1 Chron. 9:40). Whether or not a modern reader recognizes these names as evidences of syncretism, there can be no doubt that the biblical writer interpreted them this way.

Israelite inscriptions provide additional onomastic evidence of syncretism. As in the Old Testament, the Israelite personal names that have surfaced in extrabiblical sources display an overwhelming preference for Yahweh as the theophoric element. A second major contender is El, which Tigay has recognized in 77 personal names.[211] Since the Old Testament frequently identifies Yahweh with El, these names do not necessarily suggest allegiance to the head of the Canaanite pantheon by this name. However, the preponderance of Yahweh- and El-names should not blind us to the variety of pagan deities that appear as theophores in the epigraphic materials: Baal (*b'l*), Bes (*bs*), Gad (*gd*),

---

208. Cf. Fowler, *Theophoric Personal Names*, 55–56. Other names have been interpreted as contractions: *b'n'* and *b'nh*, for *b'l'nh*, "The lord has answered"; *b'r'*, for *b'lrm?* "The lord is exalted"; *b'šh*, for *b'lšm'?* "The lord has heard." See ibid., 55–57. For a paganized and syncretistic interpretation of these names see H. S. Gehman, ed., *New Westminster Dictionary of the Bible* (Philadelphia: Westminster, 1970), 84–85.

209. See further Block, *Judges and Ruth*, 269–71.

210. 2 Sam. 2:8–4:12. We learn of his real name from the Chronicler's genealogy in 1 Chron. 8:33 and 9:39.

211. Tigay, *You Shall Have*, 83–85.

Horus (*hr*), Isis (*ʾs*), Adat (*ʾdt*), Man/Min (*mn*), Mawet (*mwt*), Qos (*qws*), Shalim (*šlm*), Shamash (*šmš*), Yam (*ym*).[212] To this list we could add many more names that incorporate elements that could be interpreted as pagan theophores or as hypocoristic forms assuming Yahweh or El as the unspoken divinity.[213]

Inscriptional Evidence

The problem of Israelite syncretism is thrust into sharp relief by a series of small but significant archaeological discoveries. From the Elephantine papyri we have known for a long time that the cult of the post-exilic community in Egypt was heavily syncretistic.[214] For example, in a letter to a certain Micaiah, Giddel invokes the blessing of both Yaho and Khnub.[215] Recently several similarly syncretistic blessings have surfaced in the land of Israel. The first two, inscribed on large pithoi discovered at a ninth/eighth-century B.C. shrine at Kuntillet ʿAjrud (Horvat Teiman), read as follows:

Pithos A:
ʾmr . ʾ [. . . .]h[. .] k . ʾmr . lyhl[. .] wlywʿšh . w . . . brkt . ʾtkm lyhwh . šmrn . wlʾšrth

Thus says ʾ[. . .] (PN 1) . . . :
Say to Yehalle[lelʾ] (PN 2), Yoʿasa (PN 3) and . . . (PN 4):
I bless you (herewith—or: have blessed you)
to/before Yahweh of Samaria and his *asherah*.[216]

Pithos B

[ʾ]*mr / ʾmryw*	Thus says Amaryau:
ʾmr l.ʾdn[y]	Say to my lord:
hšlm . ʾt	Is it well with you?
brktyk . l[y]	I bless you (herewith—or: have blessed you)
hwh tmn	to/before Yahweh of Teman
wlʾšrth . yb	and his *asherah*.

212. As cited by Tigay, ibid., 65–68; idem, "Israelite Religion," in *Ancient Israelite Religion,* 164.

213. See Tigay, *You Shall Have,* 75–81.

214. Cf., for example, Papyrus 22, which records the size of contributions for Yaho (Yahweh), Ishumbethel, and Anathbethel (Cowley, *Aramaic Papyri,* 22:123–25; *ANET,* 491).

215. *ANET,* 491.

216. As transliterated and translated by O. Keel and C. Uehlinger, *Gods, Goddesses, and Images of God in Ancient Israel,* trans. T. Trapp (Minneapolis: Fortress, 1998), 225–26. One additional pithos with similar blessing invoking Yahweh of Teman and his *asherah* is published on p. 227. The authors provide full bibliography on the enormous literature on these and the following inscription. Text and translation of all these inscriptions are also provided by S. Landis Gogel, *A Grammar of Epigraphic Hebrew,* SBLRBS 23 (Atlanta: Scholars Press, 1998), 414.

rk . wyšmrk	May He bless (you) and keep you
wyhy ʿm . ʾd[n]	and be with my lord.[217]

The syncretistic nature of these documents is reinforced by the Bes figures (an Egyptian god who supposedly guarded childbirth and newborn children) sketched on the pithoi. Additional ink inscriptions mentioning alongside Yahweh not only Asherah but also El and Baal have also been found at this site.[218] A slightly later funerary inscription from Khirbet el-Qôm reads as follows:

ʾryhw . hʿšr . ktbh	Uriyahu, the honorable, has written [this] (or: this is his inscription)
brk . ʾryhw . lyhwh	Blessed is/be Uriyahu by Yahweh
wmṣrh lʾšrth hwšʿ lh	And [because?] from his oppressors, by his *asherah*, he has saved him
lʾnyhw	[written?] by Oniyahu.
lʾšrth	. . . by his *asherah* . . .
wlʾ[š]rth	. . . and by his *asherah*. . . .[219]

Among scholars the debate over the significance of *his asherah* has been intense. Many have seen in ʾšrtw the name of the goddess Asherah, here functioning as a consort for Yahweh.[220] The suffix on a proper name creates grammatical problems, however, leading many to treat the word not as a partner of Yahweh but as a cult object, presumably in the form of a tree, originally related to the goddess but here perceived as the medium through which his blessing was dispensed.[221] In either case, the syncretistic character of these inscriptions stands.

Iconographic Evidence

To this onomastic and epigraphic evidence of religious syncretism in ancient Israel we may add a growing body of iconographic evidence.[222]

---

217. Keel and Uehlinger, *Gods, Goddesses*, 226.
218. For discussion see ibid., 243–48.
219. As transliterated and translated by Keel and Uehlinger, ibid., 237, 239.
220. Cf. William G. Dever, "Asherah, Consort of Yahweh? New Evidence from Kuntillet ʿAjrûd," *BASOR* 255 (1984): 21–37.
221. The literature on the subject is vast. For recent discussions see J. A. Emerton, "New Light on Israelite Religion: The Implications of the Inscriptions from Kuntillet ʿAjrud," *ZAW* 94 (1982): 2–20; Day, "Asherah in the Hebrew Bible and Northwest Semitic Literature," *JBL* 105 (1986): 385–48; idem, "Asherah," *ABD* 1:485–86; M. S. Smith, *Early History of God*, 80–114; S. Olyan, *Asherah and the Cult of Yahweh in Israel*, SBLMS 34 (Atlanta: Scholars Press, 1988); Keel and Uehlinger, *Gods, Goddesses*, 225–48; R. H. Hess, "Asherah or Asherata?" *Orientalia* 65 (1996): 201–19.
222. Keel and Uehlinger (*Gods, Goddesses*, 182–210) provide full citation and discussion of the evidence. For a briefer survey see Tigay, *You Shall Have*, 91–96.

In the first instance we note the bronze bull figurine discovered at an open air shrine east of Dothan in the territory of Manasseh.[223] A. Mazar concluded that it was "a major object of cult, depicting or symbolizing a god, and it also expressed the attributes of a particular West Semitic storm god Hadad (Ba'al)."[224] The archaeologists' spades have also unearthed numerous female figurines with full breasts, symbolic of the mother goddess (Asherah/Astarte figures), seals with astral images, not to mention pictorial images like those of Bes found at Kuntillet 'Ajrud mentioned above.[225] Tigay's minimization of the problem of syncretism in ancient Israel is wishful thinking. The overwhelming preference for Yahweh and El as the theophores of choice does not mean that those who gave or bore these names were monolatrous or devoted exclusively to Yahweh; it means only that Yahweh was recognized as the official divine patron of the nation. The onomastic, epigraphic, and iconographic evidence suggests that even while Israelites and later Judaeans were professing primary faith in Yahweh, many were also enamored of the gods of the nations, integrating pagan beliefs and cultic practices into their own religious structures.

If the Israelites' relationship to their divine patron had been like the relationships of their neighbors to their respective gods, the syncretism they expressed would hardly receive notice. However, in sharp contrast to the religious situation outside Israel, and in stern reaction to the historical reality within, the Old Testament portrays orthodox Yahwists as consistently and vehemently opposed to the worship of any gods alongside or in competition with Yahweh. Critical scholarship today tends to question the usefulness of the Old Testament in reconstructing the religious situation in ancient Israel, treating its evidence as tendentious and polemical, the product of the "Yahweh alone" party that finally prevailed during the Babylonian exile.[226] But taken at face value, the tradi-

223. Mazar, "The 'Bull Site'—An Iron Age I Open Cult Place," *BASOR* 247 (1982): 27–42. Cf. also Mazar's less technical treatment, "Bronze Bull Found in Israelite 'High Place' from the Time of the Judges," *BAR* 9.5 (1983): 34–40. See the more recent comments by Keel and Uehlinger, *Gods, Goddesses*, 118–20. The authors amass a vast amount of additional extrabiblical evidence for syncretism in Israel.

224. Mazar, "Bull Site," 32. For other possible Israelite cult figures see O. Negbi, *Canaanite Gods in Metal: An Archaeological Study of Ancient Syro-Palestinian Figurines* (Tel Aviv: Tel Aviv University Press, 1976), 33, fig. 1361 (from Megiddo); 50–53, fig. 1454 (from Hazor). It is not certain, however, that these were actually intended as cult figures. See now the welcome caution of M. D. Fowler, "Excavated Figurines: A Case for Identifying a Site as Sacred?" *ZAW* 97 (1985): 333–44.

225. The evidence is discussed in detail by Keel and Uehlinger, *Gods, Goddesses*, 210–25.

226. See ibid., 385–91; Albertz, *History of Israelite Religion*, 2:414–26; B. Lang, *Monotheism and the Prophetic Minority: An Essay in Biblical History and Sociology*, SWBA 1 (Sheffield: Almond, 1983).

tion of the exclusive right of Yahweh to the devotion of his people dates back to the beginnings of their national history.[227] The Book of Deuteronomy is characterized by a harsh polemic against any compromise with foreigners lest they turn their hearts away from Yahweh.[228] The prophets follow in the tradition of Deuteronomy, denouncing the veneration of deities other than Yahweh with the strongest language. Idolatrous practices are treated as spiritual harlotry,[229] an abomination,[230] detestable,[231] foolishness,[232] and utterly disgusting.[233] According to the orthodox Yahwist, the God of Israel would brook no rivals.[234] In this respect the Hebrew view of Israel's relationship to its patron deity differed fundamentally from the perceptions of all the other nations around.

A related issue is the question of the openness of Yahweh to the acceptance of special gods for other nations. The Old Testament seems to reflect on this issue at several levels. At the literary level, the prophecies of Jeremiah and Isaiah speak freely of Chemosh, Milcom, Bel, Marduk, and Nebo as the gods of their respective peoples. At another level, however, Deuteronomy is emphatic about the qualitative difference between the God of Israel and the gods of the other nations. Only Israel

227. See Exod. 20:1–7; Deut. 5:1–11; 6:4–15; 7:1–11. But many scholars would date such Yahwistic claims much later. For example, Stolz ("Monotheismus," 164) suggests that it was as the exponent of the holy war against the Canaanites that Yahweh became the God of Israel. Later (p. 175), however, he dates the beginnings of the actual conflict between Yahwism and polytheism to the ninth century in Elijah's conflict with the house of Omri.

228. See esp. Deuteronomy 6–7.

229. Judg. 2:17; 8:27, 33, and many more. Cf. BDB, 275–76.

230. *tô'ēbôt*, Deut. 13:15, and many more. Cf. BDB, 1072–73. On the expression see E. Gerstenberger, "תעב," *THAT* 2:1051–55 (= *TLOT* 3:1428–31).

231. *šiqqûṣîm*, Deut. 29:16, etc. Cf. BDB, 1054–55; M. A. Grisanti, "שקה," *NIDOTTE* 5:243–46.

232. Note the satirical attacks of the prophets in Isa. 40:18–20; 41:6–7; 44:9–20; 46:1–2; Jer. 10:1–10. Cf. also Ps. 115:1–8.

233. *gillûlîm*, Ezek. 8:10 + 37 times in Ezekiel. Cf. BDB, 165, "dungy things"; *HALOT* 1:192, "droppings." This seems to have been an artificially created word derived from the root *gll*, "to roll," to which were added the vowels of *šiqqûṣîm*. Cf. H. D. Preuss, "גלולים *gillûlîm*," *TDOT* 3:1–5. Ezekiel's adoption of this expression for idolatry may have been prompted by the pellet-like shape and size of sheep feces. One can hardly imagine a more caustic remark about idolatry. Cf. D. I. Block, *Ezekiel 1–24*, NICOT (Grand Rapids: Eerdmans, 1997), 226.

234. On the surface David's response to Saul in 1 Sam. 26:18–19 seems to contradict the position of orthodox Yahwism. However, this is not presented as the stance either of the narrator or David. When David says "Go, serve other gods," he claims to be quoting cursed men who have driven him away from Yahweh. On the issue of monotheism in Israel, in addition to the works of Albright and Stolz cited above, cf. Albright, *Stone Age to Christianity*, 257–72; H. Ringgren, "Monotheism," in *IDBSup*, 602–4; D. Baly, "The Geography of Monotheism," in *Translating and Understanding the Old Testament*, 253–78.

could claim relationship to a divinity that was responsive to their prayers (Deut. 4:7); only Israel had been blessed with such a righteous set of statutes from their deity (4:8); only Israel had received such a revelation from their God (4:9–15); only Israel had experienced the mighty salvific acts of their God in such a personal way (4:32–40). Yahweh had delivered the nation from the bondage of Egypt, driven out their enemies before them, and given them their land as their inheritance (4:34–38). At a third level, we observe several strong denials of the objective reality of other national deities.[235] Accordingly, the polemical statements by Isaiah and Jeremiah on the folly of idolatry also have implications for the idolatries perpetrated by other nations as well.

The Divine Acceptance of Outsiders

Ancient Near Eastern deities' acceptance of the worship and devotion of persons other than those who identify with their subject group poses a second qualification to the notion of national deities. Examples of this situation may be adduced from all parts of the Fertile Crescent. According to Esarhaddon, an Assyrian, Marduk had specifically called him to rebuild the city of Babylon and to reinstate the proper practice of his cult.[236] In fact, this deity was venerated in this place successively by Old Babylonians,[237] Neo-Assyrians,[238] Chaldaeans,[239] Persians,[240] and Greeks.[241] In Aram and Phoenicia as well, ample evidence for the ready acceptance of the worship of aliens may be cited. I note here only Ben-Hadad of Damascus, who erected a stela in honor of Melqart, usually viewed as the divine patron of Tyre.[242]

With reference to the gods of the Transjordanian states, we have already observed that Qaus and Chemosh have been identified as far away as Egypt and Mesopotamia. Although some have suggested that the persons bearing these names may have been exiles,[243] the possibility that these were non-Edomites and non-Moabites, respectively, can-

---

235. See Ps. 96:5 (= 1 Chron. 16:26).

236. R. Borger, *Die Inschriften Asarhaddons, Königs von Assyrien,* Archiv für Orientforschung Beiheft 9 (Graz: Weidner, 1956), 16–17. In private communication A. R. Millard rightly questions whether the apparent divine acceptance of outsiders in reality involved the worship of local gods by aliens. In any case, as the (Assyrian) ruler of Babylon, Esarhaddon would want to restore Marduk in recognition of Babylon's superiority.

237. Prologue to the Code of Hammurabi, *ANET,* 164.

238. See the description of the reconstruction of Marduk's temple by Esarhaddon in Borger, *Inschriften Asarhaddons,* 16–19.

239. E.g., by Nebuchadnezzar, *ANET,* 307.

240. The Cyrus Cylinder, *ANET,* 315.

241. E.g., Antiochus Soter (280–262 B.C.), *ANET,* 317.

242. *KAI* 201; *ANET,* 65.

243. N. Avigad, "Seals of Exiles," *IEJ* 15 (1965): 222–32.

not be ruled out. The assumption of the Qaus cult by the Nabataeans, the successors to the Edomites, may point in the same direction.[244]

In this regard, the universalistic interests of Yahweh, generally known as the god of the Israelites, are equal to, if not more pronounced than, those of the deities mentioned above.[245] Genesis 12:3 and parallels place the election of Abraham within the universal context, with the statement that this person, whom Yahweh will bless, will become an agent of universal blessing. The signs and wonders accompanying the exodus of Israel from Egypt are multiplied expressly for the benefit of the Egyptians (Exod. 7:3–4), and indeed for the entire world (Exod. 9:13–16), that they might acknowledge the incomparability of Yahweh.[246] Hints of a mediatorial role for Yahweh's people (to represent the nations before God and vice versa) and his desire to relate to all the kingdoms of the earth may be recognized in his designation of Israel as "a kingdom of priests, a holy nation" (Exod. 19:4–6).

Many prophetic texts call attention to the universal recognition of Yahweh in general terms.[247] Moreover, the Israelites are not the only ones described as having received their land as "a patrimony" from Yahweh. According to Deut. 32:8 Yahweh (here identified with Elyon) has granted each nation its "patrimony."[248] None of these actions, however, annuls Israel's status as the uniquely elected people of Yahweh (Exod. 19:4–5), the special objects of his love (Deut. 4:37; 7:7–8), and recipients of his salvation (Deut. 33:26–29); they merely demonstrate that Yahweh's covenant relationship with his own people does not imply oblivion to or disinterest in the rest of humankind.

Most of the texts cited above assume that along with Israel, other peoples are also accountable in some sense to Yahweh. However, Israel's constitution contained specific provisions for the acceptance into the community of any outsider who might seek to join "the people of

244. Cf. J. T. Milik, "Nouvelles inscriptions nabatéennes," *Syria* 35 (1958): 239–40.

245. On which see R. Martin-Achard, *A Light to the Nations: A Study of the Old Testament Conception of Israel's Mission to the World,* trans. J. P. Smith (Edinburgh: Oliver & Boyd, 1962).

246. On the subject see C. J. Labuschagne, *The Incomparability of Yahweh in the Old Testament,* POS 5 (Leiden: Brill, 1966).

247. E.g., Isa. 2:1–4 = Mic. 4:1–3; Isa. 66:18–21; Zech. 2:15 (2:11 Eng.); 8:20–23; 14:16–17. Also Amos 9:12, "All the nations who are called by my name upon them." Others are quite specific. In Isa. 19:23–25 Yahweh speaks of Egypt as "my people" and Assyria as "the work of my hand," while in the same breath referring to Israel as "my inheritance." In Ps. 87:4–6 the psalmist describes Yahweh registering the "peoples," naming specifically Rahab (Egypt), Babylon, Philistia, Tyre, and Ethiopia. And, lest the Israelites should use Yahweh's special favors as occasions for spiritual complacency, Amos 9:7 reminds them that the migrations of the Philistines from Caphtor and the Arameans from Kir have been no less directed by Yahweh than has been their own exodus from Egypt.

248. Cf. Acts 17:26.

Yahweh." By the rite of circumcision the sojourner was admitted and entitled to full participation in the commemorative celebrations of Yahweh's salvation of the nation.[249] The cumulative weight of all these data dispels any doubt concerning the openness of Israel's patron deity to non-Israelites. Yahweh is identified not only as "the God of the Hebrews" and "the God of Israel," but also as "the God of all flesh" (Jer. 32:27); indeed, he is "the God of all the earth" (Isa. 54:5). It was the heresy of the false prophets to limit him to the nation of Israel.[250]

Conclusion

Jeremiah's words in Jer. 2:11 seem to reflect a theological axiom common to all the nations of the ancient Near East:

> Has a nation ever changed its gods
>   (even though they are not gods)?
> But my people have exchanged my glory
>   for "The Useless One."[251]

In the ancient Near East specific deities tended to be identified with particular nations. But does this mean that we may speak of "national deities"? From the foregoing it has become apparent that even if the expression "national deities" is not incorrect, it is somewhat misleading. In the first place, these special relationships between deity and people often involved groups much smaller or with a less sophisticated political organization than the designation "nation" would suggest. The divinities were often (if not usually) associated with specific places, rather than nations, or with tribal groups, even with households. If one requires a general phrase that would account for all levels of sociopolitical development, a functional expression like "patron" or "matron" (in the case of female deities) gods is obviously more appropriate. Nevertheless, ancient Near Easterners appear to have had difficulty contemplating a politically unified people without at the same time recognizing that people as being under the protective supervision of a particular god.

Second, the notion of "national deities" was not an absolute concept, expressing a one-to-one relationship between a god and his or her peo-

---

249. Gen. 17:9–14; Exod. 12:43–49.

250. Cf. Labuschagne, *Incomparability*, 149–51, on the comparison of Yahweh as a national deity and other gods.

251. Treating *bĕlô' yô'îl* as a proper name, a play on the name Baal, with J. A. Thompson, *Book of Jeremiah*, NICOT (Grand Rapids: Eerdmans, 1980), 166, 170. The reading "my glory" follows the note in *BHS* indicating the third masculine suffix in place of the first common suffix as a case of *Tiqqun Sopherim*.

ple. On the one hand, insofar as the gods of the nations outside Israel tolerated the worship of other divinities, even by their own people, their absolute status as national deities was diminished. On the other hand, in Israel Yahweh's position was to be unchallenged; his intolerance of rivals was total, particularly in the minds of orthodox Yahwists. However, the fact that he welcomed the worship of persons from outside the national group served as an additional limiting factor to his national deity status. While Yahweh had established a special covenantal relationship with Israel, his true devotees proclaimed him simultaneously to be the universal God.

National Territory: A Divine Estate

In the previous chapter we began to examine the ancient perceptions of the relationship between a nation and its primary deity by looking at the ways nations and peoples perceived their own association with their respective patron divinities. The examination of the epithets ascribed by the ancient Near Easterners to their patron deities suggested that titles like *ʾAdon, Baʿal, Melek,* and *Mareʾ* point to a relationship between deity and subjects analogous to the feudal association of lord and vassals. If this analogy is appropriate, then the feudal structures should involve a third factor, the land inhabited by the people. This would create a deity-nation-land triad corresponding to the lord-vassal-estate complex in feudal societies. The present discussion focuses on the third apex of this triad, seeking to determine if the feudal analogy can be maintained, and if so, what role the land played in this tripartite complex. I examine the issue from two angles: the relationship of the land to the deity, and, in the following chapter, the function of the land for the people.

The appropriateness of the feudal metaphor can be tested in various ways. This discussion focuses on two aspects of the issue: the vocabulary used to describe the relationship between the deity and his land, and the responsibilities that a patron god was expected to fulfill toward his territory.

The Feudal Vocabulary

According to the data from the ancient world, the territorial claims of divine patrons were expressed in two principal ways: by using general genitival expressions denoting ownership and by adopting a special feudal vocabulary involving *naḥălâ, yĕruššâ,* and *ʾăḥuzzâ*. I examine these forms of expression briefly in turn.

Genitival Expressions

Ancient Near Easterners employed several types of genitival expressions to express their recognition of a territory as the realm of its god. The general phrase *ʾĕlōhê hāʾărāṣôt*, "gods of the lands," occurs in 2 Kings 18:35.[1] Here the Assyrian official speaks of the patron deities' failure to deliver their respective lands (*ʾarṣām*) from the Assyrians. Second Kings 17:26–27 uses the singular, *ʾĕlōhê hāʾāreṣ*, "the god of the land."

However, the genitival form is given specific application by the introduction of place-names, rather than national names and gentilics,[2] in the genitive position, as in *ʾĕlōhê miṣrayim*, "the gods of Egypt" (Exod. 12:12). But in most cases the order of the terms is reversed, the land being described as belonging to the deity rather than vice versa. Although such expressions are rare, the territory of Israel could be identified as *ʾereṣ yhwh*, "the land of Yahweh" (Hos. 9:3), or *ʾadmat yhwh*, also "the land of Yahweh" (Isa. 14:2). It was much more common, however, simply to attach pronominal suffixes to a designation for land, so that Israel's territory is regularly referred to as "my land,"[3] "your land,"[4] or "his land."[5] Neither method is distinctly Hebrew. The Mesha Inscription from Moab describes Chemosh as having been angry with "his land" (*ʾrṣh*).[6] Eshmunazar of Sidon speaks of Dor and Joppa as *ʾrṣt dgn hʾdrt*, "the rich lands of Dagon."[7]

The Divine Naḥălâ

Of the three principal expressions employed in the Old Testament to designate Yahweh's claim to the land of Israel, *naḥălat yhwh* is the most

1. Cf. also the parallel texts, Isa. 36:20 and 2 Chron. 32:13. The latter has *ʾĕlōhê gôy hāʾărāṣôt*, "the gods of the nations of the lands." In our text the expression appears to have replaced *ʾĕlōhê haggôyim*, "the gods of the nations," found in v. 33.

2. Cf. the discussion of bound forms in chapter 2.

3. Isa. 14:25; Jer. 2:7; 16:18; Ezek. 36:5; 38:16; Joel 1:6; 4:2 (3:2 Eng.) (all *ʾarṣî*); 2 Chron. 7:20 (*ʾadmātî*).

4. Ps. 85:2 (85:1 Eng.); 2 Sam. 7:23.

5. Deut. 33:13; Ezek. 36:20; Joel 2:18; Ps. 10:16 (all *ʾarṣô*); Deut. 32:43; Zech. 9:16 (*ʾadmātô*).

6. *KAI* 181:5; *HMI* 16:5.

7. *KAI* 14:19. So translated by Gibson, *PI*, 109. Cf. F. Rosenthal, "mighty lands of Dagon," in *ANET*, 662; Donner and Röllig, "Kornländer," *KAI*, II, 23. Reference might also be made to the identification of the territory of Assyria as *mi-ṣir* ^matd^*aššur*^ki^. See A. R. Millard, "Fragments of Historical Texts from Nineveh: Ashurbanipal," *Iraq* 30 (1968): 109, lines 22′, 25′, 26′; R. C. Thompson, "The British Museum Excavations at Nineveh, 1931–32," *Annals of Archaeology and Anthropology* 20 (1933): 88–89, line 148. The ancient Mesopotamian notion of the territorial tie is reflected also in (1) some personal names, e.g., *Bēl-ana-māti-šu* (interpreted by *CAD*, 10/1, 419, as "Bel [has returned] to his country"; cf. "Bel [has shown favor] to his land," as suggested by A. R. Millard in private communication); ^d^*Sin-māti-ka-uṣur* ("Sin protect your country," *CAD*, 10/1, 416); (2) explicit statements like *ul tīdî kī ma ma-tum kaluša ša* DN *u* RN ʟᴜɢᴀʟ (*Textes cunéiformes du Musée du Louvre*, 31 vols. (Paris: P. Geuthner, 1910–67), 55:6, translated by *CAD*, ibid., "Do you know that the entire country belongs to Marduk and to King Samsuiluna?"); (3) less explicit comments like "Sin who loved Ur" (*ANET*, 617), "Ninlil who resides in Nineveh" (*ANET*, 534), and "Ninlil whose land is perished" (*ANET*, 461).

common.[8] Jeremiah, especially, found the expression useful for identifying the nature of Yahweh's claim on this territory. Several times in this book the sacred quality of the *naḥălâ* is emphasized. Thus Jer. 2:7:

> I have brought you into a fertile land
> To eat its fruit and good things.
> But you came and defiled my land (*ʾarṣî*),
> And my patrimony (*naḥălātî*) you have made an abomination.

Similarly Jer. 16:18:

> I will repay them double for their iniquity
>   and their sin,
> Because they have defiled my land (*ʾarṣî*)
>   with the carcasses of their detestable idols,
> And they have filled my patrimony (*naḥălātî*)
>   with their abominations.

This sacred nuance is not so apparent in 10:16 = 51:19[9] and 12:7–9. J. A. Soggin suggests that the last reference presupposes an allotment in which Yahweh retained Palestine/Judah as his portion, which in turn implies that other gods had received their own territories, a thought reminiscent of Deut. 32:8 (LXX, 4QD).[10] The only other text that identifies the entire land of Israel as Yahweh's *naḥălâ* is Ps. 68:10 (68:9 Eng.).[11] This psalm portrays Yahweh as a conquering divine warrior claiming his territory.[12]

In two texts the *naḥălâ* of Yahweh is localized in his dwelling place, his sanctuary. Exodus 15:17–18 brings together the notions of his residence in and his kingship over the land:

---

8. For a discussion of the term and helpful bibliography see G. Wanke, "נַחֲלָה," *THAT* 2:55–59 (= *TLOT* 2:731–34). See also C. J. H. Wright, "נחל," *NIDOTTE* 3:77–81, though Wright continues to render the term with inheritance terminology. See further below.

9. J. A. Thompson (*Book of Jeremiah*, NICOT [Grand Rapids: Eerdmans, 1980], 332, 357–58) follows J. Bright, *Jeremiah: Introduction, Translation, and Notes*, AB 21 (Garden City, N.Y.: Doubleday, 1965), 77, in identifying the *naḥălâ* here as Yahweh's people rather than his land. This latter sense is clear in many texts, e.g., Deut. 4:20; 9:26–29; 32:8; 1 Kings 8:51, 53.

10. J. A. Soggin, "Jeremias XII 10a: Eine Parallelstelle zu Deut. XXXII 8/LXX?" *VT* 8 (1958): 304–5.

11. Cf. also F. Horst, "Zwei Begriffe für Eigentum (Besitz): נַחֲלָה und אֲחֻזָּה," in *Verbannung und Heimkehr*, W. Rudolf Festschrift, ed. A. Kuschke (Tübingen: Mohr, 1961), 141.

12. On the motif see F. M. Cross, "The Divine Warrior," in *Canaanite Myth and Hebrew Epic: Essays in the History of the Religion of Israel* (Cambridge: Harvard University Press, 1973), 91–111; P. D. Miller Jr., *The Divine Warrior in Early Israel*, HSM 5 (Cambridge: Harvard University Press, 1973).

You will bring them and plant them
    in the mountain of your patrimony (*naḥălātĕkā*)
The place that you have made for your dwelling,
    O Yahweh;
The sanctuary, O Lord,
    that your hands have established.
Yahweh is king (*yimlōk*) for ever and ever.

J. Levenson observes aptly that here the land of Israel has become the sacred mountain of Yahweh, his throne and palace from which he exercises his cosmic sovereignty.[13] In later usage of this Song of the Sea, the imagery was quite naturally applied to Jerusalem/Zion and the temple.[14] This is certainly the case in Ps. 79:1:

O God, the nations have entered your patrimony (*naḥălātĕkā*)
They have defiled your holy temple;
They have laid Jerusalem in ruins.

The paralleling of *naḥălâ* with *hêkal qodšekā*, "your holy temple," recalls the Ugaritic text *ʿnt* III:25–28:

atm . wank . ibǵyh	Come and I will reveal it
btk . ǵry . il . ṣpn	In the midst of my mountain, Divine Sapan,
bqdš bǵr . nḥlty	In the holy mount of my heritage,
bnʿm bgbʿ . tliyt	In the beautiful hill of my might.[15]

Evidently, when *naḥălat yhwh* is employed in a geographic sense, the phrase reflects two lines of thought. On the one hand, it may refer to the entire land of Israel; on the other hand, it may be restricted to the sacred area associated with Yahweh's residence. These two lines need not be divergent or contradictory, if the temple precinct is considered as the divine lord's manor, and the land, the broader territory, as his large estate.

How the land as the *naḥălat yhwh* is understood depends upon the value assigned to the word *naḥălâ*. The expression has traditionally been translated with inheritance terminology. For example, von Rad recognized in the word denotations of hereditary possession of a clan or tribe.[16] After careful examination of the usage of the root in Hebrew

13. J. D. Levenson, *Sinai and Zion: An Entry into the Jewish Bible*, New Voices in Biblical Studies (Minneapolis: Winston, 1985), 136.

14. So F. M. Cross and D. N. Freedman, *Studies in Ancient Yahwistic Poetry*, SBLDS 21 (Missoula, Mont.: Scholars Press, 1975), 65.

15. Thus M. S. Smith in *UNP*, 110.

16. G. von Rad, "The Promised Land and Yahweh's Land in the Hexateuch," in *The Problem of the Hexateuch and Other Essays*, trans. E. W. Trueman Dicken (New York: McGraw-Hill, 1966), 80.

as well as in the cognate languages, however, Forshey has rightly rejected this view. He prefers to associate the expression with landed property, arguing that it points to "the practice of giving loyal servants the utilization of land as a reward for past service—fundamentally military service is involved—and in expectation of future service."[17] It is obviously out of the question to view Yahweh as a vassal who has received his *naḥălâ* from an overlord. However, the military association of the term might suggest that, as his *naḥălâ*, the land of Israel represented land that he had gained by conquest, in this case from the Canaanites. This interpretation places the term *naḥălâ* firmly within the same semantic field as *ʾăḥuzzâ* and *yĕruššâ*, discussed below, and helps to account for their occasional conjunction.[18]

The Divine Yĕruššâ

In 2 Chron. 20:11 the land of Judah is designated as Yahweh's *yĕruššâ*. The expression is surprising because in every other occurrence of *yĕruššâ* the term has reference to the land as Israel's possession.[19] The presence of *hôrîš*, "to cause to possess," in the following clause suggests the choice of *yĕruššâ* instead of *naḥălâ* or *ʾăḥuzzâ* may have been dictated by assonantal considerations. It is unlikely that the word is to be interpreted as an abstraction, "what has been dispossessed," that is, from the previous owners, even though both Qal[20] and Hiphil[21] stems are capable of bearing this sense.

The root *yrš* seems to refer fundamentally to "the transfer of property." As such it may signify "to possess," or alternatively, "to dispossess."[22] Plöger has designated the word as technical war terminology, representing the human activity, the act of taking possession involved in the transfer of territory, as opposed to the divine activity, that is, the

17. H. O. Forshey, "The Hebrew Root *NḤL* and Its Semitic Cognates" (Th.D. diss., Harvard University, 1973), 233. Cf. also idem, "Segullah and Nachalah as Designations of the Covenant Community," *Hebrew Abstracts* 15 (1974): 85–86; idem, "The Construct Chain *naḥᵃlat yhwh/ʾᵉlōhîm*," *BASOR* 220 (1975): 51–53.
18. See esp. Ezek. 44:28, where *naḥălâ* and *ʾăḥuzzâ* occur as a parallel pair. Cf. also Horst, "Zwei Begriffe," 154–55.
19. LXX has eliminated the anomaly by translating ἀπὸ τῆς κληρονομίας ἡμῶν, which assumes *mîyruššātēnû*. Cf. Deut. 2:5, 9, 19; 3:20; Josh. 1:15; Judg. 21:17; Jer. 32:8; Ps. 61:6 (61:5 Eng.). For a study of the root see H. H. Schmid, "ירשׁ," *THAT* 1:778–81 (= *TLOT* 2:578–81); C. J. H. Wright, "ירשׁ," *NIDOTTE* 2:547–49.
20. Deut. 2:12, 21, 22; 9:1; 11:23; 12:2, 29; 19:1; 31:3; Isa. 54:3.
21. Judg. 1:27–33; etc. Yahweh is the subject in Judg. 11:24; 1 Kings 14:24; 21:26; 2 Kings 16:3; 17:8; 21:2; 2 Chron. 28:3; 33:2.
22. So F. Dreyfus, "Le thème de l'héritage dans l'Ancien Testament," *Revue des sciences philosophiques et théologiques* 42 (1958): 5–8.

granting (*yāraš*) of the land.[23] This usage is attested also in the Moabite Mesha Inscription.[24]

This does not mean that *yĕruššâ* can never be associated with inheritance. This sense is attested in Hebrew,[25] Aramaic,[26] and Ugaritic.[27] At least in the Old Testament, however, this usage is the exception rather than the rule.

Remarkably, in the Hebrew texts Yahweh never appears as the subject of the Qal form of the verb *yāraš*. Furthermore, whenever the expression is employed in the sense "to dispossess," the previous owners are consistently identified as the occupants of the land, not deities. It seems best, therefore, to translate *yĕruššâ* in 2 Chron. 20:11 as "the possession of Yahweh," and thereby to recognize a military nuance. The broader context seems to support this interpretation.

The Divine *ʾĂḥuzzâ*

A third term used to identify Yahweh's claim on the land, *ʾăḥuzzat yhwh*, occurs with this significance only in Josh. 22:19. Deriving from the common Semitic root **ʾḥz*, "to seize, grasp,"[28] the present form seems to signify simply "possession."[29] The context here is instructive for the theological significance of the term, insofar as the *ʾăḥuzzat yhwh* applies only to Canaan proper, that is, the land west of the Jordan River. By contrast, the Transjordanian region is described as an unclean land (*ṭĕmēʾâ ʾereṣ ʾăḥuzzatĕkem*).[30] Should the nuance of seizure be recognized in this expression, the previous owners would again have to be understood as the Canaanites, rather than other deities.[31]

Although these genitival expressions and this special feudal terminology all reflect Yahweh's ownership of the land of Israel, the most ex-

---

23. J. G. Plöger, *Literarische, formgeschichtliche und stilkritische Untersuchungen zum Deuteronomium,* Bonner biblische Beiträge 26 (Bonn: Hanstein, 1967), 83.

24. *KAI* 181:7; *HMI* 16:7.

25. Gen. 15:3, 4; 21:10; 2 Sam. 14:7; Jer. 49:1.

26. *KAI* 222 C:24–25; *AI* 7 iC:24–25.

27. *yrṯ, Krt* 25 (//*šph*), on which see W. Johnstone, "Old Testament Technical Expressions in Property Holdings," *Ugaritica* 6 (1969): 313–14. Cf. also Late Babylonian *yāritu,* "heir," *AHw* 1:412a.

28. For Northwest Semitic occurrences of *ʾḥz* see *DNWSI* 1:35–37; Ugaritic, *ʾḫd, UT,* 355; Akkadian, *aḫāzu(m), AHw* 1:18–19. For discussions of the term see Horst, "Zwei Begriffe," 153–56; H. H. Schmid, "אחז," *THAT* 1:107–10 (= *TLOT* 1:81–83); A. H. Konkel, "אחז" *NIDOTTE* 1:354–58; also Johnstone, "Technical Expressions," 314–15.

29. Cf. Horst, "Zwei Begriffe," 153–56, who notes that *ʾăḥuzzâ* is a more general and juristic expression than *naḥălâ.* Compare also Dreyfus, "Le thème de l'héritage," 15. As noted earlier, Ezek. 44:28 conjoins *naḥălâ* and *ʾăḥuzzâ* as a parallel pair.

30. Cf. von Rad, "Promised Land," 87.

31. It is possible that the vague reference to "the gods of the Amorites in whose land you dwell" (Josh. 24:15) could be treating the land as the possession of the deities, but this is unlikely. Cf. the use of *yāraš,* above.

plicit statement is in Lev. 25:23: "The land shall not be sold permanently, for the land is mine; for you are but aliens and sojourners with me." This verse declares unequivocally that the nation's primary association is with Yahweh and not with the land. The people inhabit it and derive their sustenance from it only by the good graces of the divine lord of the manor. In the context, their responsibilities toward the land and the regulations concerning the year of Jubilee rest squarely on the deity's ownership of the territory as his estate.

This raises the question whether the territory claimed originally by Yahweh was the land of Canaan or some other region. Several alternative hypotheses have been proposed. An earlier generation of scholars proposed a Kenite or Midianite hypothesis, which made much of Yahweh's apparent original association with Sinai. Proponents of this theory observed: (1) The name of Yahweh was revealed to Moses when he was at Sinai (Exod. 3:13–15). (2) Jethro, the priest of Midian (2:16; 3:1; 18:1), invoked the name of Yahweh, acknowledging him as the greatest of all gods (18:10–11). (3) He also offered a sacrifice to Yahweh and presided at the sacred meal that followed (18:12). Combined with the identification of Horeb/Sinai as *har hā'ělōhîm*, "the mountain of God" (Exod. 4:27; 18:5; 24:13; 1 Kings 19:8), these considerations have led some to seek the origins of Yahwism among the Midianites, in which case his primary territory would be the Sinai region.[32]

Support for this hypothesis is marshaled also from ancient poetic texts such as Deut. 33:2, Judg. 5:4–5, as well as Ps. 68:8 (68:7 Eng.), all of which seem to identify the divine warrior, Yahweh, as "The One of Sinai."[33] Furthermore, it has been thought that references to *Yhw* in Egyptian inscriptions substantiate the view.[34] To respond to the evidence of the Egyptian references first, it has been demonstrated that the association of *Yhw* with Edom, the Kenites, or the Midianites is without foundation. Astour has shown that the toponym is not to be located in southern Palestine, but in the region of the Lebanon![35] Con-

32. Cf. the presentation of the hypothesis and extensive bibliography provided by M. Weippert, *The Settlement of the Israelite Tribes in Palestine,* trans. James D. Martin, SBT 2d series 21 (London: SCM, 1971), 105–6. See also J. Bright, *A History of Israel,* 3d ed. (Philadelphia: Westminster, 1981), 125–28; R. de Vaux, *The Early History of Israel,* trans. D. Smith (Philadelphia: Westminster, 1978), 332–35.

33. For this interpretation of *yhwh missînay* see Levenson, *Sinai and Zion,* 20. Cf. also Hab. 3:3, which has Yahweh coming from Teman//Mount Paran. For a discussion of these and related texts see Miller, *Divine Warrior,* 74–127.

34. Weippert, *Settlement,* 105–6; Cross, *Canaanite Myth,* 86 n. 17; R. Giveon, "'The Cities of our God' (2 Sam. 10:12)," *JBL* 83 (1964): 415–16; B. Grdseloff, "Edom, d'après les sources égyptiennes," *Revue de l'histoire juive d'Égypte* 1 (1947): 81–82.

35. M. C. Astour, "Yahweh in Egyptian Topographical Lists," in *Festschrift Elmar Edel: 12. März 1979,* ed. M. Görg and E. Pusch (Bamberg: Görg, 1979), 17–34; idem, "Yahwe," *IDBSup,* 971.

sequently an association between this place and the Israelite deity is incapable of proof.[36]

As for the biblical data, it is commonly recognized that in the traditions of Israel the self-disclosure of Yahweh, so critical for the nation's history and theology, was delivered at Sinai. It is not surprising that this place should be spoken of as the mountain of God (*har hā°ĕlōhîm*). But it is significant that only in one instance is the mountain identified as *har yhwh*, "the mountain of Yahweh" (Num. 10:33). Otherwise the generic name for God is always used.[37] Sinai may well be identified as the mountain of God, not because it represents his place of residence, nor because of any particular claims of ownership, but because it was the place of Israel's most dramatic encounter with their national deity. It represented a climactic moment in the nation's spiritual geography. Furthermore, even if Sinai should have been perceived as the original home of Yahweh, he leaves this place, going before Israel as a divine warrior, leading them to his true sanctuary (Exodus 15; Psalm 68).

The Role of the Deity in the Feudal Relationship

Understanding the deity as the patron of his people and as a feudal landlord has important consequences for the way in which the god was expected to relate to his fiefdom. Because of the privileged status of the divine lord, the function of the entire manor, the land as well as the tenants, was to serve his interests. The obverse of this privilege is found in the responsibilities placed upon the shoulders of the people and the obligations of the land. This aspect is best left for separate treatment, and I deal with it in the following chapter. For the moment my task is to survey the responsibilities assumed by the divine lord. What obligations did the ancient Near Easterners perceive patron deities to have toward them and toward the land in which they lived? Several functions may be noted.

Divine Authority and Territorial Limits

In the first place, national borders were considered to have been divinely determined. The various traditions concerning the origins of the

36. As admitted by Weippert. In view of the name's geographical and chronological proximity to Ugarit, an association of the Egyptian *Yhw* with the Ugaritic deity *Yw* (mentioned in *ᶜnt* pl. x IV:14) or *°Ieuw*, the Byblite divinity referred to by Eusebius in *Praeparatio Evangelica* 1.9.21, and whose priest, Hierombalos, was this author's authority on Sanchuniathon, is more likely. So also J. C. de Moor, *The Seasonal Pattern in the Ugaritic Myth of Baᶜlu: According to the Version of Ilimilku*, AOAT 16 (Kevelaer: Butzon & Bercker; Neukirchen-Vluyn: Neukirchener Verlag, 1971), 118–19; cf. A. Caquot, M. Sznycer, and A. Herdner, eds., *Textes Ougaritiques*, vol. 1: *Mythes et légendes* (Paris: Cerf, 1974), 309. De Moor provides an extensive bibliography of discussions of the issue.

37. Exod. 3:1; 4:27; 18:5; 24:13; 1 Kings 19:8.

deity-nation association discussed in the first chapter reflect the cosmic dimension of this notion. As noted there, according to some extrabiblical accounts, the highest god appears to have acted as a great overlord, appointing specific lands to certain lesser deities on the basis of the lot,[38] or as a reward for service rendered.[39] Orthodox Hebrews accepted Yahweh as the cosmic lord who had divided the population of the earth into nations on the basis of the number of *běnê ʾělōhîm* available, and then to have designated a certain territory for each (Deut. 32:8). In practical terms, however, patron deities themselves were acknowledged by other peoples to have been much more personally involved.

Buccellati has asserted that one of the differences between national and territorial states was the tendency of the former to be restricted to the limits of the city-states themselves.[40] National states, on the other hand, tended to expand by incorporating whatever territory the population occupied. Although this may have been the case in practice, in theory the borders that Israel, a national state, could legitimately claim were strictly limited by its deity (Num. 34:1–12).[41] It was the recognition of these restrictions that precipitated the crisis described in Joshua 22. Sensing keenly the importance of the Jordan as a territorial boundary, the two and one-half tribes that were returning to settle in the Transjordan constructed an altar of witness on the west bank of the river. They feared that in the future the residents of the west side would exploit the border to exclude them from the service of Yahweh. The purpose of the altar was to remind succeeding generations of the identification of the two and one-half tribes with Israel, and their title to "a portion of Yahweh."[42] The memory of a common heritage would not be sufficient to guarantee their continued acceptance as part of the nation.

There is no hint of expanding national territory beyond the divinely prescribed limits even during the days of empire under David and Solomon. David never engaged in conquest in order to extend the territory

38. *Atra-Ḥasīs* I:11–12; Homer, *Iliad* 15.189–93; Pindar, *Olympian Odes* 7.55–76.

39. Eusebius, *Praeparatio Evangelica* 1.10.31–38. For the Greek text and a French translation see J. Sirinelli and E. des Places, trans. and eds., *La préparation évangélique*, Sources chrétiennes 206 (Paris: Cerf, 1974), 200. For the English translation see Eusebius, *Preparation for the Gospel*, trans. E. G. Gifford (1903; reprint, Grand Rapids: Baker, 1981), 37–47.

40. Georgio Buccellati, *Cities and Nations of Ancient Syria: An Essay on Political Institutions with Special Reference to the Israelite Kingdoms*, Studi Semitici 26 (Rome: Istituto di Studi del Vicino Oriente, 1967), 108–10.

41. Note also the precise borders of Edom, Moab, and Ammon identified in Deuteronomy 2.

42. *ḥēleq bayhwh*, Josh. 22:27.

of Yahweh. This contrasts sharply with the Mesopotamian records in which Assyrian emperors annexed region after region "to the territory of Ashur" in their drive for ever expanding territorial world domination. In typical fashion, Sargon boasts, "Over his [Ashur's] entire broad land and his numerous population I installed my nobles as officials, and thus extended the territory of Ashur, king of the gods."[43] Consequently, whereas in Israel the deity was perceived to determine the national boundaries, in Assyria the kings in effect defined the limits of the territory of the god.[44]

However, the latter appears to create a discrepancy with earlier statements according to which divine-territorial associations were initiated by the gods. Two explanations may be proposed. In the first place, the original land grants by the highest deity to the lesser gods consisted only of the core area in which the worship of the respective gods was centered. Later annexations were not taken into account. Second, where territories were added to the land of the god, such conquests are consistently treated as occurring at the command, in the strength, and for the glory of the divine patron.[45]

Divine Authority and National Defense

If the gods were the ones who determined the limits of national territory, it follows naturally that it should also fall to patron deities to defend the areas over which they exercised lordship. In this respect the biblical and extrabiblical accounts agree.

The Mesha Inscription provides a clear example of the latter. In this document the interests of Chemosh, the divine patron of Moab, are presented in purely territorial terms, even though they are closely tied to the achievements of Mesha. The text refers to four regions that were viewed as legitimate parts of Moabite territory but that Omri, king of Israel, had occupied: Madeba, Ataroth, Nebo, and Jahaz. The text por-

---

43. H. Winckler, *Die Keilschrifttexte Sargons nach der Papierabklatschen und Originalen neu herausgegeben* (Leipzig: Pfeiffer, 1889), 178, lines 12–13. On the topic see M. Cogan, *Imperialism and Religion: Assyria, Judah, and Israel in the Eighth and Seventh Centuries B.C.E.*, SBLMS 19 (Missoula, Mont.: Scholars Press, 1974). On the broader topic of the role of the gods in history see B. Albrektson, *History and the Gods: An Essay on the Idea of Historical Events as Divine Manifestations in the Ancient Near East and in Israel*, Coniectanea Biblica Old Testament Series 1 (Lund: Gleerup, 1967), 42–52; W. G. Lambert, "Destiny and Divine Intervention in Babylon and Israel," *OTS* 17 (1972): 65–72; H. W. F. Saggs, *The Encounter with the Divine in Mesopotamia and Israel*, Jordan Lectures 1976 (London: Athlone, 1978), 64–92.

44. Note also Azitawadda's repeated comment, *bʿbr bʿl wᵓlm*, "by the grace of Baal and the gods," *KAI* 26 I:8; II:6, 12; III:11; IV:12; *PI* 15 Ai:8, Aii:6, 12, Aiii:11, Aiv:12; *ANET*, 653–54.

45. Cf. Albrektson, *History and the Gods*, 42–52.

trays the Israelite oppression as an expression of the anger of Chemosh "against his land."[46] Nevertheless, Mesha had been successful in reasserting Moabite control over these regions. But it is significant that the narrative describes Chemosh as having been involved in each stage of the reconquest. After Mesha took Madeba, he took up residence there (lines 8–9). In Ataroth, Mesha slew all the inhabitants as a spectacle for Chemosh and Moab. Furthermore, he presented the lion figure of David,[47] a prized object of booty, to the god at Kerioth (lines 11–13). Mesha undertook the invasion of Nebo in response to the specific command of Chemosh (line 14). Since the city was devoted to Ashtar-Chemosh,[48] the entire population was exterminated. Mesha seized the sacred vessels of Yahweh, and in a gesture symbolic of the victory of Chemosh over the Israelite patron, dutifully presented them to the Moabite deity (lines 17–18). As for Jahaz, Chemosh is supposed to have driven out the Israelite forces himself (lines 18–19). All these regions were annexed to the territory of Moab. The preserved text concludes with a command by Chemosh to Mesha to go and take the southern city of Horonaim. The Moabite king responded obediently to the charge and captured the city, permitting the patron god to establish his residence there for the duration of Mesha's reign (lines 32–33).

Two features of this text are of special interest for us. First, it is completely silent on the fate of the Moabites themselves and the relationship of Chemosh to his subjects. Inasmuch as his anger was directed "against his land," his concerns appear to have been primarily territorial. Second, the residence of the deity is not restricted to the central shrine or even to the heartland of the nation. His dwelling extends as far as the political borders of Mesha's kingdom.

The antiquity of this perspective and the extent of its pervasiveness throughout the ancient Near East is reflected in an ancient Sumerian text in which Ush, the *išakku* of Umma, violated the boundary of Lagash, only to have Ningirsu come forward to defend the land in accordance with the word of Enlil.[49]

This defensive function of the divine patron also surfaces in several Old Testament texts. The Assyrian Rabshakeh's appeal to the citizens of

---

46. *KAI* 181:5; *HMI* 16:5; *ANET,* 320.

47. The text reads *ʾrʾl dwdh*, which Gibson (*HMI*, p. 78) interprets as "lion figure of David." For a recent defense of this interpretation see A. Lemaire, "'House of David' Restored in Moabite Inscription," *BAR* 20.3 (1994): 30–37.

48. Line 17. Ashtar-Chemosh is probably a fusion of the two deities, Ashtar and Chemosh. So also Donner and Röllig, *KAI* II, 176; and Gibson, *HMI*, 81.

49. S. N. Kramer, "Sumerian Historiography," *IEJ* 3 (1953): 224. For the text see J. S. Cooper, *Sumerian and Akkadian Royal Inscriptions,* vol. 1, *Presargonic Inscriptions* (New Haven: American Oriental Society, 1986), 54–57.

Judah in 2 Kings 18:33–34 provides one of the clearest expressions of this perspective:

> Has any of the gods of the nations delivered his land from the hand of the king of Assyria? Where are the gods of Hamath and Arpad? Where are the gods of Sepharvaim, Hena, and Ivvah? Have they rescued Samaria from my hand? Who among all of the gods of the lands has delivered his land from my hand, that Yahweh should deliver Jerusalem from my hand?

However, the most dramatic demonstration of this view is in 1 Kings 20. According to this account, the Aramaean strategy against Ahab's Israelite forces was based on the assumption that Israel's divine patron was territorially bound. After an initial fiasco, supposing that Yahweh was a god of the mountains, Ben-Hadad's general advised his king to conduct the battle in the plain, where he should be out of the deity's reach. The subsequent Aramaean debacle demonstrated the error of this hypothesis.

In a later account, following the miraculous healing of Naaman, this Aramaean official confessed that there was no god in all the earth, except in Israel. Sensing some special mystical relationship between the deity and the land in which he was revered, Naaman desired to take two loads of Israelite soil with him back to Damascus. His expectation was that even if, out of duty to his master, he would need to attend the worship of Rimmon, Yahweh would pardon him because of the connection provided by the soil in his possession (2 Kings 5:15–17).

Yahweh, the divine patron of Israel, was also viewed by his people as the protector of their land. This was true despite his acknowledged universal sovereignty, a supranational authority reflected in his defense of the territorial integrity of Edom (Deut. 2:4–5), Moab (2:9), and Ammon (2:19). Nevertheless, Yahweh was especially jealous about his land. According to the oracle of Ezekiel in 36:5–7, the Edomites are condemned for their sacrilegious attempt to appropriate for themselves Yahweh's land, the mountains of Israel. Although the language is highly figurative, this is a rare passage. Yahweh's concern is seldom focused on the land rather than the people, as is the case in this text.

Interpreting history from this theological perspective brings with it another natural corollary, namely the viewing of international events as mirrors of the true occurrences that transpired in the heavens.[50] Thus the story of the exodus is presented as a contest between Yahweh and the gods of Egypt. The judgments against the land are actually attacks

---

50. Cf. the discussion by Albrektson, *History and the Gods*, 16–23.

against their gods, and the success of the venture demonstrates the superiority of Yahweh over all the gods.[51] Later reflection displays amazement that Yahweh should have invaded enemy territory to accomplish this feat:

> Has any god ever attempted to go and take a nation for himself from the midst of another nation, by trials, by signs, by wonders, and by war, by a mighty hand and an outstretched arm, and by great terrors, according to all that Yahweh your God did for you in Egypt before your eyes? To you it was shown, that you might know that Yahweh is God; there is no other besides him. . . . Because he loved your fathers and chose their descendants after them, and brought you out of Egypt with his own presence, by his great power, driving out before you nations greater and mightier than yourselves, to bring you in, to give you their land for a patrimony, as at this day. (Deut. 4:34–38)

What made the deliverance of Israel out of Egypt so remarkable was the fact that Yahweh had succeeded in invading the territory of another god and had managed, by means of a series of dramatic demonstrations of his power, to deliver a large segment of the enslaved population and call the people to himself. The gods of the land had been unable to defend their territory against the attacks of the god of Israel.

At the earthly level, this conviction underlies the common ancient Near Eastern practice of the spoliation of divine images in conquered lands. As Cogan has shown, in Neo-Assyrian times this was done to demonstrate the superior might of Ashur over the god(s) of the invaded territory.[52]

Probably nothing provides a clearer demonstration of the protective role of the patron deity than observing the consequences that were described as arising from a deity's abdication of his position as lord of the land and abandoning his territory. Not only would this inevitably precipitate moral and social disintegration; the land would be opened up immediately to invasion by foreign enemies.[53]

Divine Authority and National Government

A divine patron's sovereignty was demonstrated thirdly by his provision of human leadership for his land.[54] In the ancient Near Eastern world several avenues existed by which royal power could be gained:

51. Exod. 12:12; Num. 33:4.
52. Cogan, *Imperialism and Religion,* 40.
53. This issue is treated further in the next chapter.
54. Cf. Albrektson, *History and the Gods,* 42–52.

through selection by the citizenry,[55] through the forceful usurpation of power by means of the elimination of existing rulers,[56] through appointment by imperial overlords,[57] and perhaps most normatively through hereditary succession.[58] However, the theological explanations for a king's rise to power are remarkably consistent throughout the ancient Near East. According to the Sumerians, the office of kingship itself was lowered from heaven as if it were some tangible object.[59] Not only did the gods determine from which center kingship would be exercised;[60] from early times they were understood to have been responsible for the selection of the kings themselves.[61]

The notion of the divine election of kings seems to have become the common property of the succeeding Mesopotamian cultures as well as those of the Levant. The Neo-Assyrian kings, including those whose reigns were legitimate, generally juxtaposed divine election with royal

55. On which see the helpful studies by T. Jacobsen, "Primitive Democracy in Ancient Mesopotamia," *JNES* 2 (1943): 159–72; idem, "Early Political Development in Mesopotamia," *ZA* 52 (1957): 91–140. The latter describes how early political offices developed into monarchical institutions. These essays have been reprinted in *Toward the Image of Tammuz and Other Essays on Mesopotamian History and Culture*, ed. W. L. Moran, HSM 21 (Cambridge: Harvard University Press, 1970), 157–70 and 132–56, respectively. Cf. H. Frankfort, *Kingship and the Gods: A Study of Ancient Near Eastern Religion as the Integration of Society and Nature* (1948; reprint, Chicago: University of Chicago Press, 1978), 215–21. On the role of the people in the selection of rulers in Syria-Palestine, see T. Ishida, *The Royal Dynasties in Ancient Israel: A Study in the Formation and Development of Royal-Dynastic Ideology*, BZAW 142 (Berlin: de Gruyter, 1977), 18–25. Observe esp. 1 Kings 16:15–20.

56. Cf. 1 Kings 12; 15:27–30; 16:9–20; 2 Kings 10:1–11; 15:8–16, 25, 30 (Israelite examples); Josephus, *Contra Apion* 1.117.125 (Tyre); 1 Kings 11:23–25; and *ANET*, 280, 285 (Aram).

57. In the Amarna Age, Canaanite kings were installed by Egyptian overlords. Cf. EA 286:9–13; 288:13–15; *ANET*, 487–89. For discussions see M. Liverani, "La royauté syrienne de l'age du bronze récent," in *Le palais et la royauté*, ed. P. Garelli, RAI 19 (Paris: Geuthner, 1974), 335–38, 348–50 (hereafter this volume will be cited as RAI 19). On the relationship of Niqmad of Ugarit to the Hittite king (*UT*, 118); cf. J. Gray, "Canaanite Kingship in Theory and Practice," *VT* 2 (1952): 198; A. F. Rainey, "The Kingdom of Ugarit," *BA* 28 (1965): 102–25. For first-millennium B.C. Syria, see *KAI* 215:19–20; 216:4–7; 2 Kings 23:34; 24:17; *ANET*, 286, 287, 296, 298.

58. Cf. J. Gray, "Canaanite Kingship," 196–200; Liverani, "La royauté syrienne," 335–38; K. F. Euler, "Königtum und Götterwelt in den altaramäischen Inschriften Nordsyriens," *ZAW* 56 (1938): 277–300; Buccellati, *Cities and Nations*, 125ff.

59. On which see T. Jacobsen, *The Sumerian King List*, AS 11 (Chicago: University of Chicago Press, 1939), 70–71; A. Leo Oppenheim, trans., "The Sumerian King List," *ANET*, 265. Cf. Frankfort, *Kingship and the Gods*, 237.

60. Cf. "Lamentation over the Destruction of Sumer and Ur" (Nanna Lament), *ANET*, 617, lines 366–72.

61. Cf. Frankfort, *Kingship and the Gods*, 238–40. As a corollary to this notion, the poets emphasized also the divine parentage of kings. Cf. S. N. Kramer, "Kingship in Sumer and Akkad: The Ideal King," in RAI 19, 163–66.

lineage as the two basic pillars of their authority.[62] But it is not surprising that usurpers especially tended to place great stock in the decision of the gods. Thus Sargon recounts that he was a fatherless child, but Ishtar had chosen him to be king of Akkad.[63] In spite of the fact that Esarhaddon was the youngest in the royal family, he justified his seizure of the throne by emphasizing the role of the gods in his father's designation of him as heir.[64] In a similar vein, Cyrus's conquest of Babylon was legitimized by Marduk's pronouncing his name to become ruler of the world, taking pleasure in him, and commanding him to march against the city.[65]

Similar perceptions can be observed in Syrian texts. The Ugaritic legend of Keret emphasizes divine election in two ways. On the one hand, the provision of an heir becomes a divine concern;[66] on the other, the realm of Udum is described as "a gift of El, even a present of the Father of Man."[67] But the first-millennium B.C. records are more significant for our purposes. In the Karatepe Inscription, Azitawadda described his election in this way: "Ba⁽l made me a father and a mother to the Danunites."[68] This is reminiscent of the confession of Barrakab, king of Y⁾DY, "Because of the righteousness of my father and my own righteousness, I was seated by my Lord Rakabel and my Lord Tiglath-pileser upon the throne of my father."[69] Zakkur of Hamath wrote, "Be⁽el-shamayn [said to me]: 'Do not fear, for I made you king, and I shall stand by you and deliver you from all [these kings . . .].'"[70] Yehawmilk of Byblos introduces himself with "I am Yehawmilk, king of Byblos, the son of Yaharba⁽l, the grandson of Urimilk, king of Byblos, whom the mistress, the Lady of Byblos, made king over Byblos."[71]

The role of Yahweh in the selection of Israel's kings is emphasized in the biblical texts. Those who are specifically identified as having been chosen by him are Saul,[72] David,[73] Solomon,[74] Jeroboam,[75]

62. On the harmonization of these two principles see Ishida, *Royal Dynasties*, 6–14.
63. Cf. "Legend of Sargon," *ANET*, 119.
64. *ANET*, 289.
65. *ANET*, 315.
66. *Krt* 30–42; *ANET*, 143; *UNP*, 12–13.
67. *Krt* 133–36; *ANET*, 144; *UNP*, 17.
68. *KAI* 26:3; *ANET*, 653.
69. *KAI* 216:4–7; *ANET*, 655.
70. *KAI* 202:13; *ANET*, 655.
71. *KAI* 10:1–2; *ANET*, 656.
72. 1 Sam. 9:15–21.
73. 1 Sam. 16:1–13. This election was necessitated by the divine rejection of one previously chosen. Cf. vv. 1 and 14.
74. This is implied by the involvement of Nathan the prophet in his assumption of power, but it is explicitly recognized by David (1 Kings 1:48), Adonijah (2:15), Solomon (2:24; 3:3–9; 8:20), Hiram of Tyre (5:21 [5:7 Eng.]), and the queen of Sheba (10:9).
75. 1 Kings 11:26–39. Cf. Ahijah's announcement of Yahweh's rejection of Jeroboam (1 Kings 14:7–11).

Baasha,[76] and Jehu.[77] But this principle antedated the monarchy. The authority of the judges in an earlier era was also founded upon the principle of divine election.[78] The Hebrews even acknowledged the role of their deity in the choice of foreign kings: Hadad of Edom,[79] Rezon of Damascus,[80] and Hazael of the same city.[81]

It is clear from all these texts that regardless how a king had actually gained the throne of a nation, he was able to achieve this position because he had been appointed by the patron deity. The kingdom was a divine charge or gift to be administered on behalf of the god. The king, as vice regent, was the divinity's means of ensuring peace and prosperity in his estate.[82] This perception appears to have been common throughout the Levant.

Conclusion

In the ancient Near East all of life, be it individual or corporate, was viewed from a theological perspective. At the heart of a nation's self-consciousness was the conviction that its fate and fortune were in the hands of the gods, specifically its patron deity. The god was perceived as a type of manorial lord, whose subjects served him as vassals. The territory occupied by the vassals constituted the estate over which the god exercised supreme authority.

In most states the interests of the patron appear to have focused primarily on his territory. The identity of the vassals seems to have been incidental, being determined simply by whoever happened to occupy the land. However, the situation was quite different in Israel. Yahweh, the nation's divine patron, had entered into a covenant relationship with his people. It was after he had established them as his people that he delivered the land of Canaan over to them as their territorial grant.

Regardless of how people perceived a nation to have come to be associated with its divine patron, or how a people had come to occupy the land that was identified internally and externally as its homeland, the respective roles in the deity-nation-land association were clearly defined. Under normal circumstances, as lord of the manor the god was

---

76. 1 Kings 14:14; cf. 15:29. In 16:2–4 his rejection by Yahweh is announced.

77. 1 Kings 19:16; 2 Kings 9:1–10. Cf. 15:12, where the duration of his dynasty is set at five generations.

78. The principle is expressed in Judg. 2:16–18. Cf. the specific application in the choice of Othniel (3:9), Ehud (3:15), Barak (4:6–9), Gideon (6:11–24), and Samson (13:2–7).

79. 1 Kings 11:14.

80. 1 Kings 11:23.

81. 1 Kings 19:15; cf. 2 Kings 8:7–17.

82. Cf. the (re-)appointment of David as shepherd-king in Ezek. 34:23–24 and 37:22–24.

jealously protective about his territory. On the one hand, it was his task to maintain the integrity of a nation's borders by defending the land against external foes. On the other hand, it was the divine lord's prerogative to determine who, from among his human subjects, should govern his territory on his behalf. In this relationship of the deity to his territory, the feudal nature of the tripartite association proposed earlier receives further support.

National Territory: A Divine Grant

If I am correct in interpreting the ancient Near Easterners' perception of the relationship among deity, people, and land along feudal lines, then one might expect that the tripartite relationship would be characterized by mutually recognized privileges and responsibilities. What constituted a privilege for one member of the association would represent a responsibility for the other. For example, if the divinity assumed the role of protector of a people, then the latter would feel entitled to that protection. The possibilities involved may be depicted diagrammatically as follows (the arrows point in the direction of responsibility):

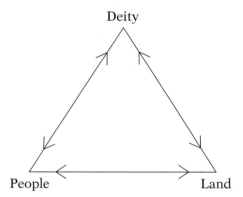

The previous chapter focused on the relationship of the land to the deity. I concluded that people looked upon a nation's territory as the estate of the divine lord. The task of the present chapter is to investigate the relationship of the land to its inhabitants. Several leading questions arise. What role did a nation's territory play in this feudal relationship? What was the people's obligation to their homeland? How did their relationship to the divine lord affect the relationship with the land? And how did their relationship to the land affect their relationship with the divine patron?

Most of the potentially helpful extrabiblical sources derive from royal circles, rather than from the "people of the land" in general. Consequently, the amount of clear information on popular ancient Levantine views of the relationship of a people to their homeland is limited. Nevertheless, the picture that emerges suggests that in general the nations viewed themselves to be related to their respective deities simply because they happened to live in his/her land.

One promising clue regarding how a particular people might have come to possess a specific territory may be found in the Ugaritic text *Krt* 135–36: *udm . ytnt . il . wušn . ab . adm*, "Udm is the gift of El, even a present of the Father of Man."[1] This statement recognizes the land as a divine grant to the inhabitants. However, the broader context of the passage indicates clearly that the basis of the people's title to the land is not in view at all. By intimating that the recipient of the grant was the king, it tells us more about kingship in Ugarit than about the territorial claims of a nation.

In fact, the general silence of extrabiblical texts on the relationship between peoples and their respective territories suggests that those responsible for preserving what records we possess were disinterested in the matter. The contrast with the Israelite perspective could hardly be more pronounced. The basis of Israel's presence in and title to the land of Canaan was a critical issue, not only for the nation's history but also for its faith. The biblical texts are permeated with the notion that, having selected Israel to be his own special people, Yahweh reserved for them a specific piece of land: his land, the land of Canaan. Moreover, according to the patriarchal traditions, this reservation was determined centuries before the Israelites appeared as a nation on their own soil.

Various stock phrases are used to describe the process whereby Yahweh delivered the land into Israel's control: he promised the land,[2] he swore to give it,[3] he prepared the land,[4] he brought Israel into it,[5] he delivered the land over to them,[6] he granted it to them,[7] he planted them

---

1. *ANET*, 144; *UNP*, 17. Cf. also *CAT* 1.14.III.31–32 for the Ugaritic text.

2. *dibbēr*, Deut. 1:21; 9:28; 19:8; 27:3; Josh. 23:5.

3. *nišbaʿ*, Gen. 24:7; 26:3; 50:24. Retrospective references to the oath are common, e.g., Exod. 6:8; 13:5, 11.

4. *hēkîn*, Exod. 23:20.

5. *hēbîʾ*, Exod. 6:8; 13:5, 11; etc.

6. *nātan lipnê*, Deut. 1:21; 2:31, 36. Cf. J. G. Plöger, *Literarische, formgeschichtliche und stilkritische Untersuchungen zum Deuteronomium*, Bonner biblische Beiträge 26 (Bonn: Hanstein, 1967), 62–63.

7. *nātan*, Gen. 15:18, and many more. Cf. *Krt* 135–36 (*CAT* 1.14.III.31), for a semantically similar expression. As has already been observed, however, because the passage does not identify the recipient of the gift (in the context it seems that King Pabel, rather than the people, is the most likely candidate), its value here is limited.

in the land,[8] and he caused them to possess it.[9] In no way is the people's presence in the land of Canaan to be credited to their own genius or to be considered their own accomplishment.[10] Nor should the people view it as a reward for their righteousness.[11] Leviticus 25:23, a text I referred to in an earlier context when discussing Yahweh's claim to the land, describes the nation's relationship to the land most concisely: "The land shall not be permanently sold, for the land is mine, for you are but aliens (*gērîm*) and sojourners (*tôšābîm*) with me."

The Responsibilities of the Land and the People in This Feudal Relationship

Ancient Israel's perception of the land of Canaan as a divine grant to them as a people carried with it several far-reaching implications. Ultimately, since both the land and the people were subject to the will of the deity, the obligations of both were to fulfill Yahweh's objectives for them. However, the degree to which this was accomplished depended in large measure upon the extent to which they served each other. It is to their respective responsibilities that we now turn.

The Role of the Land

According to the Old Testament, the territory occupied by Israel provided them with a base for national development. The land provided the context in which fullness of life could be enjoyed, a state reflected in the expressions *taʾărîk yāmîm ʿal-hāʾădāmâ*, "you will lengthen days on the land,"[12] and *yirbû yěmêkem . . . ʿal hāʾădāmâ*, "your days will multiply . . . on the land."[13] The relationship between a long life and the good life (*šālôm*) is reflected clearly in the bilingual inscription of Hadad-yisʿi of Gozan:

---

8. *nāṭaʿ*, Exod. 15:17; 2 Sam. 7:10 = 1 Chron. 17:9; Amos 9:15; Jer. 24:6; 32:41; 42:10 (cf. 45:4); Ezek. 36:36; Ps. 44:3 (44:2 Eng.).

9. *hôrîš*, Deut. 12:10; 19:3; Jer. 3:18; 12:14. Cf. also Judg. 11:24, where the Ammonites are said to possess what Chemosh has caused them to possess.

10. Deut. 6:10–11; Josh. 24:13; Ps. 44:2–4 (44:1–3 Eng.). Cf. also Jer. 49:1, "Why has Malkam taken possession of Gad and his people settled in its cities?"

11. Deut. 9:1–6. Although the extrabiblical evidence for parallels to Yahweh, the divine lord, providing his people with a land grant is scanty, in Hittite treaties the historical prologue generally concluded with a declaration granting rule and land to a vassal. For discussion see M. Weinfeld, *Deuteronomy and the Deuteronomic School* (Oxford: Clarendon, 1972), 70–74.

12. Deut. 4:40; 5:30; 11:9; 17:20; 22:7; 30:18; 32:47. Cf. 4:26, "your days will not be prolonged."

13. Deut. 11:21. On the association of the lengthening of days with "life" and "the good" see Weinfeld, *Deuteronomy*, 307–13.

mrʾ rb mrʾ	To the great lord, his lord,
hdysʿy mlk gwzn	Hadad-yisʿi, governor of Gozan,
br ssnwry mlk gwzn	Son of Sassu-nuri, also governor of Gozan:
lḥyy nbšh	For the life of his soul,
wlmʾryk ywmwh	And for the length of his days,
wlkbd šnwh	And for the increasing of his years,
wlšlm byth	And for the well-being of his house,
wlšlm zrʿh	And for the well-being of his descendants,
wlšlm ʾnšwh	And for the well-being of his men,
wlmlk mrq mnh	And for the removal of illness from him,
wlmšmʿ ṭṣ.lwth	And for the answering of his prayers,
wlmlqḥ ʾmrt pmh	And for the acceptance of the words of his mouth
knn wytb lh	He dedicated [the statue] as a gift to him.[14]

Stock phrases like *ʾereṣ zābat ḥālāb ûděbāš*, "a land flowing with milk and honey,"[15] speak of the prosperity that the land was to provide. Especially instructive is Deut. 8:7–10, which describes this function in detail:

> For Yahweh your God is bringing you into a good land, a land of brooks of water, of fountains and springs, flowing forth in valleys and hills, a land of wheat and barley, of vines and fig trees and pomegranates, a land of olive trees and honey, a land in which you will eat bread without scarcity, in which you will lack nothing, a land whose stones are iron, and out of whose hills you can dig copper. And you shall eat and be full, and you shall bless Yahweh your God for the good land he has given you.[16]

According to Deut. 11:9–17 the land is able to provide this prosperity because Yahweh exercises special care over his land. Nevertheless, it is contingent upon his blessing his people *and* his land.[17] The inscription

14. The text as provided by A. Abou-Assaf, P. Bordreuil, and A. R. Millard, *La statue de Tell Fekherye et son inscription bilingue assyro-araméenne*, Etudes Assyriologiques, Editions recherche sur les civilisations 7 (Paris: A.D.P.F., 1982), 23. For additional studies, see, among many others, A. R. Millard and P. Bordreuil, "A Statue from Syria with Assyrian and Aramaic Inscriptions," *BA* 45 (1982): 135–42; V. Sasson, "The Aramaic Text of the Tell Fakhriyah Assyrian-Aramaic Bilingual Inscription," *ZAW* 97 (1985): 86–103; J. C. Greenfield and A. Shaffer, "Notes on the Akkadian-Aramaic Bilingual Statue from Tell Fekherye," *Iraq* 45 (1983): 109–16; idem, "Notes on the Curse Formulae of the Tell Fekherye Inscription," *RB* 92 (1985): 47–59; F. M. Fales, "Le double bilinguisme de la statue de Tell Fekherye," *Syria* 60 (1983): 233–50.

15. Used in Exod. 3:8, 17 and eighteen other times, on which see S. D. Waterhouse, "A Land Flowing with Milk and Honey," *AUSS* 1 (1963): 152–66.

16. On the idealistic nature of this description see Weinfeld, *Deuteronomy*, 172–73; J. H. Tigay, *Deuteronomy*, JPS Torah Commentary (Philadelphia: Jewish Publication Society, 1996), 93–94.

17. Cf. also Deut. 7:13–15; 26:15; 28:4–6, 11–12; 30:9; 33:28.

of Azitawadda of Adana indicates that such notions were not unique to the Israelites.

> May this city possess plenty to eat and wine (to drink), and may this peo-
> ple that dwells in it possess oxen and small cattle and plenty to eat and
> wine (to drink)! May they have many children, may they be strong numer-
> ically, may they serve Azitawadda and the house of Mupsh in large num-
> bers, by virtue of Ba'l and the Gods (*El*)![18]

In 2 Kings 18:31–32 (= Isa. 36:16–17) Rabshakeh describes his native land of Assyria in similar terms:

> Make your peace with me and come out to me; then every one of you
> will eat of his own vine, and every one of his own fig tree, and every one
> of you will drink the water of his own cistern; until I come and take you
> away to a land like your own land, a land of grain and wine, a land of
> bread and vineyards, a land of olive trees and honey, that you may live,
> and not die.

Finally, ancient Near Easterners also understood the land to repre-sent the geographical context where national peace and security could be realized. This tranquillity is portrayed in several ways. In the first in-stance, it is described as rest that Yahweh gives to the people (*hēnîaḥ*), usually in association with the land.[19] In Deut. 12:9 the land as a grant (*naḥălâ*) is in fact called a "resting place" (*měnûḥâ*). The following verse defines this rest more closely as freedom from enemy oppression.[20]

In the second instance, the population is depicted as living securely in the land (*lābetaḥ*).[21] This security takes on several dimensions. Le-viticus 25:18–22 ties this security directly to the land yielding its pro-duce.[22] Other texts tie the security to freedom from the fear of enemies, as in Judg. 18:7,[23] as well as freedom from terror before wild beasts. In-deed, Lev. 26:4–8 conjoins all three of these elements in its description of the ideal secure situation. Here this state of security and well-being is identified as peace, *šālôm*.[24] Security also involves ample provision

---

18. *ANET,* 654.
19. Exod. 33:14; Deut. 3:20; Josh. 1:13, 15; 22:4.
20. Cf. also Deut. 25:19; Josh. 21:44; 23:1; 2 Sam. 7:1, 11; 1 Kings 5:18 (5:4 Eng.); Isa. 28:12; 1 Chron. 22:9, 18; 2 Chron. 14:5, 6 (14:6, 7 Eng.); 15:15; 20:30; 32:22.
21. On the word see E. Gerstenberger, "בטח," *THAT* 1:300–305 (= *TLOT* 1:226–30); A. Jepsen, "בָּטַח *bāṭach,*" *TDOT* 2:88–94; R. W. Moberley, "בטח," *NIDOTTE* 1:644–49.
22. Cf. also Deut. 33:28. 1 Kings 5:5 (4:25 Eng.) associates security with everyone from Dan to Beersheba dwelling under his own vine and his own fig tree.
23. Cf. also Deut. 12:10; 33:28 (in association with prosperity); Jer. 33:16; Ezek. 38:8–14; 39:26.
24. Cf. also Jer. 12:5, *ʾereṣ šālôm;* Isa. 32:15–20.

for the needy (Isa. 14:30), and the administration of justice in the land (Jer. 23:6; cf. Isa. 32:16–17). According to Zech. 14:11 this security implies the absence of the curse.

No text captures the importance of the land for the well-being of the people better than the beautiful eschatological vision of Ezekiel in 34:25–29:

> I will make with them a covenant of peace and banish wild beasts from the land, so that they may dwell securely in the wilderness and sleep in the woods. And I will make them and the places round about my hill a blessing. And I will send down the showers in their season; they shall be showers of blessing. And the trees of the field shall yield their fruit, and the earth shall yield its increase. *And they shall be secure in their land.* And they shall know that I am Yahweh, when I break the bars of their yoke, and deliver them from the hand of those who enslaved them. They shall no more be a prey to the nations, nor shall beasts of the land devour them. *They shall dwell securely,* and none shall make them afraid. And I will provide for them prosperous plantations so that they shall no more be consumed with hunger in the land, and no longer suffer the reproach of the nations.

This text brings together all the aspirations in one single paragraph. However, the context of the passage should be observed. The prophet foresees this new life, prosperity, and security for the nation only *after they have been regathered in the land* (34:11–14).

Even though this is an eschatological vision, it reflects the ancient Near Eastern concern for territory, a homeland. Not to have one's own territory was to be sentenced to a perpetual life of wandering, always foraging for sustenance, ever at the mercy of others (cf. Deut. 26:5–11). Nomadic tribes did not develop into strong nations.[25] For this reason, when the promise was first made to Abraham that his descendants would become a *gôy gādôl,* "a great nation,"[26] the promise of land was a natural corollary.[27] This is precisely what happened historically. Once

25. This is not to say that nomadic tribes did not develop associations with specific territories. In modern times tribal territories (*dirah*) are well-defined. Cf. G. A. Lipsky, *Saudi-Arabia: Its People, Its Society, Its Culture* (New Haven: Hraf, 1959), 71–72; C. M. Doughty, *Travels in Arabia Deserta,* new and definitive ed., 2 vols. (London: Random House, 1936), esp. 1:55, 303; 2:266.

26. J. Hoftijzer, *Die Verheissungen an die drei Erzväter* (Leiden: Brill, 1956), 13, comments, "Die Verheissung des Landes ist das Fundament des Entstehens des Volkes Israel, und dazu gehört auch das Fundament des Verhältnisses des Volkes zu seinem Gott [The promise of land, along with the relationship of the people to its God, is the foundation for the origin of the people of Israel]." For a study of the promise of the land see Claus Westermann, *The Promises to the Fathers: Studies on the Patriarchal Narratives,* trans. D. E. Green (Philadelphia: Fortress, 1980), 143–49.

27. Cf. Gen. 15:7; 17:8; etc.

the nation of Israel had established itself in the land its emergence as a dominant national force awaited only the development of more sophisticated political institutions. This was provided by the establishment of the monarchy, specifically the dynasty of David.

The Obligations of the People

The foregoing description of the prosperity and security afforded by the land represents the ideal. Even within the national homeland, however, such well-being could not be taken for granted. Viewing the territory as a feudal grant received from the deity implied that the conduct of the residents of the divine estate was subject to the lord's accounting. Thus in Israel the relationship of the nation to its land was governed by a series of guidelines given by its patron, God himself. These instructions included specific regulations for the way in which the land itself was to be treated or managed. To begin with, the land was apportioned to the tribes, the clans, and the families on the basis of the divine land grant principle. If the entire territory belonged to the nation as their *naḥălâ* that they had received from the sovereign, then the same applied to the individual parcels of land allotted to each family.[28]

The actual regulations for the treatment of the land are spelled out in Leviticus 25. Of special interest among the laws are provisions for the sabbatical rest of the land every seventh year, the year of Jubilee, at which time all lands reverted to the descendants of the original owners, the consecration of portions of the land to Yahweh, and the presentation of the tithe of its produce. In response to the faithful observance of these standards, the land, for its part, would guarantee prosperity (abundance of harvest), security (from wild beasts and enemies), and a numerous population (Lev. 26:1–12), all prerequisites for the development of the nation.[29]

Though not tied as directly to the land, other aspects of life were to have equally serious implications for the people's continued relationship to the land. Indeed, the enjoyment of its benefits was contingent

28. Joshua 13–21. Cf. Num. 26:52–56. That the procedure of allotting such patrimonies was extended to individual families is also implied by Naboth's refusal to sell his land to Ahab, 1 Kings 21:3–4. For a full discussion see H. O. Forshey, "The Hebrew Root *NḤL* and Its Semitic Cognates" (Th.D. diss., Harvard University, 1973), 188–93.

29. Deuteronomy 26:1–19 indicates that at the annual presentation of the firstfruits the people were to remind themselves of the role of Yahweh in meeting all three of these basic needs. The text concludes with a reference to Israel being above all the nations, a nation of praise, renown, and honor. Despite my reservations concerning his dating of biblical texts, J. Fager offers a helpful study of Israel's law of Jubilee in *Land Tenure and the Biblical Jubilee: Uncovering Hebrew Ethics through the Sociology of Knowledge*, JSOTSup 155 (Sheffield: JSOT Press, 1993).

upon the strict observance of all the divine lord's moral and religious demands (cf. Deut. 28:1–6). To adopt the moral practices of the previous inhabitants, the Canaanites, represented a defilement of the land itself (Lev. 18:24–30). To engage in idolatry, especially the sacrificing of children to idols, was to pollute the land.[30]

The complexity of the interrelationship among deity, land, and people is obvious. In a very real sense the land occupied by Israel was a holy land, *terra sancta*. The people were not free to treat it arbitrarily or according to their own whims. It was a divine grant, graciously bestowed on them by their divine suzerain. Their conduct within it was to reflect their gratitude for his grace and their dependence upon him.[31]

The extent to which the Israelite perception of their national territory and their own relationship to it was shared among the surrounding peoples is not clear. We may perhaps recognize a point of intersection in the practice of using special landmarks to delineate property. Old Testament references to boundary markers (*gĕbûl*) reflect the Israelite notion of the sanctity of the private patrimony.[32] Since individual Israelites, as well as the nation as a whole, considered land to be a divinely bestowed grant, to move a *gĕbûl*, or to add arbitrarily to one's property at the expense of another, was a serious offense (Isa. 5:8–9; Mic. 2:1–2). It is difficult to determine the extent to which these sensitivities were shared by other Levantine peoples. The "Instruction of Amenemope" 6 indicates that the practice of using inviolable boundary markers was known in Egypt.[33] The use of *kudurru* stones in Babylonia to mark off property also displays marked similarities with the Israelite custom.[34]

---

30. Jer. 3:2; Ps. 106:38. Cf. also Jer. 2:7; 16:18.

31. On the relationship between loyalty and obedience to Yahweh, the divine suzerain, and Israel's possession of and prosperity in the land see P. Diepold, *Israels Land*, BWANT 95 (Stuttgart: Kohlhammer, 1972), 88–104.

32. Deut. 19:14; 27:17; Hos. 5:10; Job 24:2; Prov. 22:28; 23:10. On the Egyptian practice, see A. Erman and H. Ranke, *Ägypten und ägyptisches Leben im Altertum* (Tübingen: Mohr, 1923), 101–4, 420, 594; W. Helck, "Grenze, Grenzsicherung," *Lexikon der Ägyptologie*, ed. W. Helck and W. Westendorf (Wiesbaden: Harrassowitz, 1976), 2:896–97; idem, "Grenzsteine," ibid., 897; idem, *Zur Vorstellung von der Grenze in der ägyptischen Frühgeschichte* (Hildesheim: Gerstenberg, 1951).

34. On which see A. K. Grayson, "Grenze," *Reallexikon der Assyriologie* (Berlin: de Gruyter, 1957–71), 3:639–40; W. J. Hinke, *A New Boundary Stone of Nebuchadnezzar I* (Philadelphia: University of Pennsylvania Press, 1907), 1–115; L. W. King, *Babylonian Boundary Stones and Memorial-Tablets in the British Museum* (London: British Museum, 1912); F. X. Steinmetzer, *Die babylonischen Kudurru (Grenzsteine) als Urkundeform*, Görres-Gesellschaft: Studien zur Geschichte und Kultur des Altertums 11/4–5 (Paderborn: Schöningh, 1922). The structure of *kudurru* inscriptions tends to resemble that of standard land-sale documents (thus A. R. Millard in private communication) and ancient treaties: preamble, historical prologue, border delineations, stipulations, witnesses, blessings and curses. In addition to Steinmetzer, *Die babylonischen Kudurru*, 257–58, see Weinfeld, *Deuteronomy*, 73–74.

The inviolability of these markers is stressed by the curses inveighed upon any who would dare to move them.

On the basis of this Hebrew, Egyptian, and Babylonian usage, one is tempted to assume that boundary stones were used in Phoenicia and Aram as well. That they are not attested in Assyria may yet argue against this conclusion.[35] Furthermore, Jezebel's callous seizure of Naboth's vineyard (1 Kings 21:1–16) suggests that either she, a Phoenician, had no understanding of the theological background to the custom, or she viewed herself, by virtue of her position, to be above it. The latter may account for her sharp rebuke of her husband in 21:7: "Do you not now exercise kingship over Israel?"[36]

The Effects of Feudal Infidelity

The foregoing survey suggests that the attitudes of ancient Levantine peoples toward their divine sovereign determined whether the land would fulfill its expected role and provide them with the basis for national prosperity. Two texts in particular, Lev. 26:14–38 and Deut. 28:15–68, provide a detailed description of the consequences for Israel of their failure to live up to the expectations of the patron God, Yahweh. Both descriptions are incorporated within the "blessings and curses" sections of larger documents, the structures of which have been heavily influenced by ancient Near Eastern suzerainty treaty forms.[37] Further-

35. Cf. Grayson, "Grenze," 639.

36. On the Old Testament view of property ownership see W. Johnstone, "Old Testament Technical Expressions in Property Holdings," *Ugaritica* 6 (1969): 309–17.

37. The exact relationship between the texts is not clear. M. Noth (*Leviticus: A Commentary*, trans. J. E. Anderson, OTL [Philadelphia: Westminster, 1965], 196) suggests a common origin in an older tradition, but each has been given its own special character. What differences do exist may be attributed to the present contexts in which each now occurs. The former, with its references to Yahweh as speaker and its relative brevity, appears to be a fundamental part of the treaty between the divine suzerain and the national vassal. The latter, on the other hand, is placed within the context of a sermonic address; hence the greater length, as well as the consistent reference to Yahweh in the third person. A study of both texts is provided by D. Hillers, *Treaty-Curses and the Old Testament Prophets*, Biblica et Orientalia 16 (Rome: Pontifical Biblical Institute, 1964), 30–42. Cf. Weinfeld, *Deuteronomy*, 59–157, on Deuteronomy 28.

The parallels between the Book of Deuteronomy and Hittite suzerainty treaties have received a great deal of attention since the 1950s. See G. Mendenhall, "Ancient Oriental and Biblical Law," *BA* 17 (1954): 26–46; idem, "Covenant Forms in Israelite Tradition," *BA* 17 (1954): 50–76; M. G. Kline, *Treaty of the Great King: The Covenant Structure of Deuteronomy; Studies and Commentary* (Grand Rapids: Eerdmans, 1963); idem, *The Structure of Biblical Authority* (Grand Rapids: Eerdmans, 1972); D. J. McCarthy, *Treaty and Covenant*, Analecta Biblica 21 (Rome: Pontifical Biblical Institute, 1963); J. A. Thompson, *The Ancient Near Eastern Treaties and the Old Testament* (London: Tyndale, 1964); R. Frankena, "The Vassal-Treaties of Esarhaddon and the Dating of Deuteronomy," *OTS* 14 (1965): 122–54; K. A. Kitchen, *Ancient Orient and Old Testament* (Downers Grove, Ill.: InterVarsity Press, 1966), 90–102; K. Baltzer, *The Covenant Formulary in Old Testament,*

more, both are preceded by statements of the blessings that will result from Israel's conscientious observance of the divine stipulations, namely, the economic prosperity of the land (Lev. 26:4–5; Deut. 28:8, 11b–12), the numerical increase in the population (Lev. 26:9; Deut. 28:11a), the security of the people in the face of external threats (Lev. 26:6–8; Deut. 28:7, 13), and the continuation of the relationship with Yahweh (Lev. 26:11–12; Deut. 28:9–10).

In both descriptions of the termination of the ties with the land, which is presented as the result of direct divine activity, the cancellation of the first three receives special prominence. First, Yahweh will stifle the productivity of the land by withholding rain[38] and causing disease among the crops (Deut. 28:22c) and insect plagues (Deut. 28:38–39). Indeed, all agricultural efforts will prove futile.[39] Similar curses are common in extrabiblical treaties, although these have the deities acting on behalf of human sovereigns whose authority has not been respected. This kind of futility of effort is graphically described in Part B of the Hadad-yisʿi inscription,[40] which contrasts with the blessing in Part A:

wlzrʿ wʾl yḥṣr	May he sow but not harvest,
wʾlp šʿryn lzrʿ	May he sow a thousand measures of barley,

Jewish, and Early Christian Writings, trans. D. E. Green (Philadelphia: Fortress, 1971), 1–38. Several recent commentaries have drawn heavily on these advances. See J. A. Thompson, *Deuteronomy: An Introduction and Commentary,* Tyndale Old Testament Commentary (Downers Grove, Ill.: InterVarsity Press, 1974); P. C. Craigie, *The Book of Deuteronomy,* NICOT (Grand Rapids: Eerdmans, 1976); A. D. H. Mayes, *Deuteronomy,* NCB (1979; reprint, Grand Rapids: Eerdmans, 1981); M. Weinfeld, *Deuteronomy 1–11: A New Translation with Introduction and Commentary,* AB 5 (New York: Doubleday, 1991).

For the definitive work on Neo-Assyrian treaties see S. Parpola and K. Watanabe, eds., *Neo-Assyrian Treaties and Loyalty Oaths,* State Archives of Assyria 2 (Helsinki: Helsinki University Press, 1988). For a convenient collection of Hittite treaties translated into English see G. M. Beckman, *Hittite Diplomatic Texts,* SBL Writings from the Ancient World 7 (Atlanta: Scholars Press, 1996).

38. Deut. 28:22b–24. Compare "And the heavens over your head shall be brass (*něḥō-šet*), and the earth under you shall be iron (*barzel*)," in the latter with "Just as rain does not fall from a copper sky," in *The Vassal Treaties of Esarhaddon,* #64, published by D. J. Wiseman, *Iraq* 20 (1958): 69, line 530. Cf. *ANET,* 539. (Hereafter this text will be referred to as *VTE,* followed by the number of the treaty article.) The previous article had also mentioned turning "your soil into iron so that no one may cut [a furrow] in it." Leviticus 26:19 reverses the metals, speaking of the heavens as iron and the earth as brass.

39. Lev. 26:16: "You shall sow your seed uselessly"; 26:20: "Your strength shall be spent uselessly, for your land will not yield produce and the trees of the field shall not yield their fruit."

40. Abou-Assaf, Bordreuil, and Millard, *La statue de Tell Fekherye,* 23–24. For a study of these curses, see Greenfield and Shaffer, "Curse Formulae," 47–59. Cf. also the treaty between Ashurnirari V and Matiʿilu of Arpad, *ANET,* 532–33, especially iv (hereafter referred to as Ashurnirari V followed by article number); *VTE* 47, 63–64, 85. On these see Weinfeld, *Deuteronomy,* 116–17; Frankena, "Vassal-Treaties," 122–54.

wprys lʾḥz mnh	But get only a fraction of it;
wmʾh sʾwn lhynqn ʿmr	May one hundred ewes suckle a lamb,
wʾl yrwh	But may it not be satisfied;
wmʾh swr[n] lhynqr ʿgl	May one hundred cows suckle a calf,
wʾl yrwy	But may it not be satisfied;
wmʾh nšwn lhynqr ʿlym	May a hundred women suckle an infant
wʾl yrwy	But may it not be satisfied;
wmʾh nšwn lʾpn btnwr lḥm	May a hundred women bakers bake bread in an oven,
wʾl ymlʾnh	But may it not be filled;
wmn qlqltʾ llqṭw ʾnšwh šʿrn lʾklw	From the rubbish dump may his men scavenge barley to eat;
wmwtn šbṭ zy nyrgl	May death, the rod of Nergal,
ʾl ygtzr mn mth	never cease from his land.

Second, Yahweh will decimate the population by disease[41] and by an increase in the number of wild beasts that will prey upon the people.[42] In sum, the population itself will be under the curse.[43] Third, as terrible as these disasters may be, Yahweh will send in foreign enemies who will constitute the most serious threat to the territorial association. Enemies will come in and destroy the nation by consuming its resources,[44] laying waste the countryside,[45] enslaving citizens,[46] and leaving the human corpses out in the fields for the vultures and eagles to devour.[47] Indeed, the shortages caused by the enemies' siege strategies will create a crisis so desperate that the people will resort to cannibalism.[48]

Echoes of this response of the land to the apostasy of Israel may also be heard in the prophets. In Amos 4:6–13 the prophet speaks of drought, plagues and pests, and military defeat as Yahweh's means of alerting his people to their infidelity to the covenant. Hosea 2:6–13 (2:4–11 Eng.) attributes similar disasters to the nation's "spiritual har-

41. Lev. 26:16b; Deut. 28:22a, 29, 34–35, 58–62. Cf. *VTE* 38–41, 52; Ashurnirari V Treaty iv (leprosy).

42. Lev. 26:22; *VTE* 54; Sefire I A:30–31 (*KAI* 222 A:30–31).

43. Deut. 28:18. Cf. the treaty between Suppiluliumas and Mattiwaza, *ANET*, 206, ". . . may you Kurtiwaza . . . and (you) the Hurri men with your wives, your sons and your country have no seed"; and Ashurnirari V Treaty v, "May Matiʿilu's (seed) be that of a mule, his wives *barren;* may Ishtar, the goddess of men, the lady of women, take away their 'bow,' cause their sterility." Also note the general statement in vi, "Let one thousand houses decrease to one house, let one thousand tents decrease to one tent, let one man be spared in the city to tell about my feats." Cf. also *VTE* 43–47, 61, 66–67, 105.

44. Lev. 26:16; Deut. 28:29–30, 33, 51.

45. Lev. 26:31–32.

46. Deut. 28:48. Cf. *VTE* 42, 48.

47. Deut. 28:26. Cf. *VTE* 41, 59.

48. Lev. 26:29; Deut. 28:53–57. Cf. *VTE* 69–70, 75–76; Ashurnirari V Treaty iv.

lotry."[49] Isaiah 1 is most graphic in its descriptions of the evils of the nation and their resultant catastrophes in the land. According to Jer. 12:7–13, a text that also deals with the departure of Yahweh from his people, the land harbors wild beasts that are called upon to devour the people. Mention is also made of the destruction wrought by enemies, as well as the futility of all agricultural effort.

But there was another way in which moral and cultic infidelity to the divine lord could result in the severance of the tie between the nation and its homeland, namely, the physical removal of the population from the land. In both Leviticus 26 and Deuteronomy 28 this event is presented as a final climactic catastrophic consequence. Leviticus 26:33 speaks initially in general terms of "scattering" (*zārâ*) Israel among the nations.[50] This will permit the land finally to enjoy an extended rest, as compensation for the sabbatical years that had been missed because of Israel's disregard for the covenant stipulations.[51] The purpose of the exile will be to cause the nation to perish (*ʾābad*) outside, among the nations,[52] and to evoke remorse on the part of the people for their infidelity.[53] Should the latter occur, the covenant would be renewed, as a result of which the nation's reunification with the land would ensue.

Although the Deuteronomy text reserves the fullest treatment of the exile of Israel for the end, hints of this prospect have appeared earlier. Deuteronomy 28:36–37 had indicated that Yahweh would bring his people and its king to a nation that neither they nor their ancestors had known.[54] There they would be able to serve the strange gods all they wanted, but at the same time they would be the subjects of incessant scorn and derision. The intention of vv. 62–63 seems to be to portray Israel's fate deliberately as a reversal of the process that had been described in 26:5–11. The verb *nāsaḥ*, "to tear, pull away," is used to depict the severance of the connection with the land.[55] However, the preced-

---

49. Cf. 4:1–3. On the other hand, in 2:16–25 (2:14–23 Eng.) Hosea does anticipate the day when Yahweh will renew his covenant with Israel, the effects of which will be peace with the environment, as well as security from external foes.

50. The expression is repeated frequently elsewhere. Cf. 1 Kings 14:15; Jer. 31:10; Ezek. 5:10, 12; 12:14, 15; 20:23; 22:15; Zech. 2:2–4 (1:19–21 Eng.); Ps. 44:12 (44:11 Eng.); 106:27.

51. Cf. Lev. 26:43; also 2 Chron. 36:21.

52. Lev. 26:36–39. Note the expression "the land of your enemies will consume you."

53. Lev. 26:40–45. In the text, however, the people are reminded that in view of the eternal nature of Yahweh's covenant with the people, he cannot annihilate them totally.

54. *yôlēk yhwh ʾōtĕkā . . . ʾel-gôy ʾăšer lōʾ-yādaʿtā ʾattâ waʾăbōteykā.* The same verb is used of the exile also in Jer. 32:5. Cf. the use of *nāhag*, "to drive," in Deut. 28:37. In 4:27 *nāhag* is paralleled with *hēpîṣ.*

55. Cf. the use of *pûṣ* (Hiphil), "to scatter," instead of *zārâ* in v. 64. Echoes of this usage occur in Ezek. 11:17; 20:34, 41; 28:25 (all Niphal); Deut. 4:27; Jer. 9:15 (9:16 Eng.); Ezek. 11:16; 12:15; 20:23; 22:15; 36:19; Neh. 1:8 (all Hiphil). Elsewhere the expulsion of Israel is described as Yahweh uprooting (*nātaš*) the people from the land (Deut. 29:27; 1 Kings

ing verses outlined the devastating effects of such an exile: perpetual restlessness, insecurity, despondency and despair, and the return of the slavery of Egypt. In short, this picture of the consequences of not being firmly planted in one's own homeland provides a negative image of how crucial the territorial tie was for the nation's well-being and prosperity.

This understanding of the nature of the bond between nation and territory underlies the common ancient Near Eastern practice of guaranteeing the submission of conquered states by the wholesale deportation of populations from their native soil to foreign lands. Since the biblical texts describe the experience of exile primarily from the perspective of those who were on the receiving end of the misfortune, they provide only limited information concerning the human factors upon which the policy was based. For the latter, extrabiblical sources must be consulted.

The ruthless and brutal practice of deporting en masse conquered peoples has been attested from second-millennium Egyptian,[56] Hittite,[57]

14:15; Jer. 12:14; 45:4 [opposite *nāṭaʿ*, "to plant"]; Amos 9:15 [opposite *nāṭaʿ*], cf. Akkadian *nasāḫum*, "ausreissen," also "to evacuate, deport," *AHw* 2:749–80); slinging them out (*qālaʿ*, Jer. 10:18; *ṭûl*, Jer. 16:13, to an unknown land); casting them out (*šālak*, Deut. 29:27, to another land); sending them off into exile (*higleh*, 2 Kings 17:11; Jer. 29:4, 7, 14; Ezek. 39:28; Lam. 4:22; 1 Chron. 5:41 [6:15 Eng.]). Elsewhere the subject of the verb is always human. On the development of the usage of *gālâ* see D. E. Gowan, "The Beginnings of Exile Theology and the Root *glh*," *ZAW* 87 (1975): 204–7. The root appears several times in Akkadian as *galû*, "in die Verbannung gehen," *AHw* 1:275, but omitted by *CAD*. The Hebrew noun forms, *gālût* and *gôlâ*, come to be employed as special technical terms for "exile," and collectives for "exiles." Observe also the occasional use of *šābâ*, "to take captive" (though never with Yahweh as subject): 2 Chron. 28:8; etc., and with the cognate accusative *šĕbî*, Judg. 5:12; Ps. 68:19 (68:18 Eng.); 2 Chron. 28:5, 11, 17. Cf. the Aramaic *šbh šby*, rendered "il a emmené des captifs," by André Dupont-Sommer, "L'Ostracon araméen d'Assur," *Syria* 24 (1944–45): 45 (= *KAI* 233:15–16; *AI* 20:15–16), and *šbyt zy šby*, "The prisoners you have captured," A. Cowley, *Aramaic Papyri of the Fifth Century b.c.* (1923; reprint, Osnabrück: Otto Zeller, 1967), 71:14. Also *hālak baššebî*, "to go into captivity," Deut. 28:41; Jer. 20:6; Amos 9:4; etc.

56. E.g., S. Sauneron and J. Yoyotte, "Traces d'établissement asiatiques en Moyenne-Égypte sous Ramses II," *Revue d'égyptologie* 7 (1950): 70: "He who has removed Nubia to the Northland, and the Syrians to Nubia; who has placed the Shasu-Asiatics in the Westland (= Libya), and established the Libyans on the (E.) hills." As translated by K. A. Kitchen, "Ancient Orient, 'Deuteronomism,' and the Old Testament," in *New Perspectives on the Old Testament*, ed. J. B. Payne (Waco: Word, 1970), 6. See also Kamid el-Lōz tablet 1: "Send me the Hapiru-people . . . on whose account I have written you as follows, 'I shall deliver them to the towns of Cush, that they may live in them in place of those whom I have deported.'" Cf. D. O. Edzard, "Die Tontafeln von Kammid el-Lōz," in *Kamid el-Lōz-Kumidi: Schriftdokumente aus Kamid el-Lōz*, Saarbrücker Beiträge zur Altertumskunde 7 (Bonn: Habelt, 1970), 56. Cf. M. Weippert, "Semitische Nomaden des zweiten Jahrtausends: Über die *Šśśw* der ägyptischen Quellen," *Biblica* 55 (1974): 430.

57. *ANET*, 318, 530. Cf. A. Goetze, *Die Annalen des Mursilis* (Darmstadt: Wissenschaftliche Buchgesellschaft, 1967), 21ff., 136ff.; idem, *Kulturgeschichte Kleinasiens* (Munich: Beck, 1957), 127–28, 196. Cf. Kitchen, "Ancient Orient," 6.

and Mesopotamian[58] documents. Among other objectives, the policy was designed to destroy the main pillars upon which nationalistic feelings were based, one of which was the bond of a people to its territory.[59] This treatment would not only remove the economic base of national development; since patron deities were considered to be territorially limited, it would also prevent the patron from coming to the aid of his people. Furthermore, in order to rebuild the economies of states that had been ravaged, alien peoples were brought in. The result was an eventual blending of ethnic groups and the diffusion of whatever feelings of national self-consciousness might have remained.[60] The effects of these tactics were devastating. Whereas up to the eighth century B.C. the Syrian arena had been occupied by a series of medium-sized states, by the time the Achaemenid Empire emerged in the sixth century, few vestiges of the old structures remained.[61] The territorial basis for national development and national self-consciousness had been nullified for many groups.[62]

Leviticus 26 attributes this harsh treatment of Israel to the anger of Yahweh, the divine lord whose authority had been repudiated.[63] Displaying more restraint, Deuteronomy 28 declines to attribute this emo-

---

58. See I. J. Gelb, "Prisoners of War in Early Mesopotamia," *JNES* 32 (1973): 70–98. For a comprehensive study of deportations in the Neo-Assyrian period, see B. Oded, *Mass Deportations and Deportees in the Neo-Assyrian Empire* (Wiesbaden: Reichert, 1979). Note also H. Tadmor, "Assyria and the West: The Ninth Century and Its Aftermath," in *Unity and Diversity: Essays in the History, Literature, and Religion of the Ancient Near East,* ed. H. Goedicke and J. J. M. Roberts (Baltimore: Johns Hopkins University Press, 1975), 40–42. Resettlement programs were also carried out (albeit on a smaller scale) by the Syrian kingdoms. Cf. *KAI* 215:14 (Panammuwa); 26A I:21 (Azitawadda). Cf. *ANET,* 654.

59. For a detailed discussion of Neo-Assyrian motives, see Oded, *Mass Deportations,* 41–74.

60. The Assyrian population seems to have become one massive conglomerate. Note the variations of the recurring comment, "And they were regarded as the people of his land." See A. K. Grayson, *Assyrian Royal Inscriptions,* Records of the Ancient Near East (Wiesbaden: Harrassowitz, 1972), 2:§§12, 18 (Tiglath-Pileser I); *ARAB* 1:§§617, 621 (Shalmaneser III); 1:§§763, 772 (Tiglath-Pileser III); 2:§30 (Sargon II); etc.

61. The Persian satrapies were generally much larger units than these independent states had been. For example, the fifth satrapy, Ebir-Namri, encompassed all of Aram, Phoenicia, Palestine, and Cyprus. For a full discussion, see A. F. Rainey, "The Satrapy 'Beyond the River,'" *Australian Journal of Biblical Archaeology* 1 (1969): 51–78. On Persian imperial administration, see G. Widengren, "The Persians," in *Peoples of Old Testament Times,* ed. D. J. Wiseman (Oxford: Clarendon, 1973), 332–37.

62. It is clear, however, that throughout the period ethnic self-consciousness was maintained among many peoples. Note the use of the expression "to each district, according to its script, and to each people, according to its language," in Esth. 1:22. Cf. 3:12; 8:9. On the status of some of these exiles in Babylon see I. Ephal, "The Western Minorities in Babylonia in the 6th–5th Centuries B.C.: Maintenance and Cohesion," *Orientalia,* n.s., 47 (1978): 74–89.

63. Several different expressions reflect this anger: *nātattî pānay bāhem,* "I will set my face against them" (26:17; on the expression see A. S. van der Woude, "פָּנִים," *THAT* 2:451–52 [= *TLOT* 2:995–1014]); *wĕhālaktî ʿimmākem baḥămat qerî,* "I will come toward you with wrath of hostility" (26:28); *wĕgāʿălâ napšî ʾetkem,* "My soul will abhor you" (26:30).

tion explicitly to Yahweh. The nearest the author comes is to use a positive verb, *śîś*, "to rejoice, exult," and apply it to his destructive acts. As Yahweh had formerly delighted in the nation's prosperity, so now he would delight in their annihilation.[64]

This "Deuteronomic" philosophy of history and the motif of the deity's anger with his subjects are not unique to Israel. Even though 2 Kings 17:24–40 derived from Hebrew hands, the alien perspective underlying the narrative is obvious. After the destruction of Samaria the land was populated with a variety of foreign peoples, in keeping with standard Neo-Assyrian custom. However, the rapidly increasing lion population posed a serious threat to the newcomers' welfare. The crisis was attributed to their ignorance of the custom (*mišpāṭ*) of the god of the land. The lions were interpreted as agents of judgment sent by the divine lord whose will had been affronted. To appease the anger of the deity, Israelite priests were brought back to teach the immigrants in "the custom and the fear of Yahweh."[65]

Many extrabiblical parallels, in which the land refuses to fulfill its normal functions for the inhabitants, could be cited, especially in the treaty curses.[66] Chemosh's wrath toward "his land" was expressed in the Omride oppression of Moab. The text does not identify the reason for the anger.[67] More illuminating, on account of its completeness, is the account of Esarhaddon's reconstruction of Esagila, the temple of

---

64. Deut. 28:63. References to the anger of Yahweh against his people are frequent elsewhere as well: Deut. 6:15; 7:4; 11:17; 29:26; Josh. 23:16; 2 Kings 13:3; 23:26; Isa. 5:25; Ps. 106:40 (all *ḥārâ ʾap bĕ*. . .); 1 Kings 8:46 = 2 Chron. 6:36; Ps. 85:6 (85:5 Eng.); Ezra 9:14 (all *ʾānap bĕ* . . .); 1 Kings 11:9; 2 Kings 17:18 (Hithpael of *ʾānap*); Isa. 47:6; 64:4, 8 (*qāṣap*); Hos. 5:10; 13:11; etc. (*ʿebrâ*). The anger of Yahweh is an especially prominent motif in Lamentations. Cf. 1:12–13; 2:1–10; 3:1; 4:11; 5:19–22.

65. The narrator is not oblivious to the dilemma created by the two conflicting theological positions. On the one hand, the people are anxious to pay due respect to the god of the land, but on the other, they were still tied to their respective national deities. The result was a syncretistic compromise. On the practice of re-educating deportees see *ARAB* 2:§§86, 108, 122, according to which Sargon II appointed officials to instruct the newcomers to Dur-Sharrukin "how to fear god and the king."

66. Sefire I A:21–42 (*KAI* 222 A:21–42) speaks of the herds and crops failing, devastation in the land, vicious wild beasts devouring the population, Arpad becoming the habitat of gazelles, foxes, owls, etc. Note also the prism of Ashurbanipal, *Der Alte Orient* 19.939, lines 66–71, published by J. M. Aynard, *Le prisme du Louvre Der Alte Orient 19.939* (Paris: Presses Universitaires, 1957), 56–59 and more recently analyzed by R. Borger, *Beiträge zum Inschriftenwerk Assurbanipals* (Wiesbaden: Harrassowitz, 1996), Prism F, with A, 1–76; the Ashurnirari V Treaty, *ANET,* 532–33; *VTE* 63–64, 85, *ANET,* 539. For biblical descriptions of desolation, similar in many respects to the effects of these curses, cf. Isa. 13:20–22 (Babylon); 34:10–15 (Edom); Zeph. 2:13–14 (Nineveh); Jer. 9:10–11 (9:11–12 Eng.); 10:22 (Babylon); 49:33 (Hazor); 51:37–38 (Babylon). For a discussion of these motifs, see Hillers, *Treaty-Curses,* 44–54.

67. *KAI* 181:5; *HMI* 16:5.

Marduk in Babylon. The text contains no hints whatsoever of a covenant between Marduk and the Babylonians analogous to that which existed between Yahweh and Israel. Nevertheless, the parallels to the treaty curses in Leviticus and Deuteronomy are remarkable. The Babylonian crisis had been precipitated by "evil forces" (*idâti lemnêti*[meš]), which were expressing themselves in ethical and cultic offenses by the people. They had provoked the wrath of Marduk, the divine patron,[68] who summarily determined to annihilate the Babylonians and to devastate the land. As a result of his curse, the city was flooded, its residences and temples inundated, the town was made into a desolate steppe, and its inhabitants were removed from the land. Only a change in the disposition of the god could bring about a normalization of the relationship between the people and their native soil.

Finally, and as a corollary to much of the preceding, the ancient Near Easterners acknowledged that the fate or fortune of a nation and the productivity of the land had a determinative role to play in the public reputation of a deity. The signs and wonders that had accompanied the exodus of Israel out of Egypt were readily acknowledged as demonstrations of the character of Yahweh.[69] But Israel's actual enjoyment of prosperity in the land was intended to have a similar impact. Deuteronomy 28:1–14 declares that when the nations see the prosperity of Israel in the land, they will recognize them to be called by Yahweh's name (note especially v. 10).[70] But statements like Isa. 26:15, which attaches the deity's reputation to the multiplication of the population and the extension of the nation's borders, are quite rare. With the approaching exile, however, the idea increases in prominence.

The nature of the theological crisis precipitated by the exile of Judah is expressed succinctly by Ezekiel in 36:20:

> When they came to the nations, wherever they came, they profaned my holy name in that it was said of them, "These are the people of Yahweh, yet they have had to leave his land."

Joel found the misfortune of Israel to be especially critical because it had caused the nations around to question the very existence of Israel's deity. In 2:17 the prophet urgently pleads:

---

68. R. Borger (*Die Inschriften Asarhaddons, Königs von Assyrien,* Archiv für Orientforschung Beiheft 9 [Graz: Weidner, 1956], 13, episode 5A) uses *i-gu-ug-ma*, "to be angry"; cf. *AHw* 1:14, "ergrimmen, zürnen." Variant C has *e-zi-iz lib-ba-šú ka-bat-tuš iṣ-ṣa-ri-iḫ*, "his heart became angry, his disposition was in turmoil."

69. Josh. 2:8–11; 9:9; 2 Sam. 7:23 = 1 Chron. 17:21; Isa. 63:12, 14; Jer. 32:20; Dan. 9:15; Neh. 9:10.

70. See also Deut. 26:18–19; Jer. 13:11; 33:9.

Spare your people, O Yahweh;
Do not make your patrimony (*naḥălâ*) a reproach,
a byword among the nations.
Why should they say among the nations,
"Where is their god?"[71]

As the prophet sees it, the resolution of the dilemma would come when Yahweh would once again express his zeal for the land and have pity on the people. With the resulting destruction of the oppressors and the new prosperity of the nation, the disgrace of the people would be eliminated and the name of Yahweh would be publicly vindicated (2:18–27). Ezekiel acknowledges the dependence of the reputation of Yahweh upon the return of the people to the land, that is, the restoration of the territorial tie, even more specifically:

> When I gather the house of Israel from the peoples among whom they are scattered, and shall manifest my holiness in them in the sight of all the nations, then they will live in their land that I gave to my servant Jacob. And they will live in it securely, when I execute judgment upon all who scorn them, round about them. Then they will know that I am Yahweh their God. (28:25–26)

Equally instructive is 39:21–29, according to which, out of jealousy for his holy name, Yahweh will restore the fortunes of Israel and bring them back to their land. Not only will this cause the nations to acknowledge him as their God; they will also recognize that even the exile of Israel, as well as Yahweh's withdrawal, were necessary expressions of his character.[72] But with this comment I have introduced another subject that will be the focus of attention in the final chapter.

Conclusion

If the conviction that a nation's fate and fortune were in the hands of the gods, specifically its patron deity, was at the heart of an ancient Near Eastern nation's self-consciousness, the people's sense of obligation was an important corollary. Since they had received their territory

---

71. Cf. also Ps. 42:3 (42:2 Eng.); 79:10; 115:2; Mic. 7:10.

72. Cf. also 36:22–38, according to which, out of zeal for "the holiness of his great name" (v. 23), Yahweh will restore the people of Israel to their land (v. 24), renew his relationship with them (vv. 25–28), bless the land with fertility and population (vv. 29–31), restore the land to Edenic beauty (vv. 33–36), and multiply the population (vv. 37–38). Cf. also 37:15–28, which adds that the two Israelite nations will be reunited under one Davidic king. Furthermore, Yahweh will establish his residence among the people of Israel. Then the nations will know that he is the God of Israel.

as a grant from the deity (at least in Israel), and since their occupation of his land was subject to his pleasure, they were charged with keeping the divine patron happy. This meant loyal devotion, demonstrated in careful attention to the cult and the observance of the ethical and moral expectations of the divine sovereign. They were keenly aware that ultimately their well-being was not determined by the competence of their human leaders, but by the god who exercised authority over them.

The danger of incurring the wrath of the divine patron was an ever present reality. Consequently, the subjects of nationally recognized deities took great pains to satisfy them by providing them with a manorial residence befitting their awesome splendor, by generous offering of sacrifices and oblations, and by intense prayers for mercy and forgiveness when they feared they had offended the divine lord. Nevertheless, as attested by the Sumerian "Prayer to Every God,"[73] it seems that the human subjects of the divine lords suffered from intense insecurity. They were keenly aware of their own sinfulness, but assurance that they had been favorably received often eluded them. It is perhaps in this regard that Israelite faith made its most notable contribution. Within the ancient Near Eastern context the words of Moses in Deut. 4:5–8 were revolutionary:

> See, I have taught you these statutes and ordinances, as Yahweh my God has commanded me, that you should do them in the land that you are entering to take possession of it. Keep them and do them; for that will be your wisdom and your understanding in the sight of the peoples, who, when they hear all these statutes, will say, "Surely this great nation is a wise and understanding people." For which great nation is there that has a God so near to it as is Yahweh our God whenever we call upon him? And which great nation is there that has statutes and ordinances that are as righteous as this entire Torah that I am presenting to you today?

According to this text the Israelites' knowledge of the will of their divine patron and their sense of his living presence among them were unique in their time.

In this tripartite association, the land also had a critical role to play. In providing the basis of the nation's development, prosperity, and security, it functioned as a thermometer, so to speak, of the relationship between the deity and his people. When that relationship was warm, open, and confident, the land yielded its produce in abundance. When the lord-vassal relationship was disturbed, however, the land was often the first to feel the effects. Indeed, the performance of the land was so closely tied to the reputation of the divine lord that when it would fail

---

73. *ANET,* 391–92.

to provide its inhabitants with the necessary nourishment, or even when it would spew out its inhabitants, outsiders would recognize the anger of the divine lord toward his vassals.

Theoretically, in a polytheistic world governed by capricious gods and ambitious rulers, the recognition of a divine patron, in whose care a land and its inhabitants could rest, should have provided security. In practice, however, the distance between mortal and immortal tended to constitute a perpetually frustrating barrier to true peace and shalom (Dan. 2:11). The Hebrew record of the self-disclosure of the God of Israel—who was at the same time the Lord of heaven and earth—by his mighty acts and by his revelation at Sinai, describes a unique moment in the history of the ancient Near East. This relationship, more than any other on record, offered the prospect of true shalom, which could fulfill the longings of humankind.

The End of Deity-Nation Relations

The subjects that have been discussed in the previous four chapters have an important bearing on the interpretation of the Old Testament. As I have attempted to lay this theological groundwork, some of the most fundamental Israelite beliefs have been examined, specifically their understanding of themselves as a nation, as the people of Yahweh. By setting the biblical data alongside extrabiblical records we have observed that in many respects the Israelite approach to their own relationship to their patron deity resembled that of their neighbors. In some very significant respects, however, their perspective differed drastically from those of the peoples around. One more dimension of the deity-nation-land association requires examination, namely, the possibility and nature of the termination of such relationships. This will be pursued once more by juxtaposing information derived from the Old Testament with that which the archeologist's spade and the historian's research have revealed from the world of which Israel was a part.

The subjects that have been discussed in the foregoing chapters have required the gathering and synthesizing of information from a great variety of sources. The Old Testament texts to which I have referred have not been uniform with respect to genre and have often been separated by hundreds of years of national development. Inasmuch as my treatment of these documents seems to disregard the evolution and progression that occurred in the nature and sophistication of Israel's faith and in their national self-understanding down through the centuries, some will judge my approach naive. Surely the ideological and theological understanding of Jeremiah and Isaiah exceeded that of the patriarchs and even of Moses. From the standpoint of method, one should not skip back and forth so freely from one century to another as if there had been no growth. I recognize this weakness, but the limits of the present study have precluded a thorough diachronic investigation of each of the subjects that has been raised. I will leave that for another occasion, or for another scholar.

The same charge may be leveled at my use of the extrabiblical sources. The limits of the investigation have prevented separate analysis of the various literary genres that have been encountered. Nor have I sought to trace any historical evolution of these notions. I have been operating deductively, identifying critical problems and then searching for the answers from whatever source. Having collected the information, I have attempted to synthesize it in a coherent and understandable presentation. The nature of the discussion that follows resembles that of the first chapter in that it becomes more focused, exploring a single narrower theme and concentrating on fewer biblical texts. By ending this volume with the consideration of a theme that represents the antithesis to the first chapter, I have created a chiastic structure to the overall investigation.

The objective of the present chapter differs from the preceding four in another way. In the foregoing discussions I have sought to understand some prominent concepts in the Old Testament in the light of the ancient Near Eastern cultural and religious milieu out of which they derive. I now continue this comparative approach by examining how extrabiblical perceptions of divine abandonment compare with biblical accounts of the same notion.

Ancient Near Eastern Accounts of Divine Abandonment

Like the Israelites, ancient Near Easterners in general feared the prospect of divine abandonment, whether from the individual, the clan, or the state. My concern is with the departure of titular deities from their cities and/or states. The extrabiblical accounts available to us for an examination of this issue may be divided into three groups: Sumerian accounts, second-millennium B.C. Akkadian accounts, and first-millennium Akkadian accounts.[1] I deal with each in turn.

Sumerian Accounts

Time and space constraints preclude a detailed discussion of the Sumerian literature, but I may summarize the perspectives reflected in

---

1. To date no Northwest Semitic text describing the departure of a deity from his/her land or city with such detail has been discovered. The most promising text is the ninth-century B.C. stele inscription of Mesha, the Moabite king, commemorating his victory over the Israelites. For English translations of the text see *ANET*, 320–21; *HMI*, 71–83. Some such event may be implied in the comment, "Omri, king of Israel, had oppressed Moab many days, for Chemosh was angry with his land" (lines 4–5). The statement creates the impression that the deity had been absent during the Omride occupation, but had now returned. In any case, the text provides no hint concerning the cause of Chemosh's anger.

two types of texts represented by the "Curse of Agade" and the Sumerian lament literature.

The Curse of Agade

Classified as a "historiographic" document by Samuel Kramer,[2] the "Curse of Agade" describes Inanna abandoning her cult shrine in Agade, apparently at the command of Enlil because of the crimes of Naram-Sin (2254–2218 B.C.) in sacking Nippur, and turning on her own subjects. The first fifty lines of the document describe the prosperity of Agade during the early reign of Naram-Sin. With lines 54–65, however, a drastic change occurs:

> (But then) in the palace of Agade—what prostration!
> Holy Inanna accepted not its gifts,
> Like a princely son who . . . , she *shared* not its wealth,
> The "word of the Ekur" was upon it like a (deathly) silence,
> Agade was all atremble,
> The Ulmash was in terror,
> She who had lived there, left the city,
> Like a maiden forsaking her chamber,
> Holy Inanna forsook the shrine Agade,
> Like a warrior hastening to (his) weapon,
> She went forth against the city in battle (and) combat,
> She attacked as if it were a foe.

The reasons for Inanna's departure are only obliquely hinted at. The reference to "the word of Ekur" in line 57 suggests that Enlil had commanded this in retaliation for Naram-Sin's iniquities, particularly his sacking of Nippur and the desecration of Enlil's temple there.[3] Significant for my purposes is the description of Inanna attacking her own city after her departure from the Ulmash, her cult shrine. Joining forces with Enlil and the other gods in avenging the desecration of the shrine of the highest deity, she turned on her own subjects. In Ezekiel, Yahweh is portrayed similarly, leaving his shrine and then sending Nebuchadrezzar to attack Jerusalem as an agent of his wrath. Reflective of Akkad's total eclipse, however, not a word is said about Inanna's eventual return. The point of view of the "Curse of Agade" is attributable to the Nippurian interests of the author.

2. *ANET*, 646–51. So also J. S. Cooper (*The Curse of Agade* [Baltimore: Johns Hopkins University Press, 1983], 7), who provides the most detailed study of the text.

3. So S. N. Kramer, *ANET*, 646. According to Cooper (*Curse of Agade*, 17), as in the Cuthean legend, this attack on Ekur was precipitated by Naram-Sin's frustration at and disrespect for omens.

Lamentations over the Destruction of Sumer and Its Cities

With the passing of the Sargonid dynasty of Akkad, the political center of gravity in Mesopotamia shifted to the Sumerians in the south, centering in Ur. The period of Sumerian dominance lasted slightly less than one century, coming to an end with the fall of Ur in 2004 B.C. at the hands of invaders from the east. This event is commemorated in a series of laments bewailing the destruction of major cities in the Sumerian region of lower Mesopotamia. Two of these laments, the "Nippur Lament" (*LN*)[4] and the "Uruk Lament" (*LW*),[5] name Išme-Dagan, the fourth ruler in the Isin Dynasty (1953–1935 B.C.), who was responsible for rebuilding the cities. These texts, as well as the "Eridu Lament" (*LE*)[6] and the "Lament over the Destruction of Ur" (*LU*),[7] seem to have been inspired by an earlier piece, the "Lamentation over the Destruction of Sumer and Ur" (*LSUr*).[8] This lament appears to have been composed earlier in the Isin-Larsa period, perhaps during the reign of Išbi-Erra, the founder of the dynasty, to legitimize his rule by showing that he and his successors were the true sovereigns of Sumer and Akkad.[9]

Although these laments are not homogeneous literarily or in content, they share several motifs important to our discussion. *LSUr* portrays all of Sumer as languishing from the effects of a series of catastrophes, including political disintegration, Elamite/Gutian invasions, and famine. After cataloguing the cities whose titular gods had abandoned their respective shrines,[10] the lament focuses on the fate of Ur. Because the

4. On the "Nippur Lament" see S. N. Kramer, "Lamentations over the Destruction of Nippur: A Preliminary Report," *EI* 9 (1969): 89–93; idem, "Lamentation over the Destruction of Nippur," *Acta Sumerologica* 13 (1991): 1–26.

5. For the "Uruk Lament" see M. W. Green, "The Uruk Lament," *JAOS* 104 (1984): 253–79. Uruk is otherwise known as Warka, hence the use of *LW* as the standard abbreviation for this document. *LU* is used for "The Lament over the Destruction of Ur." See below.

6. For the "Eridu Lament" (*LE*) see M. W. Green, "The Eridu Lament," *JCS* 30 (1978): 127–67.

7. For the "Lament over the Destruction of Ur" (*LU*) see S. N. Kramer, *Lamentation over the Destruction of Ur*, AS 12 (Chicago: University of Chicago Press, 1940). For a more recent translation see J. Klein, "Lamentation over the Destruction of Sumer and Ur," in *CCBW*, 535–39.

8. So also P. Michalowski, *The Lamentation over the Destruction of Sumer and Ur*, Mesopotamian Civilizations 1 (Winona Lake, Ind.: Eisenbrauns, 1989), 4–8, who offers the most recent translation and commentary on the text. For an earlier translation see S. N. Kramer, *ANET*, 611–19.

9. Cf. Michalowski, *Lamentation*, 6; idem, "Charisma and Control: On Continuity and Change in Early Mesopotamia," in *The Organization of Power: Aspects of Bureaucracy in the Ancient Near East*, ed. M. Gibson and R. D. Biggs (Chicago: University of Chicago Press, 1987), 55–68.

10. *LN, LE*, and *LW* may represent expansions of *LSUr* lines 140–42, 149–54, and 231–50, respectively.

plight of his beloved city is more than Nanna, the divine patron, can bear, he appeals to Enlil on its behalf. But Enlil declares his own impotence in the situation. Although Ur had been granted kingship by the gods, this was not an eternal decree. The divine assembly has decided that it must now pass from Ur; its glory days are over. Accordingly Enlil advises Nanna to resign himself to reality and leave the city, which he proceeds to do with painful heart.[11] The text continues by describing the disastrous consequences for the city (lines 377–448). Finally Sin approaches Enlil again, begging for a reconsideration of the sentence of death on the city (lines 451–56). Enlil responds immediately, announcing the restoration of Ur for Nanna and authorizing the god to return, whereupon Nanna reenters his shrine, the Ekišnugal (lines 461–77). The city mourns, but it has been spared.

LSUr cites no human causation behind Nanna's departure from his shrine. Enlil's decision to destroy "the righteous houses," to decimate righteous Sumer as a whole, seems purely arbitrary. The kingship, and with it the well-being of the city, must depart. The focus is entirely on divine causation; the time for a new order has been decreed, no doubt an allusion to the ascendancy of the Isin Dynasty founded by Išbi-Erra.

LU commemorates the same events as *LSUr*, but with a slightly different focus. After placing the annihilation of Ur within the context of the broader Sumerian catastrophe, the first of ten songs lists a long series of cities that have been abandoned by their titular deities. The second song then takes up the lament over the destruction of Ur, calling attention to Nanna's weeping for his city. But the focus shifts to Ningal, Nanna's divine consort, who shares the supervision of the city. Moved by Ur's plight, she determines to give Nanna no rest until he comes to the city's aid. Her efforts at stopping the "storm" fail to save Ur. Finally, in the fourth song, she appeals to Enlil to rescind his decree determining its destruction, but to no avail. The disaster continues unabated through the next two songs. From the perspective of this chapter, the critical moment occurs after a recital of the effects of the calamity, with this brief note:

> Its lady like a flying bird departed from her city;
> Ningal like a flying bird departed from her city;
> On all its possessions that had been accumulated in the land,
> a defiling hand was placed.
> In all its *storehouses* that abounded in the land,
> fires were kindled. (lines 237–40)

11. Lines 340–76 (Michalowski, "Charisma and Control," 57–61; *ANET*, 617).

The remainder of the lament consists primarily of a description of Nin-gal's weeping for her city, concluding with the poet's own plea to Nanna not to let the city perish.

This text is of interest for several reasons. First, at the outset the tit-ular deity refuses to leave the city (lines 143–44), but he is finally forced out because Ur has been destroyed. The abandonment of the city is the consequence rather than the cause of its destruction.[12] Second, remi-niscent of *LSUr*, this lament emphasizes the powerlessness of patron gods to defend their own territories when the highest deity, Enlil, has decreed their end. In the end, he controls historical events. Third, like *LSUr*, this song says nothing about human actions provoking these de-cisions by the gods. Lamentations of this sort focus on divine causation and on the divine basis of hope for the future.

While *LSUr* and *LU* lament the fall of Ur, politically the most impor-tant Sumerian city, the extant laments commemorate the fall of outly-ing cities. *LW* laments the fall of Uruk and the departure of Inanna, the titular deity, from Eanna, her shrine. This composition is unique in that, by opening with a mythological introduction announcing the gods' decision to destroy humankind as a whole, presumably because the noise of humans had disturbed the divinities' sleep, it ascribes a cos-mic dimension to the Sumerian crisis.[13] In the context of the devasta-tion of the city, along with the flight of the rest of the gods:

> The city's patron god turned against it;
> Its shepherd [abandoned] it;
> Its guardian (spirit) though not an enemy,
> was exiled to (?) a foreign place. (2.23′–25′)

Meanwhile Enlil struck the land with relentless ferocity and ground Uruk into dust. The text breaks off with a fragment of the sixth stanza (*kirugu*), leaving the reader to speculate on how the city was rebuilt, ap-parently the subject of stanzas 7–11. When it is resumed in stanza 12, Inanna has returned to her Eanna and is receiving the worship of Išme-Dagan, who pleads with her to intercede for him and Uruk to the great gods so they will act favorably toward him.

Apart from allusions to Mesopotamian creation accounts in which human noise provokes the wrath of the gods, this document is silent on human causation behind the collapse of Sumer. As in the previous la-ments, Enlil determines the fate of the city, and Inanna appears help-less to ward off his fury. Again the departure of the titular deity occurs

---

12. Cf. lines 230–43.
13. Cf. Green, "Uruk Lament," 254.

in the context of the general devastation of the city rather than prior to it. But the lament concludes on a positive note, with the deity back in her shrine and a dutiful king on the throne. Together they are expected to restore peace and prosperity to the land.

For my purposes, *LE* is less instructive.[14] This lament opens with a storm, and the image of Enki outside, weeping for his city Eridu, and his consort Damgalnunna flying away like a bird (1.1–15).[15] Meanwhile the city and the Abzu, Enki's shrine, feel the full force of Enlil's fury. Stanzas 6–7 are taken up with Damgalnunna's impassioned plea to Enki to return to his shrine, to be joyful, followed by the poet's request that he respond favorably to this lament and prayer. The remainder of the composition is missing. It probably described the return of Enki and the restoration of Eridu.

LN may be the most significant Sumerian lament. If Ur was the most important Sumerian city politically, religiously pride of place belonged to Nippur, which was home to the Ekur, the sacred shrine of Enlil, the highest divinity in the Sumerian pantheon. *LN* is a lengthy composition (326 lines) consisting of twelve stanzas (*kirugus*).[16] It opens with a picture of once glorious Nippur now devastated and abandoned by gods and humans. In the second stanza the city herself is portrayed as wailing over her condition and that of the Ekur, which lay in ruins because the lord of the city (Enlil) had turned away from his shrine. The third stanza asks how long the enraged Enlil will remain away,[17] but in the fourth a glimmer of hope appears. In response to the persistent prayers of Nippur's poets and musicians bemoaning the fate of the city, Enlil, father of all the "blackheaded," was moved to pity and commanded her restoration. Stanza 5 is addressed to the city, joyfully announcing Enlil's change of heart and his merciful promise to restore the pride of Nippur. According to the sixth stanza, Enlil's promises to Nippur are fulfilled. There is no need to lament any more since he has brought joy to the city, appointed Ninurta as its divine guardian, and commissioned Išme-Dagan, his beloved shepherd, to reconstruct the Ekur and to reinstitute all its rituals. The restoration is completed in stanza 7, with Enlil and his consort Ninlil taking their places in their shrines, and Enlil's return of Nippur's population from all the directions in which they had been scattered. The picture of restoration is extended to all of Sumer-Akkad in stanza 8, including Isin, whose reign the gods set for

14. See Green, "Eridu Lament," 127–61.
15. Ibid., 133.
16. For text, translation, and commentary see Kramer, "Lamentation," 1–26.
17. Note esp. line 89 (ibid., 16), "He [Enlil, its lord] has abandoned it," and lines 95–97, "Lo, he has let the enemy do bitter things there,/Its lord has turned it over to the hand of the evil wind,/It destroyed that city. . . ."

a long time. Stanzas 9–11 describe in detail the utopia Enlil has ordained for his people—a day characterized by prosperity in field and
flocks, enthusiastic worship of Enlil in the Ekur, and perfect order and
harmony among the citizens. The poem concludes with praise for
Išme-Dagan's acts of piety and glorification of Enlil by all the people of
Sumer.

Opening with the picture of Nippur's desolation, *LN* is silent on the
human factors behind the tragedy. The composition is emphatic, however, in its portrayal of the well-being of the city as depending upon the
presence and favorable disposition of the patron deity. Especially in-
teresting is the order of events involved in the restoration of Nippur:
(1) The city's ruin is associated with the absence of the patron divinity.
(2) The deity takes pity on the city and orders its restoration, and appoints a divine guardian for the city. (3) He appoints a human shepherd to reconstruct the Ekur and reinstitute the rituals. (4) Enlil returns to his shrine. (5) He regathers the scattered population of
Nippur. (6) The restoration is extended to all of Sumer, including the
return of the titular deities to their respective cities. (7) With the restoration of the deity-people-land relationships, peace and prosperity return. (8) All Sumer and Akkad join in glorifying Enlil, "the great mountain, the ruler of heaven and earth."

The Sumerian laments seem to have been written as "congregational
laments" mourning the destruction of a city and its temple at the hands
of enemies and the departure of the disaffected patron deity. Apparently they served a ritual purpose, to ward off the fury of the respective
gods when the remaining ruins were leveled to make way for the new
structure on the same site. By attributing the destruction of the home
of the deity to hostile hands the ruler absolved himself of charges of sacrilege for having demolished a sacred shrine.[18]

Akkadian Accounts

In their radical theological interpretation of historical events Amorites, Babylonians, and Assyrians were all heirs of the Sumerians. Allusions and explicit references to the abandonment of their shrines by tit-

---

18. For helpful discussions of these laments see W. W. Hallo, "Lamentations and
Prayers in Sumer and Akkad," in *Civilizations of the Ancient Near East*, ed. J. M. Sasson,
4 vols. (New York: Scribners, 1995), 3:1876–81; idem, "Sumerian Literature," *ABD* 6:235–
36. Elsewhere Hallo comments that these Sumerian laments were composed "as liturgical accompaniments to the royal rebuilding of the destroyed temples, which involved the
inevitable razing of their remains—a potential sacrilege against their gods" (idem, *Origins: The Ancient Near Eastern Background of Some Modern Western Institutions*, Studies
in the History and Culture of the Ancient Near East 6 [Leiden and New York: Brill, 1996],
224–25).

ular deities are ubiquitous in the Akkadian texts of these cultures. The texts selected for the following discussion represent a variety of times, contexts, and literary genres.

A Prophetic Letter from Mari

A precursor of more complex texts to follow may be found in the Mari correspondence from the time of Zimri-Lim (eighteenth century B.C.), specifically *ARM* X No. 50. This tablet contains a letter of a prominent woman of the court in which she communicates a prophetic dream she had:

> Say to my lord: Thus Addu-dāri, your maidservant. Since the fall of your father's house I have never had such a dream. My earlier omens were like this. In my dream I entered the temple of Bēlet-ekalim. Bēlet-ekalim was not there, and the statues standing in front of her were not [there]. When I saw this I began to weep. This was the dream of the first watch of the night. [In another dream] I saw Dada, the priest of Ištar-pišrā, standing at the temple door of Bēlet-ekalim. A hostile voice kept calling out in the following manner: "Come back, Dagan! Come back, Dagan!" This is what it called.[19]

With respect to the issues that concern us in this chapter, the text is silent on the causes (divine or human) and effects of Dagan's absence, and says nothing about the prospects for his return.

The Tukulti-Ninurta Epic (Middle Assyrian)

The Tukulti-Ninurta Epic is a lengthy historiographic "victory song" composed to celebrate the victory of Tukulti-Ninurta I of Assyria (1244–1208 B.C.) over the Kassite king Kaštiliaš IV (1242–1235 B.C.).[20] After opening with a laudatory introduction of the protagonist (now largely unintelligible), the text presents the Kassite king and a theological ex-

19. This is an adaptation of the translation provided by D. Bodi, *Ezekiel and the Poem of Erra*, Orbis biblicus et orientalis (Freiburg: Universitätsverlag; Göttingen: Vandenhoeck & Ruprecht, 1991), 207. For other translations see those of W. L. Moran in *ANET*, 631, and H. Schmökel in *Near Eastern Texts Relating to the Old Testament*, ed. W. Beyerlin, trans. J. Bowden, OTL (Philadelphia: Westminster, 1978), 126–27. Schmökel compares the dream account with Ezekiel 8–11. For the transliterated full text see G. Dossin, *La divination en Mésopotamie ancienne*, RAI 14 (Paris: Presses Universitaires de France, 1966), 77–86. Cf. also F. Ellermeier, *Prophetie in Mari und Israel* (Herzberg: Jungfer, 1968), 64–66.

20. The most thorough study of the text is provided by P. B. Machinist, "The Epic of Tukulti-Ninurta I: A Study in Middle Assyrian Literature" (Ph.D. diss., Yale University, 1978). See also his "Literature as Politics: The Tukulti-Ninurta Epic and the Bible," *CBQ* 38 (1976): 455–82. For a more recent translation of the text see *BM* 1:209–29 (further bibliography is provided on pp. 228–29); idem, *From Distant Days: Myths, Tales, and Poetry of Ancient Mesopotamia* (Bethesda, Md.: CDL Press, 1995), 178–96.

planation for his defeat. The segment of text of interest to us, I:32'-46',
reads as follows:

32' [The gods were angry at] the treachery/ies of the king of the
     Kassites (committed) by the stand[ard *of Šamaš*   .]
33' ⌜Against the oath-breaker,⌝ Kaštiliaš, the gods of heave[n (and)
     earth *decided to send* punishment   .]
34' ⌜They⌝ developed wrath against the king, the land, and the pe-
     opl[e   .]
35' With the forceful/obstinate one, the shepherd over them, they
     were angry and . [   ]
36' The Enlilship of the lord of all the lands became distressed, so
     that Nippu[r he *cursed/abandoned*   ,]
37' So that the habitation of Dur-Kurigalzu he *no longer* ap-
     proaches . .[.]
38' Marduk abandoned his august sanctuary, the city .[.]
39' He cursed the city of his love, Kar- .[   ]
40' Sin left Ur, [his] cult center [.]
41' With Sippar and Larsa, Š[amaš *became wroth*   .]
42' Ea [abandoned] Eridu, the house of wisdom .[.]
43' Istaran became angry w[ith Der   .]
44' Anunitu *no longer* approaches Agade[.]
45' The mistress [of] Uruk gave up [*her city*   .]
46' The gods were extremely angry and .[.][21]

This account differs from the Sumerian laments in several important
respects. First, it attributes the departures of the deities to human
causes. The king of the Kassites is accused of treachery (*saliptu*, line 32'),
breaking his oath with the gods (*etiq mamiti*, line 33'),[22] being obstinate
(*parriku*, line 35'). Second, it highlights the gods' emotional response,
with expressions like "wrath" (*rašu*, line 34'), "anger" (*šabsu*, lines 35',
43'), "distress" (*ašašu*, line 36'), and "extreme anger" (*kamālu*, line 46').
Third, Marduk's abandonment of his sanctuary is associated with a
curse (*arāru*) that he invokes on his beloved city (lines 39'–40'). Fourth,
the role of the deities changes. According to the Sumerian laments the
collapse of the Ur III period occurred because the high god had decreed
that the kingship that had been granted to Ur be transferred to another
state, and the destruction of the rest of the cities of Sumer and Akkad
was part of this decree. The gods of the respective cities tried to intervene
on behalf of their shrines, but to no avail. Reluctantly and with great

21. Thus Machinist, "Epic," 62–65; cf. Foster, *BM* 1:212.
22. Cf. Yahweh's accusation against Zedekiah in Ezek. 17:19–20.

lamentation they abandoned their shrines. In this epic, fury over the crimes of Kaštiliaš has spread to all the gods of Sumer and Akkad. Far from defending their shrines, the gods take the side of the invader and unleash all the forces of destruction upon their respective cities.[23]

The differences in the roles of the titular deities is undoubtedly due to the changes in points of view of the authors of the respective texts.[24] The Sumerian laments were composed by victims of the disaster— poets of Ur and the other cities trying to give a theological explanation for the political and economic collapse of the Ur III civilization. Composed to laud the accomplishments and character of Tukulti-Ninurta I, the epic reflects the perspective of the conquerors. The gods have abandoned their subjects and transferred their support to the invader.

The Marduk Prophecy (Middle Babylonian)

The "Marduk Prophecy," composed with reference to the reign of Nebuchadnezzar I of Babylon (1125–1104 B.C.), represents the only extant autobiography by a deity in cuneiform sources.[25] In this purportedly divine speech Marduk reminds his hearers of the three occasions in which he had left his city, traveling successively to Hatti,[26] Assyria, and Elam. These departures appear to correspond to the conquests of Babylon by Mursilis I (1620–1590 B.C.), Tukulti-Ninurta I, and Kudur-Naḫḫunte (ca. 1160 B.C.), respectively. On the human plane, the events in question apparently involve the successive forceful entrances of these enemies into the temple of Marduk and the dragging off of his statue. The composition itself glorifies the achievements of Nebuchadnezzar in reconstructing the Ekursagila in Babylon and his restoration of Marduk's image to its proper place.

For the purposes of the present study, the significance of Marduk's prophetic speech lies in its portrayal of divine involvement in the series of catastrophes that struck Babylon. The spoliations of Marduk's image are presented as journeys undertaken by Marduk of his own volition. In each instance he continued to function as the divine patron of the Babylonians, serving as ambassador in the foreign land, promoting the in-

---

23. *Signaturen der Vorderasiatschen Abteilung der Berliner Museen* (unpublished), 31– 56. Machinist, "Epic," 118–22.

24. So also Machinist, "Epic," 153–54.

25. So also R. Borger, "Gott Marduk und Gott-König Šulgi als Propheten: Zwei prophetische Texte," *BiOr* 28 (1971): 21. Borger provides a full transcription, translation, and commentary on the text. For English translations and discussions of the text see T. Longman III, *Fictional Akkadian Autobiography: A Generic and Comparative Study* (Winona Lake, Ind.: Eisenbrauns, 1991), 132–42, 233–35; idem, *CCBW,* 480–82; Foster, *BM* 1:304–7.

26. The return of the cult statue and reconstruction of Esagila from Hatti is commemorated in an autobiographical account by the Kassite king Agum-Kakrime (mid-fifteenth century B.C.). See Foster, *BM* 1:273–77, for translation and bibliography.

terests of his city by establishing transportation connections between his place of sojourn and his home city.

The Elamite exile is described most fully. Marduk portrays himself as having ordered the termination of the temple cultus and the expulsion of the gods of the herds and grain. Like the Sumerian laments, this text offers no hints of human causation. Nevertheless, the effects of the departure of the divine patron from his city are catastrophic and graphically described (II:1–11). A change in the fortunes of the city follows, however, when the disposition of the deity changes. When Marduk had fulfilled *his* days in exile, he yearned for his city and recalled all the goddesses. The text does not speak specifically of the god's appointment of a new king (Nebuchadnezzar I), but this is implied in the "prophetic" portion (II:19–32). With the predicted arrival of the new ruler a dramatic transformation within the city will occur, and prosperity, peace, and security will return.

The Seed of Kingship (Middle Babylonian)

A fragmentary "historiographic" bilingual (Sumerian/Akkadian) text, K 4874, derives from the same general period and deals with the same spoliation of the statue of Marduk by the Elamites.[27] Unlike the "Marduk Prophecy," this text explicitly attributes the anger of the gods to human evil, as the following excerpt demonstrates:

> At that time, in the reign of a previous king,
> conditions changed.
> Good departed and evil prevailed.
> The lord became angry and got furious;
> He gave the command and the gods of the land abandoned it [. . .]
> The guardians of peace (*ra-bi-[ṣu] šul-me*) became furious,
> and went up to the dome of heaven.
> The spirit of justice stood aside,
> . . ., who guards living beings, prostrated the peoples.
> They all became like those who have no god.
> Evil demons filled the land, the namtar-demon [. . .]. . . .
> They penetrated the cult-centres,
> The land diminished, its fortunes changed.[28]

The text goes on to describe the awesome intensity of Marduk's fury. Unfortunately the end is too mutilated to determine if it originally recounted the return of the divine patron.

27. For transliteration, translation, and commentary of the text see W. G. Lambert, "Enmeduranki and Related Matters," *JCS* 21 (1967): 128–31. Compare the more recent translation by Foster in *BM* 1:290–93, and in *From Distant Days*, 197–201.
28. Lines 15–22, adapted from Lambert, "Enmeduranki," 130.

The Poem of Erra and Ishum (Neo-Babylonian)

Although the circumstances are extraordinary, the composition of "Erra and Ishum" offers one of the fullest portrayals of divine abandonment of any ancient Near Eastern document.[29] The date of this text is disputed. Since the poem reflects the historical events surrounding the decline of Babylon and refers to the Sutu on several occasions,[30] the Sutu invasion around 1050 B.C. provides a firm terminus a quo. Since the poem envisions the restoration of Babylonian power, it must have been composed prior to the Assyrians' ascent to supreme political power in Mesopotamia in the mid-eighth century B.C.[31]

In stark contrast to the independence of Marduk depicted in the "Marduk Prophecy," this composition portrays the divine patron of Babylon as an apparently weak-willed, if not senile, personality.[32] He seems unaware of the state of his domain and powerless before Erra. It is Erra who must ignite Marduk's anger over his people, cause him to abdicate his throne, and make him leave the city to Erra's destructive fury.

"The Poem of Erra and Ishum" deliberately and explicitly presents the rebellion of the inhabitants of Babylon as the catalyst for all these divine schemes. Hear Erra's provocative report in I:120–29:

> "All the (other) gods are afraid of battle,
> So that the black-headed people despise (them).
> But I, because they no longer fear my name,
> And since prince Marduk has neglected his word and does as he
>   pleases,
> I shall make prince Marduk angry, and I shall summon him from
>   his dwelling, and I shall overwhelm (his) people."
> Warrior Erra set his face towards Shuanna, city of the king of the
>   gods.

---

29. For the transliterated text see L. Cagni, *Das Erra-Epos, Keilschrifttext*, Studia Pohl 5 (Rome: Pontifical Biblical Institute, 1970); for English translation and commentary see idem, *The Poem of Erra*, SANE 1/3 (Malibu: Undena, 1973). See also Foster, *BM* 2:771–805; idem, *From Distant Days*, 132–63; S. Dalley, *Myths from Mesopotamia: Creation, the Flood, Gilgamesh, and Others* (Oxford: Oxford University Press, 1989), 282–315; idem, *CCBW*, 404–16. For a discussion of the portrayal of divine abandonment in this text and its relation to Ezekiel see Bodi, *Ezekiel and the Poem of Erra*, 191–97.

30. See IV:54,69,133; V:27.

31. W. von Soden ("Entemenanki vor Asarhaddon nach der Erzählung vom Turmbau zu Babel und dem Erra-Mythos," *UF* 3 [1971]: 255–56) proposes a precise date of composition between the end of 765 B.C. and the beginning of 763 B.C. For further discussion and bibliography on the date, see Bodi, *Ezekiel and the Poem of Erra*, 54–56.

32. Cf. the discussion by Cagni, *Poem of Erra*, 19, following B. Landsberger, "Akkadische-hebräische Wortgleichungen," in *Hebräische Wortforschung*, Walter Baumgartner Festschrift, VTSup 16 (Leiden: Brill, 1967), 198. For a contrary opinion, see Bodi, *Ezekiel and the Poem of Erra*, 193–94.

> He entered Esagila, palace of heaven and earth,
>   and stood in front of him (Marduk),
> He made his voice heard and spoke (to) the king of gods,
>   "Why does the finery, your lordship's adornment which is full of
>   splendor like the stars of heaven, grow dirty?
> The crown of your lordship which made E-halanki shine like
>   E-temen-anki—its surface is tarnished."[33]

Marduk's initial response is to recall how, many years ago, he had become angry (the cause is not indicated), risen from his seat, and contrived the deluge. His suspension of rule had precipitated the upsetting of the entire natural order and produced total chaos on earth. Even the statue of Marduk was damaged. But Marduk had had it repaired in a way that could never be duplicated. In fact, the human and material resources employed in the previous refurbishing have all been sent down to the Apsû. But now the image had been sullied once again. However, the only way to retrieve the needed resources from the Apsû is for Marduk to get them himself. Erra promises to watch over the world order while he is away (I:190–93).

Marduk concedes to Erra's plan. Unfortunately, the description of his departure is poorly preserved. But sufficient text remains to link the ensuing cosmic disturbance predicted by the king of the gods and his abandonment of his throne:

> He rose up from his inaccessible dwelling
> and set his face towards the dwelling of the Anunnaki.
> He entered his . . . and st[ood before them,]
> [Discarded] his radi[ance] and let his rays fall [. . .]
> [Because(?)] he had set his face towards another place
> and no longer [. . .] the earth,
> [The winds(?)] rose up,
> and bright day was turned into darkness.[34]

Tablets II–IV go on to expound in great detail the havoc that Erra and his evil forces wreak on Babylon in Marduk's absence. In Tablet V Erra's fury is finally placated through the mediation of his herald Ishum. He resolves to bring back the prosperity of Akkad and to reprovision Babylon and Esagila. Although Erra orders Ishum to restore to their temples all the gods who had fled their shrines (V:31), the absence of any reference to the return of Marduk, and of the restoration of the city without him, are striking.

33. As translated by Dalley, *CCBW*, 407.
34. II A:1–10, as translated by Dalley, *CCBW*, 408.

Esarhaddon's Rebuilding of Babylon (Neo-Assyrian)

The description of the reconstruction of Babylon by Esarhaddon (680–669 B.C.) provides the most helpful account for our discussion, not only because it was composed within one century of Ezekiel's ministry, but also because it offers the most complete extrabiblical account of the cycle of divine abandonment and return. The story, preserved in several different versions,[35] must be interpreted against the background of the fall of the city and the demolition of Esagila in 689 B.C. by Esarhaddon's predecessor, Sennacherib. Like the "Marduk Prophecy" and the "Poem of Erra and Ishum," Esarhaddon's account is generally interpreted as an apologia, intended to gain the favor of the Babylonians[36] by emphasizing that this Assyrian ruler had been specially chosen by Marduk, the patron deity of Babylon, to govern his city and to restore its prosperity.

1. The reasons for Marduk's departure from Babylon. Esarhaddon's account attributes Marduk's abandonment of Babylon to several factors. At the cosmic level, during the reign of the previous king "evil forces" (*idâti lemnêti*[meš]) appeared in Sumer and Akkad (2 A:18–21). This malaise was reflected at the human level by a series of offenses. Text A speaks of moral crimes like deceit and falsehood; texts B and G of a "murderous trap" (*naḫ-ba-lu šag-ga-šu*) expressed by the exploitation of the weak and their deliverance into the hands of the mighty, oppression and bribery, thievery, sons publicly cursing their fathers, and insubordination on the part of male and female servants (3 G:4–16; B:2). Equally reprehensible were the cultic misdemeanors. Not only were taboo foods introduced, the regular offerings were suspended, and conspiracies plotted (against the cult?). Texts A and D speak of sacrilegious treatment of Esagila, Marduk's shrine. Out of bounds for laypersons, the palace of the god was invaded and its treasures stolen and squandered off to Elam as the price for assistance against Assyria (4

---

35. These have been edited, transliterated, and translated by R. Borger, *Die Inschriften Asarhaddons Königs von Assyrien*, Archiv für Orientforschung Beiheft 9 (Graz: Weidner, 1956), 10–29, episodes 1–41. For a valuable, though older, English translation see *ARAB* 2:242–47, §§640–51. For a helpful discussion of segments of the text, see M. Cogan, *Imperialism and Religion: Assyria, Judah, and Israel in the Eighth and Seventh Centuries B.C.E.*, SBLMS 19 (Missoula, Mont.: Scholars Press, 1974), 12–13. See also J. Brinkman, "Through a Glass Darkly: Esarhaddon's Retrospects on the Downfall of Babylon," *JAOS* 103 (1983): 35–42. A. R. Millard kindly reminds me that several additional texts dealing with Esarhaddon and Babylon are provided in translation and discussed by B. N. Porter, *Images, Power, Politics: Figurative Aspects of Esarhaddon's Babylonian Policy* (Philadelphia: American Philosophical Society, 1993).

36. Cf. Cogan, *Imperialism and Religion*, 12; also H. Tadmor, "Autobiographical Apology in the Royal Assyrian Literature," in *History, Historiography, and Interpretation*, ed. H. Tadmor and M. Weinfeld (Jerusalem: Magnes, 1984), 36–57.

A:28–33). The local divinities also seemed to be involved in the general disintegration as gods and goddesses abandoned their normal functions (3 B:25–27). This degenerate state of affairs in Babylon infuriated Marduk.[37]

In response "he plotted evil (*ik-ta-pu-ud lemuttim*), determining to level the land and to bring its population to ruin" (5 A:34–37). An "evil curse" (*ar-rat ma-ru-uš-ti*) was found in his mouth (5 B:10).

2. *The effects of Marduk's anger toward Babylon.* Marduk's fury had disastrous consequences for Babylon. The evil forces in heaven and earth persisted, the symmetry (*mit-ḫur-tim*) of the cosmos disappeared, the orbits of the stars were altered, all of which signified impending doom for Babylon (6 B:11). On earth the mighty and reliable Arahtu canal overflowed its banks in a flood reminiscent of the great deluge, leveling the city with a mighty torrent. The residences and temples of Babylon, including Esagila, were turned into a wasteland, the resulting swamp providing refuge for innumerable fish and fowl. Simultaneously, all the deities in the city flew to heaven like birds (7 A:38–8 A:47; 7 E:9–8 E:14). As for the people, they were scattered in foreign lands, fleeing either as exiles seeking a place to hide (9 A:46–48; B:18), or as captives destined to a life of slavery (9 D:8–11).

3. *Marduk's change of heart toward Babylon.* The turning point in the story occurs in episode 10:

> Although he had written down (on the tablets of destiny) 70 years as the duration of its desolation, after his heart had been calmed (*lib-ba-šu i-nu-uḫ-ma*) he forthwith inverted the digits and commanded its (Babylon's) rebuilding in the eleventh year.[38]

37. The texts describe his anger in several ways:
    5 A:34–35 *i-gu-ug-ma* [d]*en-líl(-la₅) ilâni*[meš] [d]*Marduk*
           "Marduk, the lord of the gods, grew furious."
    5 B:8 *e-zi-iz lib-ba-šú ka-bat-tuš iṣ-ṣa-ri-iḫ*
           "His heart fumed; his liver raged."
    5 E[1]:11–14 *bêlu rabû* [d]*Marduk i-gu-ug i-ru-um-ma* [*it*]-*ti E-sag-gil*
           "The great lord Marduk shook with rage against Esagila."
    5 E[2]:4–6 *ù Bâbili*[ki] *e-zi-iz libba-šú zi-nu-tu ir-ši*
           "and (against) Babylon his heart raged."

38. 10 A:2–9; B:19–20. This remarkable numerical effect may be achieved by transposing the cuneiform symbols for 70 (𒐋), which yields 11 (𒐋). See the discussion by J. Nougayrol, "Textes hépatoscopiques d'époque ancienne conservée au Musée du Louvre II," *RA* 40 (1946): 65. Cf. Borger, *Die Inschriften Asarhaddons*, 65. Jeremiah's prophecy in 29:10 suggests that a seventy-year period of exile as a result of an angered divinity was a well-known motif in the ancient Near East. Cf. C. F. Whitley, "The Term Seventy Years Captivity," *VT* 4 (1954): 60–72; A. Orr, "The Seventy Years of Babylon," *VT* 6 (1956): 304–6; P. R. Ackroyd, "The 'Seventy Year' Period," *JNES* 17 (1958): 23–27; R. Borger, "An Additional Remark on P. R. Ackroyd, *JNES* XVII, 23–27," *JNES* 18 (1959): 74.

Esarhaddon's rebuilding of Babylon represents the effect of Marduk's change of disposition toward his own city. The reconstruction transpired in a series of discreet stages. (a) Esarhaddon is appointed "shepherd" of the Assyrians for Marduk's sake and commissioned to rebuild the city (11 A:9–23; cf. 12 B:21–22a). (b) The astrological signs indicate an alteration in the disposition of the forces (*idât*^meš), as a result of which the angered gods are reconciled to Akkad (12 A:29–40; D:9–14). (c) An omen is given, indicating the imminent return of Marduk to Esagila (14 B:5–8), and Esarhaddon is commissioned to prepare the way by rebuilding his temple (14 A:41–15 A:49). (d) Fearing to begin the reconstruction of Marduk's temple, Esarhaddon pays homage to the god and receives confirmation of his commission (16 A:7–17 A:17). (e) The project is completed with the help of the citizens of the land who had previously been taken captive, but whom Esarhaddon had regathered (episodes 19–31). (f) The cult statues are duly redecorated and the rituals reinstituted (episodes 32–35). (g) The state images that had been removed to other lands are returned (episode 36). (h) The king restores the oppressed citizenry of Babylon to free and secure status, and the transportation routes to other lands are reopened (37 A:16–40).

4. Interpretation. The departure of Marduk from Babylon is not explicitly mentioned but it is implied in episode 8, which describes the flight of the gods to heaven, and is required by the reference to the reentry of Marduk into Esagila in episode 14. Of special interest to us is this account's depiction of the correlation between human and divine causation in the city's calamity, the effects of divine abandonment on the city, and Marduk's later return to Babylon. Consistent with the extrabiblical witness elsewhere, Marduk's change of heart is motivated primarily by his concern for a geographic site and apparently occurs independently of any alteration in the citizens' behavior. The text suggests that Marduk was simply homesick for his city.

The Autobiography of Adad-Guppiʾ

Chronologically even nearer Ezekiel's lifetime than the Esarhaddon inscription is the autobiography of Adad-guppiʾ, the one-hundred-and-four-year-old mother of Nabonidus, king of Babylon (555–539 B.C.).[39] Classified by Longman as fictional royal autobiography,[40] the prayer recalls the destruction of Harran by the Babylonians in 609 B.C., to

---

39. For the primary edition, with Akkadian text, translation, and commentary, see C. J. Gadd, "The Harran Inscriptions of Nabonidus," *AnSt* 8 (1958): 35–92. For more recent translation and discussion, see Longman, *Fictional Akkadian Autobiography*, 97–101, 225–28; idem, *CCBW*, 477–78. Cf. also *ANET*, 560–62.

40. *Fictional Akkadian Autobiography*, 97–101; idem, *CCBW*, 477–78.

which the departure of Sin, the city's patron deity, correlates. Sin's abandonment of his residence is described in one short statement:

> Whereas in the sixteenth year of Nabopolassar, king of Babylon, Sin, the king of the gods, became angry (*iz-nu-ú*) with his city and his house, and went up to heaven (with the result that) the city and its people were transformed into a ruin.[41]

Again of special interest for us is the motive for Sin's departure: the anger of the deity toward his people. No human offenses are cited as reason for the departure, though the reference to the temple might suggest some cultic misdemeanor. As expected, the divine abandonment resulted in the destruction of the city. The text goes on to describe the penitential intercession of Adad-guppiᵓ, as the result of which Sin's "wrathful heart quieted down" (*ug-ga-ti lib-bi-šú i-nu-uḫ-ma*, I:36–37), and he became reconciled with Ehulhul, his divine residence (I:29–39). Expressive of his change of heart, Sin appointed Nabonidus, Adad-guppiᵓ's son, to the kingship of Sumer and Akkad. This king's primary task would be to reconstruct the temple of Sin in Harran and then to reinstitute his worship in the city (II:1–11).

The Cyrus Cylinder

The final text to be considered here is the well-known inscribed clay cylinder in which Cyrus, the Persian king (557–529 B.C.), gloats over his conquest of Babylon without a fight.[42] Although the first part of the text is incompletely preserved, A. L. Oppenheim's translation makes the general sense sufficiently clear:

> . . . a weakling has been installed as the *enû* of his country; [the correct images of the gods he removed from their thrones, imi]tations he ordered to be placed upon them. A replica of the temple Esagila he has . . . for Ur and the other sacred cities appropriate rituals . . . daily he did blabber [incorrect prayers]. He (furthermore) interrupted in a fiendish way the regular offerings, he did . . . he established within the sacred cities. The worship of Marduk, the king of the gods, he [chang]ed into an abomination, daily he used to do evil against his (i.e. Marduk's) city. . . . He [tormented] its [inhabitants] with corvée-work (lit.: a yoke) without relief he ruined them all.

---

41. I:6–9, as translated by Longman, *CCBW*, 478.

42. For the text in transliteration, German translation, and commentary see P.-R. Berger, "Der Kyrus-Zylinder mit dem Zusatzfragment BIN II Nr. 32 und die akkadischen Personnenanmen im Danielbuch," *ZA* 64 (1975): 192–234. Cf. the earlier edition by F. Weissbach, *Die Keilinschriften der Achämeniden*, VAB 3 (Leipzig: Hinrichs, 1911), 2–3. For the text in English, see *ANET*, 315–16.

> Upon their complaints the lord of the gods became terribly angry (*ez-zi-iš i-gu-ug-ma*) and [he departed from] their region, (also) the other gods living among them left their mansions, wroth that he had brought (them) into Babylon.

The sins committed by the king, which precipitated Marduk's departure, included both cultic (inappropriate rituals, incorrect prayers, dispensing with the regular sacrifices, general sacrilege against Marduk) and moral crimes (oppression of the citizens). Again the divinity's departure resulted in the ruination of the temples and the city, along with the annihilation of the population, as the following lines indicate. A return to good fortune in Babylon occurred only after Marduk's anger had subsided and he had displayed mercy toward the city. This was expressed concretely by calling out Cyrus as the righteous king who should lead Marduk once more in the annual procession.

Summary Observations

To synthesize the findings on the Mesopotamian descriptions of divine abandonment I may tabulate the elements in the accounts that have been relevant to the discussion as in table 1.

While the wrath of Enlil is expressed in the Sumerian laments, the emotions of the titular deities of the cities of Sumer is the opposite of fury. Reflecting the perspective of the victims of conquest, the gods of the respective cities defend and intercede on behalf of their subjects and their shrines. Intent on glorifying Tukulti-Ninurta, the "Epic" highlights him as an agent of divine fury against the Kassites. The positive tone of the "Marduk Prophecy" is striking, lacking any hint of human causation behind the abandonment, or of divine anger. Marduk departs of his own will, but even in his absence from Babylon he serves the city's interests. The "Seed of Kingship" seems to promise the entire sequence of events involved in accounts of divine abandonments. Unfortunately it breaks off at a critical point, leaving us to speculate whether Marduk had a change of heart and the city was restored. The "Erra Epic" goes its own way in presenting Marduk, the divine patron, as a passive figure, leaving the fate of the city in the hands of Erra, the divine agent of disaster. The failure of the text to mention the appointment of a new ruler over Babylon who will institute a new era of peace may be attributed to the fact that the poem focuses on Erra, not on the divine patron of Babylon.

In terms of the motifs that concern us, the last three texts are the most complete. Like the "Tukulti-Ninurta Epic," each one functions as an apologia for the current ruler. All three contain mythological fea-

Table 1. A Comparison of Ancient Near Eastern Accounts of Divine Abandonment

Text	Date (B.C.)	Genre	Cause: Human Provocation	Motive: Divine Anger	Effect: Disaster	Deity's Altered Disposition	Deity's Return to City	Divine Selection of a Ruler	Final Peace and Prosperity
Curse of Agade	2100	Historiographic Poem	X(?)		X				
Sumer and Ur Lament	1940(?)	Poetic Lament			X^a		X^b		X
Ur Lament	1940(?)	Poetic Lament			X^a				
Uruk Lament	1940(?)	Poetic Lament	X^c		X^a		X	X^d	
Eridu Lament	1940(?)	Poetic Lament			X^a				
Nippur Lament	1940(?)	Poetic Lament		X	X	X	X	X	X
Prophetic Letter from Mari	1700	Dream Report							
Tukulti-Ninurta Epic	1230	Victory Song	X	X	X				
Marduk Prophecy	1110	Divine Autobiography				X	X	X	X
Seed of Kingship	1110	Historiographic Poem	X	X	X				
Erra and Ishum	800	Mythic Poetry	X	X	X	X^e			X^f
Esarhaddon Account	670	Annalistic Apologia	X	X	X	X	X	X	X
Adad-guppi?	540	Royal Autobiography		X	X	X	X	X	X
Cyrus Cylinder	530	Autobiographical Annal	X	X	X	X	X	X	X
Ezekiel	593–570	Prophetic Vision	X^g	X^h	X^i	X^j	X^k	X^l	X^m

Notes to Table 1

a. To be precise, in the Sumerian laments the disaster struck prior to the departure of the gods. Their leaving was the result of, rather than the cause of, the catastrophe. The latter had been decreed by the supreme deity, Enlil, against whose will the titular gods of the respective cities were powerless to act.

b. Nanna does indeed return to the city with Enlil's permission, meaning the city will be spared, but the residents mourn.

c. The noise of humans.

d. The election of the ruler is not described, but the naming of Išme-Dagan assumes it.

e. The change of heart is experienced by Erra, the god of such calamities, rather than the patron of the city who has departed.

f. Expressed as a hope by Erra, rather than an accomplished fact.

g. 8:5–18.

h. 8:17–9:10.

i. Predicted in 9:5–8 and 10:6, but fully developed in Ezekiel's judgment oracles in chaps. 4–24.

j. Never formally mentioned in the visions, but see 11:16–21, a disputation speech inserted in the vision narrative. This prophecy promises the divine presence, in limited measure, to the exiles and their eventual restoration to the homeland. See also 39:25–29, placed immediately prior to the concluding vision.

k. 43:1–5.

l. Not within the vision accounts, but see 34:23–24 and 37:21–25.

m. 47:1–48:35; cf. also 34:25–32; etc.

tures and reflect fully the theological perspective on history common throughout the ancient world. Being more closely tied to history than most of the earlier texts, however, they also deal more fully with the earthly implications of divine abandonment.

M. Cogan has established that underlying the notion of divine abandonment was the ancient Near Eastern political-military policy of the spoliation of divine images. By examining the inscriptions of a series of new-Assyrian emperors, he established that:

> [Neo-Assyrian] spoliation of divine images was meant to portray the abandonment of the enemy by his own gods in submission to the superior might of Assyria's god, Ashur. Accordingly, foreign gods were not treated as captives nor displayed in Assyrian temples as trophies, but were held, at times not far from their homes, for as long as it took Assyria to secure guarantees of loyalty from the defeated.[43]

Since the statue of a god was perceived to be indwelt by the spirit of the divinity,[44] no experience could be more devastating psychologically than to lose the image. Without the god the people were doomed. It is in the light of such notions that Ezekiel's visions of the departure of Yahweh from (chaps. 8–11) and his eventual return to (43:1–5) the temple must be interpreted, a subject to which we now turn.

The Motif of Divine Abandonment in the Old Testament

References to deities abandoning their lands are relatively rare in the Old Testament. However, the few that may be cited indicate that the Hebrews were generally familiar with the concept. The most explicit statement is provided in Isa. 46:1–2, in the context of a satirical attack on the impotence of Babylon's gods:

> Bel bows down, Nebo stoops,
> their idols are on beasts and cattle;
> these things you carry are loaded
> as burdens on weary animals.
> They stoop, they bow down together;
> they cannot save the burden,
> but themselves go into captivity. (NRSV)

---

43. *Imperialism and Religion*, 40. See also J. F. Kutsko, "Turning Swords into Plowshares: Ezekiel's Response to Imperial Rhetoric" (paper presented at the annual meeting of the Society of Biblical Literature, Theological Perspectives on the Book of Ezekiel Seminar, San Francisco, November 1997), 2–3 (in response to my essay).

44. See T. Jacobsen, "The Graven Image," in *Ancient Israelite Religion: Essays in Honor of Frank Moore Cross*, ed. P. D. Miller Jr. et al. (Philadelphia: Fortress, 1987), 15–32.

Jeremiah expressed similar notions in Jer. 48:7:

> And Chemosh will go into exile,
> Together with his priests and his princes.

The same action is attributed to Milcom, the god of the Ammonites, in Jer. 49:3:

> For Milcom will go into exile,
> Together with his priests and his princes.[45]

Given the polemical nature of these prophetic utterances, the absence of any reference to infidelity on the parts of the deities' subjects as a precipitating factor in the gods' departure is not surprising. Nor is any offer of hope for the eventual return of the deity and the consequent restoration of the respective nations to be expected.

But Israelite reflection on divine abandonment did not limit this notion to the nation's enemies. On the contrary, the Israelites also feared the consequences of their own God, Yahweh, leaving them. The possibility of such an event is assumed in the oft-repeated question, "Where is your/their God?"[46] But in tracing the history of this motif more specifically we may recognize five dimensions of Yahweh's abandonment contemplated in the Old Testament: (1) Yahweh's absence from an individual, devotee or otherwise;[47] (2) Yahweh's absence from his people, the nation of Israel;[48] (3) Yahweh's absence from the land of Is-

45. Cf. also Amos 1:15, which Emile Puech argues should be read *milkōm*, not *malkām*, "their king" ("Milcom, le dieu Ammonite, en Amos I 15," *VT* 27 [1977]: 117–25).

46. Mic. 7:10; Joel 2:17; Ps. 42:4, 11 (42:3, 10 Eng.); 79:10; 115:2.

47. This notion is expressed directly with the verbs *ʿāzab*, "to leave, abandon" (2 Chron. 12:5; 15:2; Ps. 9:11 [9:10 Eng.]; 22:2 [22:1 Eng.]; 27:9, //*nāṭaš* //*histîr pānāw;* 37:25, 28; 119:8; cf. Gen. 28:15, where Yahweh promises Jacob not to abandon him until he returns to the land of Canaan; in Isa. 41:17 Yahweh promises not to forsake the afflicted and needy), and *nāṭaš*, "to give one up" (Ps. 27:9, //*ʿāzab* //*histîr pānāw;* the sense is different in Ezek. 29:5 and 32:4, where Yahweh threatens to abandon an adversary [Pharaoh] in the desert), and paraphrastic expressions like *histîr pānāw*, "to hide his face" (Ps. 13:2 [13:1 Eng., //*šākaḥ*, "to forget"]; 22:25 [22:24 Eng.]; 27:9; 30:8 [30:7 Eng.]; 69:18 [69:17 Eng.]; 88:15 [88:14 Eng., //*zānâ*, "to reject"]; 102:3 [102:2 Eng.]; 143:7; Job 13:24; 34:29; Ps. 10:11 contemplates God hiding his face [//*šākaḥ*] from the wicked, and in 51:11 [51:9 Eng.] from one's sin; for a full study of the motif in the Old Testament see S. E. Balentine, *The Hidden God: The Hiding of the Face of God in the Old Testament* [Oxford: Oxford University Press, 1983]), or *ʿāmad bĕrāḥôq*, "to stand far away" (Ps. 10:1, //*ʿlm*, Hiphil, "to close [one's eyes] to"; cf. Lam. 3:56, "to close one's ears to"). Cf. Jer. 23:23, which contemplates Yahweh being distant (*mērāḥôq*) from a person.

48. This notion is expressed similarly with the verbs *ʿāzab*, "to leave, abandon" (Deut. 31:6, 17, //*nāṭaš;* Josh. 1:5; 1 Kings 6:13; 8:57, //*nāṭaš;* Lam. 5:20; Ezra 9:9; Neh. 9:28; 2 Chron. 24:20; Ps. 94:14, //*nāṭaš*), *nāṭaš*, "to give up" (Judg. 6:15; 1 Sam. 12:22; 1 Kings 8:57, //*ʿāzab;* 2 Kings 21:14; Isa. 2:6; Jer. 7:29, //*māʾas;* 23:33, 39; Ps. 94:14, //*ʿāzab*), *nûaḥ,*

rael;[49] (4) Yahweh's absence from Jerusalem/Zion;[50] (5) Yahweh's absence from his sanctuary.[51] The present study is not concerned with the first.

The references cited in the preceding notes demonstrate that the possibility of Yahweh's absence from his people/land/sanctuary was widely recognized in the Old Testament. Even so it is remarkable that, although the covenant curses list a host of disastrous consequences for persistent rebellion against Yahweh, neither version hints at this eventuality. Leviticus 26 warns that Yahweh will set his face against,[52] he will act with hostility toward,[53] he will send a host of agents of destruction against, and his soul will loathe Israel,[54] and he will expel them from the land, but there is no mention of abandoning them.[55] On the contrary, Yahweh affirms that he will not reject (*mā'as*) or loathe (*gā'al*) them to destroy them. Deuteronomy 28 is similar, emphasizing even more strongly Yahweh's direct (even if destructive) involvement in the nation's fate from the onset of the curses to the people's expulsion to foreign lands to their return from exile.

It has long been recognized that in the main Ezekiel's pronouncements of judgment upon his own people were based upon the covenant curses in Leviticus 26 and Deuteronomy 28. This being the case, it is remarkable that in Ezekiel 8–11 the prophet offers the fullest development of the motif of Yahweh's abandonment of land and people, a notion that is absent from those curses. One may speculate that the motif was more important to him than to other Israelite prophets because he lived in Mesopotamia, where he was surrounded by images of deities

---

Hiphil, "to leave someone somewhere" (Jer. 14:9), and *histîr pānāw*, "to hide his face" (Deut. 31:17–18, //'āzab; 32:20; 44:25 [44:24 Eng., //šākaḥ]; Isa. 8:17; 54:8; 59:2, //hibdîl, "to divide, separate"; 64:6 [64:7 Eng.]; Ezek. 39:23, 24, 29; Mic. 3:4; Ps. 104:29 contemplates Yahweh hiding his face from animals, removing their breath [*rûaḥ*] so that they die).

49. Expressed directly with the verb *'āzab*, "to leave, abandon." This notion is extremely rare, being explicitly declared only in Ezek. 8:12 and 9:9. However, the geographic sense is not far from Jeremiah's mind when he asks in 14:8, "Why are you like a stranger (*gēr*) in the land, or like a traveler (*'ôrēaḥ*) who has pitched his tent for the night?" Nevertheless, v. 9 reflects the more common emphasis: "Yet you, O Yahweh, are in the midst of us, and we are called by your name; do not abandon us!"

50. This notion is also expressed directly with the verbs *'āzab*, "to leave, abandon" (Isa. 49:14, //šākaḥ; 54:7), and paraphrastically with *histîr pānāw*, "to hide his face" (Jer. 33:5).

51. This notion is expressed directly with the verbs *'āzab*, "to leave, abandon" (Jer. 12:7, //nāṭaš), and *nāṭaš*, "to give up" (Jer. 12:7, //'āzab; Ps. 78:60, his *miškān* at Shiloh).

52. Lev. 26:17, *wĕnātattî pānāw bākem*.

53. Lev. 26:24, *wĕhālaktî 'ap-'ănî 'immākem*. Cf. vv. 28, 41.

54. Lev. 26:30, *wĕgā'ălâ napšî 'etkem*.

55. The verb *'āzab* does indeed occur, but only of Israel leaving the land. Cf. Lev. 26:43.

and where stories of divine abandonment had flourished for two mil-
lennia. Ezekiel was undoubtedly familiar with Babylonian interpreta-
tions of catastrophes such as Jerusalem experienced. Nevertheless, although the accounts discussed above follow a certain pattern,
especially the later texts, the Israelite prophet could not adopt the Mesopotamian model wholesale. In contrast to the idolatrous cults, in
which the deity was thought to indwell the image of him-/herself, Yahwism was a spiritual religion.[56] The temple in Jerusalem housed no
image of Yahweh; his presence was represented by his glory, the *kābôd*, which under normal circumstances rested above the sacred ark of
the covenant inside the most holy place.[57] Furthermore, in the mind of
orthodox Yahwists of Ezekiel's day, Yahwism was also an exclusive religion. The "Yahweh-alone" party,[58] to which he belonged, could not
accept that historical events were merely reflections and/or the consequences of capricious and arbitrary decisions by the gods, nor of feuds
between members of the heavenly realm. Accordingly, one expects
Ezekiel's presentation of the motif to go its own way. At the same time,
one must remember that he was dealing with an Israelite audience that
had to a large extent bought into the pagan perspectives on historical
and spiritual reality. He knew his audience well, and his rhetorical
strategy was carefully designed to expose both the heresy and the futility of their beliefs. For this reason, in Ezekiel's representation of
Yahweh's departure from his temple in Jerusalem one may expect to
find features that were common to other ancient Near Eastern accounts. But he exploits these elements polemically, to expose the bank-
ruptcy of pagan religious notions: Yahweh will defeat the gods at their
own game.[59]

The notion that Ezekiel's portrayal of the departure of the glory of
Yahweh should be interpreted in the light of the ancient Near Eastern
environment in which the prophet ministered is not new. Sixty years ago

---

56. Cf. Helmer Ringgren, *Israelite Religion*, trans. D. E. Green (Philadelphia: Fortress,
1966), 66–71.

57. Cf. R. de Vaux, *Ancient Israel* (New York: McGraw-Hill, 1961), 297–302.

58. On which see B. Lang, *Monotheism and the Prophetic Minority: An Essay in Biblical History and Sociology*, SWBA 1 (Sheffield: Almond, 1983); idem, "No God but Yahweh!
The Origin and Character of Biblical Monotheism," *Concilium* 177 (1985): 41–49; idem,
"Zur Entstehung des biblischen Monotheismus," *Theologische Quartalschrift* 166 (1986):
135–42.

59. Kutsko has recently argued that Yahweh's restoration of his people, who are his
image, represents another way in which the Mesopotamian ideology is turned on its
head. See his brief treatment in "Turning Swords into Plowshares," 3–7, but especially his
detailed study, *Between Heaven and Earth: Divine Presence and Absence in Ezekiel*, Biblical
and Judaic Studies from the University of California, San Diego (Winona Lake, Ind.:
Eisenbrauns, 2000).

Herbert G. May linked this vision with the Babylonian Tammuz (= Marduk) myth, comparing the departure of Yahweh to Erra's (= Nergal's) dethronement of Marduk and the latter's departure to heaven.[60] However, May erred in his interpretation on two counts; first, in identifying Yahweh with Marduk (= Tammuz), and second, in finding the *Sitz im Leben* of the vision in a ritual involving the procession of the ark from the temple at the time of the summer solstice.[61] Rather than reflecting an *identification* of Yahweh *with* Marduk in the ritual, the vision functions as a deliberate *polemic against* the typical Mesopotamian understanding of divine abandonments. William Brownlee recognized the polemical significance of the vision. Following Theodor Gaster, however, he misinterpreted the portrayal of the departure of Yahweh (8:12; 9:9) cosmically, seeing in the vision the proclamation of Yahweh's enthronement over all the forces of nature at the time of the autumnal equinox.[62] Moshe Greenberg's recent attempts at interpreting the movement of the divine *kābôd* against the backdrop of Mesopotamian culture and iconography are much more satisfactory, and his appeal to extrabiblical parallels to the departure of Yahweh from Jerusalem is on the right track.[63] However, I have taken the brevity of his discussion as an invitation to investigate the notion further.

Scholars have long recognized the centrality of the "travels" of the glory of Yahweh in the prophecy of Ezekiel. The prophet himself receives a harbinger of things to come in the opening vision, when the heavenly chariot bearing the divine glory suddenly appears to him by the Kebar canal in Babylon (1:1–28). As the initial element in a lengthy and complex call narrative, the overwhelming magnificence of the glory of Yahweh represents the first in a series of volleys by which Yahweh seeks to break down Ezekiel's resistance to the call to prophetic ministry.[64] As Ezekiel will discover, however, the vision also introduces him to one of the fundamental motifs in his prophetic proclamation: the movements of the glory of Yahweh. In fact, visions of the divine *kābôd* will appear twice more in the prophet's ministry. Fourteen months after the inaugural vision Ezekiel observed in visionary form the glory of Yahweh move by stages out of the temple and then disappear over the

60. "The Departure of the Glory of Yahweh," *JBL* 56 (1937): 309–21, esp. 312.
61. Ibid., 317–21.
62. William H. Brownlee, *Ezekiel 1–19*, WBC 28 (Waco: Word, 1986), 125–68.
63. *Ezekiel 1–20*, AB 22 (Garden City, N.Y.: Doubleday, 1983), 164–206; idem, "The Vision of Jerusalem in Ezekiel 8–11: A Holistic Interpretation," in *The Divine Helmsman: Studies on God's Control of Human Events, Presented to Lou H. Silberman*, ed. J. L. Crenshaw and S. Sandmel (New York: Ktav, 1980), 146–64.
64. See my comments in D. I. Block, *Ezekiel 1–24*, NICOT (Grand Rapids: Eerdmans, 1997), esp. 11–12.

horizon east of Jerusalem (8:1–11:25).[65] Almost two decades later the vision returned.[66] During a visionary tour of the temple he saw the *kābôd* of Yahweh return from the east, pass through the east gate, and enter the temple, apparently never to leave again (43:1–9).

But our primary concern is the vision of the departure of the *kābôd* in chapters 8–11.[67] That Yahweh's abandonment of his temple is the central idea in these chapters is clear not only from the general drift of the narrative but also from several explicit statements. The literary complexity of this text is apparent even to a casual reader, but from beginning to end the motif of divine abandonment provides a unifying thread.[68] With glorious irony, explicit declarations of Yahweh's departure from Jerusalem come only from the lips of those whose religious ideas have been contaminated by notions borrowed from neighboring peoples, and whose actions are characterized as abominable (*tôʿēbôt*, 8:9). Twice, in what turns out to be a self-fulfilling prophecy, Yahweh's abandonment of the land is declared to be an event that has already transpired:

ʾên yhwh rōʾeh ʾōtānû	Yahweh does not see us;
ʿāzab yhwh ʾet-hāʾāreṣ	Yahweh has abandoned the land. (8:12)
ʿāzab yhwh ʾet-hāʾāreṣ	Yahweh has abandoned the land;
wĕʾên yhwh rōʾeh	And Yahweh does not see. (9:9)

The implications the people draw from Yahweh's apparent absence are disturbing. Instead of confessing their sin and pleading for his return, as did the mother of Nabonidus, they use Yahweh's absence as a pretense for rationalizing their evil actions: all kinds of cultic offenses in chapter 8, moral and social crimes in chapter 9. The form of Ezekiel's presentation exposes the perversion of the people. Pagans would have assumed that the event had been precipitated by their sin and responded to the departure of Yahweh with confession and prayer. But in the minds of Ezekiel's audience, cause and effect have been reversed. To the Babylonians a deity's abandonment of his temple and his city was provoked by the sins of the people; to the people of Judah, the

---

65. The inaugural vision is dated the fifth day of the fourth month of the fifth year of Jehoiachin's exile (1:1–2 [= July 31, 593 B.C.]); the first temple vision, the fifth day of the sixth month of the sixth year of the exile (8:1 [= September 18, 592 B.C.]).

66. According to 40:1, the concluding vision occurred on the tenth day of the first month of the twentieth year of the exile (= April 28, 573 B.C.).

67. For interpretation of the details of Ezekiel 8–11, see Block, *Ezekiel 1–24*, 272–360.

68. Cf. P. R. Ackroyd, *Exile and Restoration: A Study of Hebrew Thought of the Sixth Century B.C.*, OTL (Philadelphia: Westminster, 1968), 40–41.

former justified the latter. Having formerly based their security on Yahweh's unconditional commitment to them, they now treat his abandonment as betrayal, absolving them of any moral and spiritual obligation
to him. The statements made by these residents of Jerusalem are indeed
false—Yahweh has not yet left—and the implications they draw are
quite erroneous. But the prophet utilizes their declarations to an-
nounce his own theme in the pericope: Yahweh's departure is imminent. Ezekiel's vision elaborates in great detail on the causes and consequences of such perversion. But placing this account alongside other
ancient accounts of divine abandonment calls forth several additional
observations.

First, the repeated references to the evils being committed in Jerusalem emphasize that Yahweh's abandonment of the temple is provoked
by human action. The offenses described in 8:3–16 are primarily cultic
in nature: the introduction of the idol of jealousy into the court of Yahweh's temple, the worship of carved images of every sort, the women
weeping the Tammuz,[69] and twenty-five men paying homage to the sun.
In 8:17 Yahweh, through the prophet, accuses the people of social and
moral crimes—they have provoked the ire of Yahweh[70] by filling the
land with violence. This is reiterated in 9:9, which speaks of a land filled
with blood and a city filled with perversion (*muṭṭeh*). These evils are de-
nounced with the sharpest language as abominable (*tôʿēbâ*, 8:6a, 9, 13,
15, 17; 9:4), detestable (*šeqeṣ*, 8:10), wicked (*rāʿâ*, 8:9). It is no wonder
that Yahweh's passion (*qinʾâ*, 8:3, 5) and ire have been provoked (*hakʿîs*,
8:17). Twice Yahweh declares his response in terms reminiscent of the
extrabiblical accounts:

> Therefore I will deal in wrath (*ḥēmâ*); my eye will not spare, nor will I
> have pity (*ḥûs*); and though they cry in my ears with a loud voice, I will
> not hear them. (8:18)

> As for me, my eye will not spare, nor will I have pity, but I will bring their
> conduct upon their own heads. (9:10)

69. Although most translations have them weeping "for" Tammuz, the definite article
on Tammuz suggests that Tammuz denotes a special genre of lament, rather than the
deity himself. Since this scene follows immediately after the elders' assertion that Yahweh had abandoned the land, it appears that these women have either equated Yahweh
with Tammuz, or they are expressing their grief at their own deity's departure by adapting
a Tammuz ritual. In either case, Ezekiel observes the people in Jerusalem replacing the
vital worship of the living God with lamentations for the dead. See further Block, *Ezekiel
1–24*, 294–96.
70. "Sticking the branch to the nose" describes a physical gesture that is not only
painful but also extremely insulting. Here the expression is employed idiomatically, referring to the entire complex of crimes portrayed in the foregoing scenes. See further
Block, *Ezekiel 1–24*, 297–300.

Second, Yahweh leaves his temple of his own volition. Although the ancient Near Eastern accounts of divine abandonment generally create the impression that in a crisis the gods left their shrines voluntarily,[71] as noted earlier, underlying these accounts are enemy invasions and the spoliation of divine images. In Ezekiel's mind, Yahweh's departure does indeed coincide with the destruction of Jerusalem and the temple at the hands of Nebuchadnezzar. Since the temple contained no image of the deity, however, such spoliation with respect to Yahweh is impossible. On the contrary, Ezekiel highlights Yahweh's independence at each stage of his departure. (1) The *kābôd* rises from the cherub over the ark of the covenant within the holy of holies and moves over to the threshold of the temple, filling the entire court with its emanating brightness (9:3; 10:4). (2) A magnificent vehicle,[72] with total and absolute freedom of movement, appears bearing an object resembling a throne (10:1–13). (3) The *kābôd* moves from the threshold and rests above the vehicle (10:18). (4) The vehicle, bearing the *kābôd*, rises from the earth and pauses at the entrance of the east gate of the temple (10:19).[73] (5) The *kābôd* departs from the midst of the city and stands over the mountain to the east (11:23). Like the sudden termination of a dream, at this climactic moment the vision breaks off. But the description of the vehicle bearing the throne, with its absolute freedom of movement and limitless maneuverability, sends a clear and unequivocal message: Yahweh will not be transported like any other image from his dwelling place by any human monarch.

Third, the vision describes the disastrous effects that would attend the departure of the deity from the city. Yahweh would turn upon his subjects, delivering them into the hands of strangers who would execute them with the sword (11:7–11) within the border of Israel (*gĕbûl yiśrā᾿ēl*), which had, ironically, been viewed as sacrosanct. This description is reminiscent of extrabiblical texts in which divinities abandon their shrines and then turn on their subjects as if they were the enemy.[74]

Fourth, Ezekiel's vision holds out the prospect of an eventual normalization of relationship between Yahweh and his people (11:14–21), but with an extraordinary twist. In keeping with common oriental per-

71. Though the Sumerian laments portray local deities as subject to the will of Enlil. Marduk's freedom in the "Erra Epic" seems more limited than in the "Marduk Prophecy."

72. According to 10:15, 20, the prophet recognizes it as the same one he had seen in his inaugural vision (1:4–28).

73. For a consideration of the relationship between the *merkābâ* vision in chap. 1 and chaps. 9–10 see D. I. Block, "Text and Emotion: A Study on the 'Corruptions' in Ezekiel's Inaugural Vision (Ezekiel 1:4–28)," *CBQ* 50 (1988): 427–33; idem, *Ezekiel 1–24*, 90.

74. Cf. Inanna in the "Curse of Agade"; the gods of Sumer and Akkad in the "Tukulti-Ninurta Epic."

ceptions, those among Ezekiel's compatriots who had not been exiled interpreted their continued presence in Jerusalem as a mark of divine favor. Because the exiles had been expelled from the land, they had obviously been rejected by Yahweh. "Go far from Yahweh," the non-exiles declare heartlessly. "This land has been given to us as a possession" (*môrāšâ*, 11:15). But the prophet pulls the rug out from under their feet by announcing that the opposite is in fact the case. Breaking with convention Yahweh promises to follow the exiles and become a sanctuary for them in small measure (*miqdāš mĕ'aṭ*) "in the lands where they have arrived" (11:16). Ironically, the ones who are rejected by the deity are those who remain at home. As a sign (not precondition) of his continued interest in the exiles, Yahweh promises to regather them from their scattered locales and return them to the land of Israel. The prophet would have undoubtedly interpreted Yahweh's appearance to him in Babylon as a deposit and confirmation of this divine commitment, to be reported to his fellow exiles (cf. 11:25).

Fifth, whereas extrabiblical texts tend to emphasize the deity's change of heart prior to his/her return to the shrine, Ezekiel emphasizes that by a divine act the subjects' hearts will be changed (11:18–21).[75] Instead of having his subjects polish the exterior of a dirtied image (as in the "Erra and Ishum" composition), Yahweh declares that he will cleanse his subjects of their iniquity from the inside out, giving them a new heart so they will walk in his ways, and he may renew the covenant.[76] Those who insist on going their own way he will reject.

But this does not mean that Ezekiel will not recognize a change in Yahweh's disposition. On the contrary, intensely jealous for his land, in 35:1–36:15 Yahweh directs his wrath against those who had tried to capitalize on Israel's misfortune, and comes to the defense of the land where he is at home (35:10) and that he claims as his own (36:5). Yahweh had previously been against Jerusalem, the capital of the land of Judah,[77] and had threatened to impose all the covenant curses upon her (5:7–17). In the sequel he had set his face against the *land* of Judah, determined to destroy it completely. But in 36:1–15, Yahweh adopts the very opposite stance, announcing that he has turned toward Judah.[78] He will restore prosperity to the land and defend it in the face of the insults of the nations.

---

75. Cf. 36:16–32.

76. Kutsko ("Turning Swords into Plowshares," 3–4) argues that in this presentation Ezekiel assumes that the Israelites function as the image of Yahweh.

77. 4:1–17. Note the hostile orientation formula, *hinĕnî 'ālayik gam-'ănî*, "Behold, I myself am against you," in 5:8.

78. The formula *hinĕnî 'ălêkem*, "Behold, I am for you," followed by *ûpānîtî 'ălêkem*, "and I will turn toward you," in 36:9 deliberately reverses Yahweh's disposition.

In 36:16–38 Ezekiel announces the change of Yahweh's disposition toward the *people* of Israel. Whereas previously he had poured out his wrath on them, now he will regather the scattered population, bring them back to their ancestral homeland, cleanse them of their sin, and cause them to walk in new obedience to him. The text is emphatic, however, that this will not be done for the sake of Israel or because Israel deserves it. Yahweh's actions are driven by a concern for the sanctity of his name (vv. 19–23, 31–32).

Sixth, the links between Ezekiel's vision of Yahweh's departure from the temple in chapters 8–11 and extrabiblical accounts of divine abandonment suggest to the reader that the prophet's story cannot end with Yahweh's exit from the land (11:22–23). The pattern of the Mesopotamian accounts leads one to expect the regathering of the people to their homeland, the appointment of a new king, the institution of peace and prosperity to the people, and the return of Yahweh to his temple. Although Ezekiel is silent on these matters in this context, in long-range terms he does not disappoint. Indeed, these four elements represent major motifs in his restoration oracles proclaimed after Jerusalem had fallen in 586 B.C. (33:21–22).

1. The return to the land. In chapters 34 and 37 Ezekiel describes the return of the people to the land of Israel. Verses 34:11–19 highlight Yahweh's personal role seeking his scattered sheep, caring for them, delivering them from the hostile lands that hold them, bringing them to their own land and feeding them on the mountains of Israel. Yahweh himself will seek the lost, bind up the broken, strengthen the sick, and administer justice (v. 16). Chapter 37 divides into two parts. In the first (vv. 1–14), Yahweh resurrects the nation, infusing the dead bones with his own "breath" (*rûah*) and placing the people on their own land (v. 14). In the second (vv. 15–28), the promise of restoration is extended to the scattered remnants of all twelve tribes that originally made up the nation (vv. 16–21). Of course, this affirmation is based on Yahweh's own ancient promise to Abraham that he and his descendants should have eternal title to the land of Canaan (Gen. 15:7–18; 17:7–8).

2. The appointment of a shepherd. In 34:23–24 and 37:22–24 Yahweh announces his appointment of a new ruler. Although Yahweh had presented himself as the divine shepherd and Israel as his flock in 34:1–22, vv. 23–24 introduce another (under)shepherd, one appointed by Yahweh to care for his people:

> Then I will set over them one shepherd, my servant David, and he shall feed them; he will feed them himself and be their shepherd. And I, Yahweh, will be their God, and my servant David will be prince (*nāśîʾ*) among them. I am Yahweh. I have spoken.

In 37:22–25 Yahweh reiterates his promise to appoint a shepherd over his regathered flock, highlighting this person's role in canceling the centuries-old division of Israel into two kingdoms and unifying all twelve tribes into one nation:

> And I will make them a single nation in the land, on the mountains of Israel, and one king will be king for all of them. They will no longer be two nations, nor be divided any longer into two kingdoms. . . . And my servant David will be king over them, and they will have a single shepherd. . . . They shall live on the land that I gave to Jacob my servant, in which your ancestors lived. They and their sons and their grandsons will live on it forever, and David my servant shall be their prince forever.

The link between Ezekiel's identification of this person as "shepherd of Yahweh's people" and the use of similar titles in the extrabiblical texts examined above is striking.[79] Nevertheless, Ezekiel's present utterances were inspired primarily not by his cultural environment but by Israel's indigenous Davidic tradition. In keeping with Yahweh's eternal promise to David (2 Samuel 7), this person had to be identified as a (new) David. The present declaration serves as a reminder to Ezekiel and his audience that he had not forgotten that covenant commitment.

   3. The return of peace and prosperity. References to ultimate peace and prosperity are missing entirely in the original vision of the departure of Yahweh from the temple in chapters 8–11. Since ancient Near Easterners in general would have expected the return of the deity to be accompanied by a return of shalom, however, it is not surprising that Ezekiel should pick up the theme in his restoration oracles. In the "Divine Shepherd" oracle of chapter 34, the scene in the land of Israel after the appointment of David the *nāśîʾ* as shepherd is painted in most extravagant and glowing terms:

> I will make a covenant of peace with them, and eliminate harmful beasts from the land, so that they may live securely in the desert and sleep in the forests. And I will make them and the areas around my hill a blessing. And I shall send down the rain in its season; they shall be showers of blessing. And the trees of the field shall produce their fruit, and the earth shall yield its produce, and they shall be secure on the land. And they shall know that I am Yahweh, when I have broken the bars of their yoke, and have delivered them from the power of those who enslaved them. No longer shall they be booty for the nations, nor shall the beasts of the land devour them, but they shall live securely with no one terrifying them. And I will estab-

---

79. The "Nippur Lament" (*kirugu* 6, line 174) calls Išme-Dagan Enlil's "beloved shepherd" (Kramer, "Lamentation," 18); the "Esarhaddon Account" (episode 11 A:22) declares that Marduk endowed Esarhaddon with "shepherd-ship" over Assyria.

lish for them a planting place of renown. They shall no longer be victims
of famine in the land; nor shall they endure the insults of the nations any
more. Then they shall know that I, Yahweh, their God, am with them, and
that they, the house of Israel, are my people. (34:25–30)

In the survey of the effects of Yahweh's appointment of his "shepherd"
in 37:24–28, the final statement highlights the eternality of the new
peace and concludes with a note on the foreign recognition of the renewed relationships:

My servant David shall be king over them; and they shall all have one
shepherd. They shall follow my ordinances and observe my statutes dili-
gently. They shall reside in the land that I granted to Jacob, my servant,
in which your fathers lived. They shall reside in it, they and their sons,
and their grandsons, forever; and my servant, David, shall be their prince
forever. I will make a covenant of peace with them. It shall be an eternal
covenant with them. I will establish them and cause them to multiply. I
will place my sanctuary in their midst; my dwelling place shall be with
them. I will be their God, and they shall be my people. Then the nations
will know that I am Yahweh who sanctifies Israel, when my sanctuary is
eternally in their midst.[80]

4. The return of Yahweh to his temple. The account of Ezekiel's vision
in chapters 8–11 had left no hint that Yahweh's abandonment of his
temple was not permanent and that his rejection of his people was not
final. But the book cannot close without every thread that had been un-
raveled in the earlier vision being restored and reunited. In a dramatic
reversal of the movements of the *kābôd* in chapters 10–11, Ezekiel observes the symbol of divine presence return from the east, move into the
temple complex through the east gate, enter the temple, and fill the
house with his radiant glory (43:1–5). The description of the event is followed by Yahweh's own interpretation of the event:

Son of man, this is the location of my throne, and the place of the soles of
my feet, where I will reside in the midst of the children of Israel forever.
And the house of Israel will not defile my holy name again. . . . They have
defiled my holy name by their abominations that they have committed.
For this reason I have consumed them in my anger. Now let them put
away their harlotry and the corpses of kings far from me, and I will reside
in their midst forever. (43:7–9)

The sequel notes that the return of Yahweh will be accompanied by the
reestablishment of the cultic and moral orders (43:10–46:24), the heal-

---

80. Cf. also 36:28–38.

ing of the landscape (47:1–12), and the equitable distribution of the land among the twelve tribes (47:13–48:29). Although not functioning as the shrine of Yahweh, nonetheless the central city proclaims the new order in its name: *yhwh šāmmâ*, "Yahweh is there!" Deity, nation, and land exist once more in a state of eternal shalom.

The restorative motifs presented in these later texts were not even hinted at in Ezekiel's original vision of the departure of Yahweh from his temple. However, two factors render the conclusion described almost inevitable: first, the eternality of Yahweh's covenant promises with Israel and their king, and second, common ancient Near Eastern expectations in particular. Ezekiel's restoration oracles and visions fill out a picture that had been begun earlier, but whose completion could not be announced prior to the climactic moment, the fall of Jerusalem.[81] Before this event, the prophet's messages needed to concentrate on Israel's need for judgment. Only when the judgment has passed does Ezekiel begin to flesh out his vision of hope for the future.

Conclusion

Recent scholarship has recognized that the interpretation of biblical texts involves a conversation between the written text and the reader. The disposition of the reader plays a vital role in the establishment of the significance of a passage. We must indeed be ever mindful of the assumptions and expectations we bring to the text. At the same time, however, we must recognize the danger of imposing modern, and for the most part alien, Western definitions of literary and semantic propriety upon ancient texts. This is particularly true of the Book of Ezekiel. This is an ancient Near Eastern literary document that must be interpreted according to the literary standards and conventions of the world in which it arose. Many of the riddles in the book can be understood only in the light of the cultural and literary contexts from which this written record derives. A comparison of the shape of Ezekiel's message with similar accounts from Mesopotamia has important implications not only for the unity of the book as a whole and individual pericopes in particular, but also for the very nature of the prophetic task. Moreover, that Ezekiel's later oracles pick up themes begun earlier, but never completed, should caution against drawing the distinctions between the various modes of prophetic utterance too sharply.

We should not be surprised if the content of Ezekiel's vision bears striking links with Mesopotamian literature. After all, the prophet re-

---

81. The announcement of the fall of Jerusalem in 33:21–22 represents a turning point not only in the personal life of the prophet but especially in the nature of his message.

sided in Babylon and his message was directed primarily to exiles in Babylon. The picture the book paints of the spiritual condition of the Judaeans in Babylon is far from complimentary. They are in revolt against Yahweh, their own divine patron (2:3–4; 3:7–8), cynical toward the prophetic messages directed their way (12:17–28), defiled by idolatry (14:1–11), immoral and exploitative in their ethical conduct, in general perpetuating the abominations of the ancestors (20:1–44). Indeed, his audience had been infected by many of the prevailing religious ideas among Israel's neighbors. It is appropriate, therefore, that the account of the vision of impending destruction of their own beloved city should be cast in terms and employ motifs with which they had become fascinated. Even without Israel's own long-standing traditions of Yahweh's association with Zion, his portrayal of Yahweh leaving Jerusalem would have had a familiar ring.

On the other hand, his vision of Yahweh's departure could no more fit the pattern of the religious beliefs of the native Mesopotamians than could the representation of Yahweh in his temple. The God of Israel remained sovereign not only over the fate of his people but over his own destiny as well. Nebuchadnezzar would not forcibly drag him from his residence. Yahweh would leave of his own will, under his own power, and for his own reasons. Furthermore, even after he had left, his primary interest would remain with his covenant people. The land would serve this relationship.

Both Ezekiel and his contemporary Jeremiah attacked with great vigor official temple theology, according to which Yahweh's commitment to his people and his residence in the temple were treated as firm guarantees of the security of the people. Nevertheless, one may recognize a certain irony in that even as Nebuchadnezzar's battering rams were beating at the walls of the city, the very theology that the prophets were challenging was being confirmed. So long as Yahweh remained in his temple the city stood. Once he had left, however, neither gods nor humans could prevent the mighty Babylonian conqueror from storming in.

Conclusion

It has become apparent that the ancient Israelites' perception of the world, and in particular of political realities, had much more in common with that of their neighbors than with our own. The theological framework through which all of life was interpreted is especially alien to many moderns. For this reason it is often difficult to understand the motives that underlay the actions of nations and their leaders, and to grasp the significance of their reports of those actions. The latter applies whether one is dealing with visual artistic documents or literary accounts. My investigation of the role of divinities in ancient Near Eastern perceptions of national identity and history has attempted to examine several crucial issues from the perspective of the ancients themselves. I may now summarize my conclusions in seven main points. As I do so I will note the extent to which the Israelite perspective shared or deviated from the prevailing viewpoints of their neighbors.

1. Although several different elements contributed to ancient Near Eastern feelings of national unity (common genealogical descent, a shared history, a unifying language, occupation of an identifiable geographic territory, etc.), all nations recognized specific deities as having jurisdiction over them. For several reasons, however, such gods are better identified as patron rather than national divinities. First, this special affinity between god and people was often felt by groups that were not recognized as nations. On the one hand, individual households, clans, and tribes within a nation had their own favorite gods. On the other, some deities were associated with specific places: mountaintops, cities, the seas, and so on. Second, their veneration often extended beyond the borders of a particular nation. Gods that were recognized as supreme in one nation were often secondary or tertiary members of other people's pantheons. Third, the involvement of a specific god with a specific people was frequently shared with other gods. Specific functions in relationship to a nation were distributed among several. Nevertheless, in the latter part of the second and the first two-thirds of the first millennium B.C. the tendency toward henotheism was strong. Among most peoples one divinity eventually emerged as the god especially responsible for the welfare of that group.

As for the Israelites, their fundamentally theological approach to national affairs was of a piece with the perspectives of their neighbors. Nevertheless, in several crucial respects their attitude (in particular that of the doctrinaire Yahwists) toward their own divine patron, Yahweh, differed radically from these. Whereas the population never seemed to rid itself entirely of syncretistic religious perspectives, the spokespersons for orthodoxy in Israel became more and more intolerant of any rivals to Yahweh. He alone was the God of Israel. Since the nation owed its very existence to his mighty acts of salvation, the people were to worship no one else beside or in place of him. He would share his glory with none. In fact, the Hebrews alone of all of the peoples of the ancient Near East developed a doctrine of monotheism. Other gods, even those worshiped by other nations, were nonentities. They were railed upon as nothing but the figments of human imagination portrayed in carvings of wood and stone or molten images of gold and silver. Yahweh was the only God in heaven and on earth.

One corollary of this theological position was the universal jurisdiction of Yahweh and the accountability of all nations to him. To be sure, his election and deliverance of Israel, his appointment of them to a special status among the nations, and his establishment of his covenant demonstrated that their relationship with him was unique. Nevertheless, all the nations of the earth belong to him. Their fates and fortunes are in his hands alone. Ultimately they too must answer to him.

2. The deity-nation association was intricately tied to territorial considerations. Gods were associated with specific lands as well as peoples. Indeed, their concern with the geographic entity often appears to have overridden their real interest in the people. Like human monarchs, they had staked out their territorial claims. Their role was that of divine lords who owned property of varying size, dependent upon their power to seize and control it. The temples represented the manors where these divine lords lived and from which their authority emanated to the far corners of their domain. It was the responsibility of their human subjects to maintain the integrity of those claims. Whoever those subjects happened to be was often immaterial. The basis of the latter's subjugation to given deities was simply their presence in his land.

The God of the Israelites had his special fiefdom as well, the land of Canaan. Jerusalem was his manor, his dwelling place. However, the witness of the Old Testament is consistent in its portrayal of Yahweh as a God primarily of the people and only secondarily of the land of Canaan. He called Israel to himself long before they were in the land. Furthermore, his assurance of them as his people remained steadfast even when they were divorced from it. The land represented a special grant to them, providing them with a geographic context in the midst of the rest of the nations in which they would showcase the benefits of covenant relationship. But ultimately the whole world belonged to him. Just as he was sovereign over all nations and peoples, so his domain extended to the four corners of the earth.

3. The role of patron deities was to maintain the welfare and prosperity of their subjects. This was achieved by defending them against foreign enemies, by providing them with human shepherds whose task it was to maintain social harmony and justice, and by causing the land to yield its fruit in abundance for the prosperity of the inhabitants. The reputation of divine patrons depended upon the fate or fortune of a nation. Failure to provide for their well-being constituted a public demonstration of incompetence and impotence.

This was also the role of Yahweh in relationship to Israel. He was their divine warrior who went before them in battle. He appointed rulers for his people. He established the nation's principles of justice and righteousness, and functioned as divine judge when those standards were violated. His glory was at stake when the nation suffered defeat, and in particular when the population was expelled from the national homeland.

Although declarations of Yahweh acting for the sake of his glory and for the honor of his name are common, it is perhaps the gracious nature of his dealings with his own people that distinguishes him from all other deities. He is not capricious, egotistical, or self-indulgent, as are his rivals. The history of biblical revelation is a history of merciful condescension. Yahweh rescues a helpless people from Egyptian slavery (through no merit of their own). At the slightest hint of repentance he extends his grace and forgiveness to those who have rebelled against him. Yahweh assures his people that his covenant with them is eternal, for he is distinctively one who keeps his word. The creedlike proclamation to Moses in Exod. 34:6 sets him apart from all other gods:

> Yahweh! Yahweh!
> A God compassionate and gracious,
> slow to anger,
> abounding in kindness and faithfulness,
> extending kindness to the thousandth generation,
> forgiving iniquity, transgression, and sin;
> yet he does not remit all punishment,
> but visits the iniquity of parents
> upon children and grandchildren,
> to the third and fourth generation.

4. The role of the people in this tripartite relationship was to fulfill the will of the deity. This was achieved by providing the god with a res-

idence commensurate with his divine glory, the conscientious supervision and performance of the cult devoted to his worship and celebrating his lordship, and the maintenance of his standards of social justice. Prosperity and peace would be the rewards of faithfulness and the demonstrations of divine pleasure.

All this was true in Israel as well. From the perspective of the Israelites, however, what was unique was the clarity of Yahweh's revelation concerning his will and the righteous nature of his standards. According to Deut. 4:8 no other nation enjoyed such a privilege. Whereas they were viewed as floundering about seeking to appease the wrath of the gods by whatever means they thought appropriate (without any assurance of having achieved those ends), Yahweh had spoken verbally and personally to Israel. When his wrath was provoked by their behavior, they could never plead ignorance. In his grace he had revealed to this people the limits and dimensions of acceptable and pleasing conduct. When the nation forgot the fundamental instructions given through Moses, Yahweh repeatedly engaged official spokespersons, prophets, to call the people back to their covenant relationship. When the nation finally fell to the Babylonians, it was not because they had not known the will of God. It was because they had stubbornly refused to do it.

5. The function of a nation's territory was to respond to the deity's blessing by yielding abundant harvests for the inhabitants. The land provided a basis for economic security and population growth. Not to have possession of one's own land was to be sentenced to a life of restlessness and vagrancy, ever at the mercy of the elements and enemies. On the other hand, a land with fertile soil and abundant rainfall should have ensured a nation's prosperity and stability. But the territory's fulfillment of this role was dependent upon the blessing of the deity. The latter in turn were dependent upon the people's fulfillment of the pleasure of the god. Failure to satisfy the deity would inevitably incur his wrath, which would be expressed by all kinds of disasters: drought, disease, famine, flood, invasion, and so on.

To a large extent, this view of their national territory was also held by the Israelites. The land of Canaan was Yahweh's gracious gift to them. It was a good land, a rich land flowing with milk and honey, eager to yield its bounty for Yahweh's people. But their moral and spiritual failures led to the stifling of the soil's productivity. Droughts, disease, and famine were not only punitive actions by an offended deity but appeals to repentance and return to the covenant Lord. When such appeals failed, Yahweh had to inflict the ultimate punishment: divorce from the land. The Assyrian and Babylonian policies of exiling entire populations were employed to remove Israel from its land. Although the land was promised to the patriarchs as an eternal privilege, title to it was not automatic for each generation. The enjoyment of the privilege of living in Yahweh's land was conditional upon faithfulness to him.

6. The severance of the ties between patron deities and their land/people constituted the ultimate disaster. So long as the patron god was present in the land, the people could look to the god for protection and support. When a god would depart, either voluntarily or involuntarily, however, the theological basis on which national security was founded would be removed. The abandonment by a deity became a signal for whatever forces were on hand to wreak their destructive fury on the nation.

In essence, Israel's experience was no different. When Yahweh abandoned his land the divine support left and Nebuchadnezzar was able to move into the sacred city and the temple. The nation that had staked its security on his presence stood naked and defenseless before the conqueror. In Israel, however, Yahweh's departure did not reflect the supremacy of the deity of the Babylonians. He would not be dragged out of his temple. He abandoned his people of his own free will. In fact, Nebuchadnezzar and the Babylonians were *his* agents, not Marduk's. The persistent apostasy of the people had rendered Israel his enemy. The nation that had been the object of his grace now had become the target of his wrath. The nation that had abandoned its god now experienced the worst of all fates: abandonment by its own divine patron.

7. I conclude with one final observation that demonstrates how radically different was Israel's perception of their relationship to their deity from those of the nations around. In light of the emphasis on the permanent nature of Yahweh's covenant with Israel, the people, it is not surprising perhaps that the prophets should hold out hope for the nation beyond the dissolution of the deity-nation-land association effected with the fall of Jerusalem in 586 B.C. However, this study has helped us understand why the picture of the restored nation painted by the prophets has been given its present shape. If the restoration of the nation was to be complete, it had to be expressed in terms of: (a) a fundamental spiritual renewal of the people and the restoration of the covenant relationship; (b) the involvement of the entire house of Israel; (c) a return to the national homeland; and (d) the restoration of an indigenous (messianic) monarchy. Without any one of these elements, the process of restoration would have been perceived as incomplete, aborted. However, the hope witnessed in the prophets rested upon the conviction that in the end Yahweh would reinstitute the deity-land-nation association, and each member of the triad would faithfully fulfill its functions within the complex. When that great day would arrive, then the state of shalom and prosperity would return.

Bibliography

Abou-Assaf, Ali, Pierre Bordreuil, and Alan R. Millard. *La statue de tell Fekherye et son inscription bilingue assyro-araméenne.* Etudes Assyriologiques, Editions recherche sur les civilisations 7. Paris: A.D.P.F., 1982.

Ackroyd, Peter R. *Exile and Restoration: A Study of Hebrew Thought of the Sixth Century B.C.* Old Testament Library. Philadelphia: Westminster, 1968.

Albertz, Rainer. *A History of Israelite Religion in the Old Testament Period.* Trans. John Bowden. 2 vols. Old Testament Library. Louisville: Westminster/John Knox, 1994.

Albrektson, Bertil. *History and the Gods: An Essay on the Idea of Historical Events as Divine Manifestations in the Ancient Near East and in Israel.* Coniectanea Biblica Old Testament Series 1. Lund: Gleerup, 1967.

Albright, William F. *From the Stone Age to Christianity: Monotheism and the Historical Process.* 2d ed. Garden City, N.Y.: Doubleday, 1957.

———. *Yahweh and the Gods of Canaan: A Historical Analysis of Two Contrasting Faiths.* Jordan Lectures 1965. Garden City, N.Y.: Doubleday, 1968.

Block, Daniel I. *Ezekiel 1–24.* New International Commentary on the Old Testament. Grand Rapids: Eerdmans, 1997.

———. *Ezekiel 25–48.* New International Commentary on the Old Testament. Grand Rapids: Eerdmans, 1998.

———. *The Foundations of National Identity: A Study in Ancient Northwest Semitic Perceptions.* Ph.D. diss., University of Liverpool, 1981. Ann Arbor, Mich.: University Microfilms, 1983.

———. "Nations." In *New International Dictionary of Old Testament Theology and Exegesis,* ed. W. VanGemeren, 4:966–72. Grand Rapids: Zondervan, 1997.

———. "Table of Nations." In *International Standard Bible Encyclopedia,* ed. G. W. Bromiley, rev. ed., 4:707–13. Grand Rapids: Eerdmans, 1988.

Bodi, Daniel. *Ezekiel and the Poem of Erra.* Orbis biblicus et orientalis. Freiburg: Universitätsverlag; Göttingen: Vandenhoeck & Ruprecht, 1991.

Borger, R. "Gott Marduk und Gott-König Šulgi als Propheten: Zwei prophetische Texte." *Bibliotheca Orientalis* 28 (1971): 3–24.

Bright, John. *A History of Israel.* 3d ed. Philadelphia: Westminster, 1981.

Buccellati, Giorgio. *Cities and Nations of Ancient Syria: An Essay on Political Institutions with Special Reference to the Israelite Kingdoms.* Studi Semitici 26. Rome: Institute di Studi del Vincino Oriente, 1967.

Cogan, M. *Imperialism and Religion: Assyria, Judah, and Israel in the Eighth and Seventh Centuries B.C.E.* Society of Biblical Literature Monograph Series 19. Missoula, Mont.: Scholars Press, 1974.

Cross, Frank M. *Canaanite Myth and Hebrew Epic: Essays in the History of the Religion of Israel.* Cambridge: Harvard University Press, 1973.

Cross, Frank M., and David N. Freedman. *Studies in Ancient Yahwistic Poetry.* Society of Biblical Literature Dissertation Series 21. Missoula, Mont.: Scholars Press, 1975.

Dalley, Stephanie. *Myths from Mesopotamia: Creation, the Flood, Gilgamesh, and Others.* Oxford: Oxford University Press, 1989.

Day, John. "Asherah." In *Anchor Bible Dictionary,* ed. D. N. Freedman, 1:483–87. New York: Doubleday, 1992.

———. "Asherah in the Hebrew Bible and Northwest Semitic Literature." *Journal of Biblical Literature* 105 (1986): 385–408.

Driver, Godfrey R. *Canaanite Myths and Legends.* Old Testament Studies 3. Edinburgh: Clark, 1956.

Foster, Benjamin J. *From Distant Days: Myths, Tales, and Poetry of Ancient Mesopotamia.* Bethesda, Md.: CDL Press, 1995.

Fowler, Jeaneane D. *Theophoric Personal Names in Ancient Hebrew: A Comparative Study.* Journal for the Study of the Old Testament Supplement 49. Sheffield: Sheffield Academic Press, 1988.

Frankena, R. "The Vassal-Treaties of Esarhaddon and the Dating of Deuteronomy." *Oudtestamentische Studiën* 14 (1965): 122–54.

Frankfort, H. *Kingship and the Gods: A Study of Ancient Near Eastern Religion as the Integration of Society and Nature.* Chicago: University of Chicago Press, 1948.

Gadd, C. J. *Ideas of Divine Rule in the Ancient East.* Schweich Lectures 1945. London: British Academy, 1948.

Gibson, John C. L., ed. *Canaanite Myths and Legends.* Old Testament Studies 3. Edinburgh: Clark, 1977 (revision of 1956 edition by Godfrey R. Driver).

Gray, John. "Canaanite Kingship in Theory and Practice." *Vetus Testamentum* 2 (1952): 193–220.

———. *The Legacy of Canaan: The Ras Shamra Texts and Their Relevance to the Old Testament.* Vetus Testamentum Supplement 5. Leiden: Brill, 1957.

Greenberg, Moshe. *Ezekiel 1–20: A New Translation with Introduction and Commentary.* Anchor Bible 22. Garden City, N.Y.: Doubleday, 1983.

———. "The Vision of Jerusalem in Ezekiel 8–11: A Holistic Interpretation." In *The Divine Helmsman: Studies on God's Control of Human Events, Presented to Lou H. Silberman,* ed. J. L. Crenshaw and S. Sandmel, 143–64. New York: Ktav, 1980.

Heider, George C. *The Cult of Molek: A Reassessment.* Journal for the Study of the Old Testament Supplement 43. Sheffield: JSOT Press, 1985.

Höfner, Maria. *Die Religionen Altsyriens, Altarabiens, und der Mandäer.* Ed. Hartmut Gese, Maria Höfner, and Kurt Rudolph. Religionen der Menschheit 10.2. Stuttgart: Kohlhammer, 1970.

Hübner, Ulrich. *Die Ammoniter: Untersuchungen zur Geschichte, Kultur und Religion eines transjordanischen Volkes im 1. Jahrtausend v. Chr.* Abhandlungen des Deutschen Palästina-Vereins 16. Wiesbaden: Harrassowitz, 1992.

Jacobsen, Thorkild. "The Graven Image." In *Ancient Israelite Religion: Essays in Honor of F. M. Cross*, ed. P. D. Miller Jr. et al., 15–32. Philadelphia: Fortress, 1987.

Keel, Othmar, and Christoph Uehlinger. *Gods, Goddesses, and Images of God in Ancient Israel*. Trans. Thomas H. Trapp. Minneapolis: Fortress, 1998.

Kitchen, Kenneth A. *Ancient Orient and Old Testament*. Downers Grove, Ill.: InterVarsity Press, 1966.

Kramer, Samuel N. "Kingship in Sumer and Akkad: The Ideal King." In *Le palais et la royauté*, ed. P. Garelli, 163–66. XIXe Rencontre assyriologique internationale. Paris: Geuthner, 1974.

——— "Lamentation over the Destruction of Nippur." *Acta Sumerologica* 13 (1991): 1–26.

———. "Sumerian Historiography." *Israel Exploration Journal* 3 (1953): 217–32.

Kraus, Hans-Joachim. *Die Königsherrschaft Gottes im Alten Testament*. Tübingen: Mohr, 1951.

Lambert, W. G. *Babylonian Wisdom Literature*. Oxford: Clarendon, 1960.

———. "Destiny and Divine Intervention in Babylon and Israel." *Oudtestamentische Studiën* 17 (1972): 65–72.

Lambert, W. G., and Alan R. Millard. *Atra-Ḫasīs: The Babylonian Story of the Flood*. Oxford: Clarendon, 1969.

Lang, Bernhard. "No God but Yahweh! The Origin and Character of Biblical Monotheism." *Concilium* 177 (1985): 41–49.

Longman, Tremper, III. *Fictional Akkadian Autobiography: A Generic and Comparative Study*. Winona Lake, Ind.: Eisenbrauns, 1991.

Machinist, Peter. "The Epic of Tukulti-Ninurta I: A Study in Middle Assyrian Literature." Ph.D. diss., Yale University, 1978.

McCarthy, Dennis J. *Treaty and Covenant: A Study in Form in the Ancient Oriental Documents and in the Old Testament*. Analecta Biblica 21. Rome: Pontifical Biblical Institute, 1963.

Noth, Martin. *Die israelitischen Personennamen im Rahmen der gemeinsemitischen Namengebung*. Beiträge zur Wissenschaft vom Alten und Neuen Testament 3/10. Stuttgart: Kohlhammer, 1928. Reprint, Hildesheim: Olms, 1980.

Oded, Bustenay. *Mass Deportations and Deportees in the Neo-Assyrian Empire*. Wiesbaden: Reichert, 1979.

Ollenburger, Benjamin C. *Zion the City of the Great King*. Journal for the Study of the Old Testament Supplement 41. Sheffield: Sheffield Academic Press, 1987.

Olyan, Saul. *Asherah and the Cult of Yahweh in Israel*. Society of Biblical Literature Monograph Series 34. Atlanta: Scholars Press, 1988.

Orlinsky, Harry. "Nationalism-Universalism and Internationalism in Ancient Israel." In *Translating and Understanding the Old Testament: Essays in Honor of Herbert Gordon May*, ed. H. T. Frank and W. L. Reed, 206–36. Nashville: Abingdon, 1970.

Parpola, S., and K. Watanabe, eds. *Neo-Assyrian Treaties and Loyalty Oaths*. State Archives of Assyria 2. Helsinki: Helsinki University Press, 1988.

Rad, Gerhard von. "The Promised Land and Yahweh's Land in the Hexateuch." In *The Problem of the Hexateuch and Other Essays,* trans. E. W. Trueman Dicken, 79–93. New York: McGraw-Hill, 1966.

Ringgren, Helmer. *Israelite Religion.* Trans. D. E. Green. Philadelphia: Fortress, 1966.

———. *Religions of the Ancient Near East.* Trans. John Sturdy. Philadelphia: Westminster, 1973.

Saggs, H. W. F. *The Encounter with the Divine in Mesopotamia and in Israel.* Jordan Lectures 1976. London: Athlone, 1978.

———. *The Greatness That Was Babylon: A Sketch of the Ancient Civilization of the Tigris-Euphrates Valley.* London: Sidgwick & Jackson, 1962.

Schmökel, Hartmut. "Mesopotamian Texts." In *Near Eastern Religious Texts Relating to the Old Testament,* ed. Walter Beyerlin, trans. John Bowden, 68–145. Old Testament Library. Philadelphia: Westminster, 1978.

Smith, Mark S. *The Early History of God: Yahweh and Other Deities in Ancient Israel.* San Francisco: Harper & Row, 1987.

Stamm, Johann J. *Die akkadische Namengebung.* Mitteilungen der vorderasiatisch-ägyptischen Gesellschaft 44. Leipzig: Hinrichs, 1939.

Stolz, F. "Monotheismus in Israel." In *Monotheismus im alten Israel und seiner Umwelt,* ed. Othmar Keel, 144–89. Biblische Beiträge 14. Fribourg: Schweizerisches Katholisches Bibelwerk, 1980.

Tadmor, Hayim. "Assyria and the West: The Ninth Century and Its Aftermath." In *Unity and Diversity: Essays in the History, Literature, and Religion of the Ancient Near East,* ed. Hans Goedicke and J. J. M. Roberts, 36–48. Baltimore: Johns Hopkins University Press, 1975.

———. "Autobiographical Apology in the Royal Assyrian Literature." In *History, Historiography, and Interpretation: Studies in Biblical and Cuneiform Literatures,* ed. Hayim Tadmor and Moshe Weinfeld, 36–57. Jerusalem: Magnes, 1983.

Teixidor, Javier. *The Pagan God: Popular Religion in the Greco-Roman World.* Princeton: Princeton University Press, 1977.

Tigay, Jeffrey H. "Israelite Religion: The Onomastic and Epigraphic Evidence." In *Ancient Israelite Religion: Essays in Honor of Frank Moore Cross,* ed. P. D. Miller Jr. et al., 157–94. Philadelphia: Fortress, 1987.

———. *You Shall Have No Other Gods: Israelite Religion in the Light of Hebrew Inscriptions.* Harvard Semitic Studies 31. Atlanta: Scholars Press, 1986.

Vaux, Roland de. *Ancient Israel.* New York: McGraw-Hill, 1961.

Weinfeld, Moshe. *Deuteronomy and the Deuteronomic School.* Oxford: Clarendon, 1972.

Weippert, Manfred F. "'Heiliger Krieg' in Israel und Assyrien: Kritische Anmerkungen zu Gerhard von Rads Konzept des 'Heiligen Krieges im alten Israel.'" *Zeitschrift für die alttestamentliche Wissenschaft* 84 (1972): 460–93.

Westermann, Claus. *The Promises to the Fathers: Studies on the Patriarchal Narratives.* Trans. D. E. Green. Philadelphia: Fortress, 1980.

Wiseman, Donald J. *Nebuchadnezzar and Babylon.* Schweich Lectures 1983. Oxford: University Press for the British Academy, 1985.

———, ed. *Peoples of Old Testament Times.* Oxford: Clarendon, 1973.

Zyl, Anton H. van. *The Moabites.* Pretoria Oriental Series 3. Leiden: Brill, 1960.

Index of Scripture

159

Index of Extrabiblical Materials

Index of Authors

Index of Subjects

wild beasts, 103, 104, 107 n. 66
worship, 152
wrath, of deity, 110, 152

Yaho, 67
Yahweh, 26–27, 32
  abandonment of Israel, 135–42
  as Adon, 49
  claim to land of Israel, 76–79, 80, 86–87
  covenant with Israel, 90, 153
  disposition to people, 143
  glory, 137–38
  as God of Israel, 29, 37, 38
  gracious nature, 151
  as king, 53–54
  as lord of heaven, 56
  as "our God," 39

reputation, 108–9
residence, 77–78
return to his temple, 145
selection of Israel's kings, 89–90
as shepherd, 57–58
theophoric, 40–41
universal jurisdiction, 54, 72–73, 150–51
wrath, 106–7, 140, 142
Yahwists, 33, 63, 65, 69, 74, 137, 150
Yam, 67
Yamm, 19
Yariḥ, 64
Yehawmilk, 37, 89

Zakkur, 89
Zeus, 19, 21–23
Zimri-Lim, 121